ESSENTIALS OF
BAKING

WILLIAMS-SONOMA

ESSENTIALS OF
BAKING

RECIPES AND TECHNIQUES FOR SUCCESSFUL HOME BAKING

RECIPES

CATHY BURGETT, ELINOR KLIVANS, LOU SEIBERT PAPPAS

GENERAL EDITOR

CHUCK WILLIAMS

PHOTOGRAPHY

NOEL BARNHURST

Contents

If you are timid about baking, or just rarely undertake the making of cookies or cupcakes because you are disappointed in the results, do not walk past Williams-Sonoma *Essentials of Baking*.

This book does not assume that you know the many details of how to bake. Indeed, most of the recipes even give you choices—with your hands, with an electric mixer, and, in some cases a food processor—for mixing doughs and batters. The opportunity of mixing with your hands is a very good option if you are a beginner. The feel of the dough instructs you to know what to expect when the recipe is repeated in the future, and also encourages you to make it even if you do not have all the fancy equipment.

The recipes are well thought-out, with step-by-step instruction and splendid photographs that, rather than making your efforts appear unrealistically glamorous, clearly show you how your results should look. There are also suggestions for the most practical tools to use at every step, as well as photographs of all the basic equipment you will need. Ingredients are discussed and pictured, too, so you will know what to buy.

Between the instructions and the photographs in this book, nothing in the baking process is left to the imagination or to guesswork. You will find that you are able to re-create such classics as apple turnovers, chocolate soufflé, éclairs, popovers, and the supper favorite, quiche Lorraine, as well as many others, old and new. Simply put, Williams-Sonoma *Essentials of Baking* will quickly become an "essential" part of your cookbook collection.

Marion Cunningham

Basic Equipment

This detailed list of common baking equipment and tools will help get you started on the road to becoming an experienced home baker. Look for these items in the cookware section of department stores, in kitchenware shops, and in specialty-baking or restaurant-supply stores.

Biscuit Cutters

A set of round, metal biscuit cutters, either plain or fluted, can be used for cutting out not only biscuits but also cookies and scones.

Bowls

Choose a good-quality nesting set of stainless-steel bowls, which are durable and can be heated. A set of nesting ceramic bowls is an excellent option. They are heavy, which keeps the bowl in place when mixing, and durable. Other alternatives include Pyrex or glass bowls, which are also heavy and easy to clean. Avoid aluminum bowls, which react to acidic foods, and plastic bowls, except for rising yeast dough or storage, which absorb odors and fats.

Cake Turntable

With its rotating platter raised above the work surface, a cake turntable, also known as a cake stand, allows you to frost and decorate layer cakes quickly and accurately. An already-on-hand lazy Susan is a great alternative.

Cardboard Cake Rounds

If you bake layer cakes often, these cardboard rounds are very useful. They are great for moving individual cake layers when decorating and for transporting whole cakes. They also contribute stability when decorating cakes on a cake turntable or a serving platter.

BAKING SHEETS AND PANS

The most fundamental components of a baker's kitchen are baking sheets and pans. Invest in good-quality commercial baking pans. They are heavier and retain heat better than lighter pans, and they will cost you less in the long term because they will not warp or buckle. Dark metal pans, which conduct, retain, and distribute heat well, are good for fruit pies or other baked items that need more crispness. Glass baking dishes and pie dishes are also a good option for fruit-based desserts. Ceramic dishes should be reserved for cobblers, crisps, or other crustless fruit desserts. Pale or shiny metal pans, such as heavy-gauge aluminum, deliver a tender, delicate crust, which is good for breads and cookies. Some bakers prefer nonstick pans, which they appreciate for their easy release and cleanup, but many nonstick pans warp easily. Always use the pan size and type called for in a recipe, or the quality of your finished product may be disappointing.

The following pans will allow you to bake many of the recipes in this book:

■ two rimless baking sheets (also known as cookie sheets)

■ two 11-by-17-inch (28-by-43-cm) half-sheet pans

■ two 12-cup muffin pans

■ two 9-by-5-inch (23-by-13-cm) loaf pans

■ two 9-inch (23-cm) round cake pans

■ 9- or 10-inch (23- or 25-cm) Bundt pan and/or tube pan

■ 9-inch (23-cm) springform pan

■ 9-inch (23-cm) metal pie pan

■ 9-inch (23-cm) fluted metal tart pan with removable bottom

■ 8- or 9-inch (20- or 23-cm) square metal baking pan

Left to right, from top left: COOLING RACKS, BISCUIT CUTTERS, ASSORTED KITCHEN KNIVES, BOX GRATER-SHREDDER, PARCHMENT (BAKING) PAPER, MELON BALLER, COOKIE PRESS, CAKE TURNTABLE.

Cherry Pitter

When fresh cherries are in season, this small, easy-to-use tool is indispensable for pitting a mound of fruits. You simply place a cherry in the little metal cup and depress the plunger, pushing the pit out and leaving the fruit whole.

Cookie Press

Dough is slipped into this cylindrical tool and then pressed out through an assortment of design plates into beautiful, uniform cookie shapes. Cookie presses range in quality from inexpensive and flimsy to costly and sturdy. Look for a good-quality metal press that will hold up to stiff cookie doughs.

Cooling Racks

For the best results, always cool baked goods on sturdy wire racks that allow air to circulate on all sides. They will cool faster and are less likely to become soggy from condensation. Have available a variety of racks in various sizes, all with feet of at least ¹/₂ inch (12 mm) that raise them above the work surface.

Cutting Boards

Have on hand at least two cutting boards, one for sweet and one for savory. Solid, durable plastic cutting boards are ideal, as they can be easily cleaned. Buy different-colored boards to make it easy to tell them apart.

Grater

A sturdy box grater-shredder with a handle has multiple uses. It allows you to shred cheese and carrots, zest citrus, and grate Parmesan cheese safely and with ease. A handheld Microplane grater, which comes in multiple sizes, is indispensable for extra fine grating.

Knives

A set of good-quality sharp kitchen knives will last you many years. The following knives are indispensable: a paring knife with a 3- to 4¹/₂-inch (7.5- to 11.5-cm) blade, a chef's knife with a 10-inch (25-cm) blade, a serrated bread knife with at least a 10-inch (25-cm) blade, and a thin, serrated slicing knife with at least a 12-inch (30-cm) blade.

Measuring Cups and Spoons

Metal measuring cups and spoons, in graduated sizes, are best for measuring dry ingredients, as metal is more durable than plastic, which can crack, melt, or warp. For measuring liquid ingredients, 1-cup (8–fl oz/250-ml) and 4-cup (32–fl oz/1-l) glass pitchers are standard.

Melon Baller

This handy little tool, which comes in a variety of sizes, has more uses than creating melon balls for fruit salads. Use one that has a small bowl about 1 inch (2.5 cm) in diameter for coring apples and pears, for forming truffles, and for shaping small balls of cookie dough.

Parchment Paper

Moisture- and grease-resistant parchment paper, also known as baking paper, is the professional baker's secret weapon. It is used primarily for lining pans to prevent sticking, and for folding into cones for piping delicate decorations out of chocolate.

TO LINE A ROUND CAKE PAN, fold a piece of parchment larger than the cake pan into quarters. Place the point of the parchment into the center of the pan and press the parchment into the pan, so that it creases along the edge. Cut along the crease, unfold, and press the parchment round into the pan.

TO MAKE A PIPING CONE, start with a rectangle that measures about 6 by 8 inches (15 by 20 cm). Cut the rectangle in half on the diagonal, forming two triangles. Roll one triangle into a cone, so that the center of the long side of the triangle becomes the tip of the cone. Bring the tail up to the top of the cone and tuck it inside. The cone should have a small opening at the tip. If the opening is not large enough, use scissors to cut a small hole.

Pastry Blender

This simple tool consists of a set of sturdy, curved steel wires attached to a handle. Also called a dough blender, it is used for cutting butter or other fat into dry ingredients.

Pastry Brushes

Three pastry brushes are essential. Label one brush for glazing, and use to brush baked goods with milk, cream, or egg wash before baking. Label a second brush for sugar, and use to wash down the sides of the saucepan when melting and caramelizing sugar. And label the third brush for fats, and use with butter or oils. Purchase high-quality brushes (not paint brushes) with natural bristles.

Peeler

A sturdy, swivel-bladed peeler nicely follows the contours of foods. Look for one with a comfortable handle.

Ramekins

These small, round ceramic or glass molds, usually 3 to 4 inches (7.5 to 10 cm) in diameter, can be used for baking individual soufflés, custards, bread puddings, crisps, cobblers, and more. They are also handy containers for readying ingredients for recipes.

Reamer

This inexpensive handheld wooden or plastic tool, with its deeply ridged surface, is great for juicing citrus fruits. Countertop versions with built-in strainers are also available.

Rolling Pin

If you have only one rolling pin, make it a heavy French-style pin. This long, wooden dowel without handles might take some getting used to, but once you do, you will discover that it gives you greater control over your pastry dough. Care for it properly, and you will have it for years: Never soak it in water or wash it with soap. To clean, wipe it with a soft, clean cloth, and remove any stubborn dough bits with a plastic pastry scraper.

Ruler

It might surprise you, but a ruler is extremely handy in the kitchen. You'll find many uses for it: measuring baking pans and rolled-out pastries and doughs; marking various doughs

Left to right, from top left: TONGS; RAMEKINS; PLASTIC PASTRY SCRAPER AND BENCH SCRAPER; SMALL AND BALLOON WHISKS; INSTANT-READ, CANDY, AND OVEN THERMOMETERS; FRENCH ROLLING PIN; SIEVES; SIFTER.

Left to right: PASTRY BRUSHES, VEGETABLE PEELER, PASTRY BLENDER, REAMER.

and pastries for folding, cutting, or shaping; and cutting straight lines. Metal is best, with both centimeters and inches indicated.

Scrapers

Two basic types of scrapers are invaluable to every baker: a bench scraper, or dough cutter, and a plastic pastry scraper, or bowl scraper. The bench scraper consists of a stainless-steel, rectangular blade with a griplike handle on one edge. It makes quick work of dividing dough into portions and scraping dough off a work surface. The plastic pastry scraper is a piece of flexible plastic that fits in the palm of your hand and allows you to easily scrape batter from a bowl or off your rolling pin.

Sifters and Sieves

Two tools allow you to sift dry ingredients, such as flour, cocoa powder, or confectioners' (icing) sugar: a sifter, which consists of a canister with at least two mesh screens and a rotating blade controlled by a rotary or squeeze handle; and a sieve, a mesh bowl with a handle. The mesh can range from very fine to large, depending on the intended use.

Spatulas

A baker's kitchen is incomplete without a good range of rubber and metal spatulas. Purchase sturdy, commercial-quality spatulas with silicone rubber blades that won't melt during stove-top use. Rubber spatulas are ideal for scraping down the sides of bowls, for folding lighter ingredients into heavy batters, and for stirring stove-top custards.

Two basic types of metal spatulas are available: the offset spatula, for lifting baked items and smoothing batters in a pan, and the icing spatula or palette knife, for frosting cakes, dislodging pastry dough from work surfaces, and smoothing fillings.

Spoons

Have on hand one or two good-quality wooden spoons with long handles that fit comfortably in your hand. Wooden spoons stay safely cool when used on the stove top and are more durable than plastic.

Thermometers

Maintaining the correct temperature is critical to successful baking. Three basic types of thermometers will help you do that. An oven thermometer measures the temperature inside the oven. Choose a mercury type (rather than a spring type) that either hangs or sits on the rack. Check the temperature after you have preheated the oven, then adjust the control knob as needed if the actual temperature varies from the original setting. An instant-read thermometer is handy for checking water temperatures and for stove-top custards and curds. Candy thermometers, the best of which have a mercury bulb and column attached to a metal casing with a clip that slips over the pan side, register very high temperatures and are used for boiling sugar for candy, caramel, and other uses.

Timer

The sign of a good baker is the ability to determine when an item is perfectly baked by color, smell, and feel. But it's a good idea to keep a portable digital kitchen timer on hand for when your attention is diverted from what is happening in the oven.

Tongs

Long handled metal tongs are perfect for lifting hot items such as ramekins or custard cups out of a water bath.

Whisks

You will find that owning two different whisks will cover all your basic whipping needs. A medium-sized, sturdy metal wire whisk is perfect for whipping up batters and stirring yeast into warm water. The rounded shape of a balloon whisk is good for whipping egg whites and cream. Purchase professional-quality whisks with wooden or metal handles and sturdy loops of wire.

Ambitious Equipment

Once your love of baking has been awakened, you will want to build your equipment collection. These items have specific functions, but you may find you cannot live without some of them. They can be purchased at kitchenware shops and in specialty-baking or restaurant-supply stores.

Baking Sheets and Pans

Above and beyond the pans listed in the basic equipment section is a whole range of specialty pans that will allow you to become more creative in your baking and put your own individual stamp on each item. As with the basics, buy good-quality, heavy-duty sheets and pans, and they will last for years. Some specialty items include nontraditional cake pan shapes, such as hearts, flowers, squares, and diamonds; a variety of cake pan sizes, from small 6-inch (15-cm) pans to large 18-inch (45-cm) pans; specialty Bundt pans in elaborate designs; popover pans; specialty muffin pans, with miniature, jumbo, or heart-shaped cups; and a variety of tart pans, such as individual, rectangular, and square.

Baking Stones

For finer, crisper crusts when baking yeast breads, flatbreads, and pizzas, use a baking stone (also called a pizza stone) or unglazed quarry tiles, which simulate a brick oven. While baking stones are sold in a variety of shapes and sizes, quarry tiles tend to be less expensive and offer more flexibility in lining the oven rack. Stones and tiles retain heat and distribute it efficiently.

Banneton

A banneton is a basket, sometimes lined with heavy cloth, that is used for proofing yeast breads in their final stage of rising. Available in many shapes and sizes, it is an expensive but worthwhile tool for any serious bread baker.

Brioche Mold

A butter-rich brioche just isn't the same if it is not baked in its traditional circular, fluted metal mold. The molds are available in various sizes, from petite to family size.

Copper Bowl

A copper bowl is the best choice for beating egg whites. A chemical reaction that occurs between the egg protein and the copper gives the egg whites greater volume and stability and a more satiny finish than when they are beaten in a stainless-steel or other bowl. Copper is also an excellent conductor of heat and is often used when making candy and for sugar work.

Food Processor

Although an expensive investment, this versatile machine can quickly and efficiently chop nuts, purée ingredients, mix pastry dough, and more. Look for a respected brand with a capacity of at least 11 cups (88 fl oz/2.75 l).

Left to right, from top left: ROUND AND OVAL BANNETONS, PASTRY (PIPING) BAG AND TIPS, NONSTICK LINER, MADELEINE PLAQUE, KITCHEN TORCH, BAKING STONES, BRIOCHE MOLDS, PEEL.

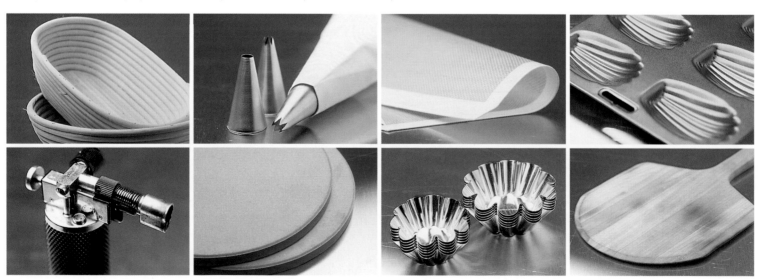

Left to right: PIZZA CUTTER; ZESTER; TAPERED, MARBLE, AND BALL-BEARING ROLLING PINS; NONTRADITIONAL CAKE AND TART PANS.

Kitchen Torch

A small kitchen torch makes creating a caramelized topping on your crème brûlée easy and fast. It is also handy for browning meringues and glazing tarts.

Madeleine Plaque

Few baked items are as distinctive as a madeleine. A cross between a cake and a cookie, these little shell-shaped delights are baked in a special pan called a madeleine plaque. The plaques, which usually have 8 or 12 shallow molds, come in tinned steel, metal with a nonstick finish, and pliable silicone. If you are going to bake madeleines, a madeleine plaque is a necessity.

Marble Surface

A marble slab or marble-topped table is the ideal surface for handling, rolling, and cutting out pastry, as it keeps the pastry cool. On particularly hot days, you can cool the marble down quickly by placing a bag of ice on the surface for 15 minutes before working with your dough. Marble is also excellent for chocolate or sugar work.

Nonstick Liner

Silicone-coated fiberglass baking mats, widely known by the brand name Silpat, are reusable nonstick liners that may be used any time a recipe calls for a greased pan or a pan lined with parchment (baking) paper. They work well for baking thin, delicate cookies.

Pastry Bags and Tips

Pastry (piping) bags and pastry tips are more functional than might first be imagined. Choose a larger pastry bag for piping cookies, choux, and even filling for cakes. A smaller bag is ideal for finer decorating work. The best pastry bags are made from durable plastic-coated canvas. Wash and air-dry them thoroughly immediately after use. Pastry tips come in many shapes and sizes, and it is generally more economical to buy a standard set. Start with a set of professional-quality plain tips and star tips for the most versatility.

Peel

A baker's peel, a wide, flat, usually long-handled wooden board, is used to slide yeast breads, flatbreads, and pizzas into a hot oven onto a baking stone. Peels come in many sizes and levels of quality. Choose a sturdy peel, and never immerse it in water or wash it with soap, or it may warp.

Rolling Pins

Once you have mastered your French rolling pin, you might want to add more styles to your baker's tool kit. A hefty wooden pin with ball bearing–loaded handles is both a classic and a very useful addition. It makes rolling easy and is great for stiff doughs. A marble rolling pin is ideal for pastries, such as croissant and Danish pastry, that need to remain cold, and a tapered handleless pin is helpful for rolling rounds of dough, such as pie or tart dough.

Pizza Cutter

Used widely by professional bakers, a pizza cutter, also known as a pizza wheel or pastry wheel, consists of a sharp metal disk, with plain or fluted edges, attached to a handle. It is the ideal tool for cutting shapes out of or trimming pastry doughs.

Stand Mixers

Serious bread bakers swear by stand mixers. While a good-quality mixer is a big investment, you will be rewarded with the versatility and functionality of this sturdy machine. Choose a mixer with a 4$\frac{1}{2}$- to 5-quart (4.5- to 5-l) mixing bowl. The mixers come with paddle, whip, and dough hook attachments, and can be used to knead doughs, beat meringues, and fold batters together smoothly.

Zester

This handheld metal tool has a row of small holes that, when drawn across a citrus peel, results in perfect strips of zest.

Ingredients

This section explores the main ingredients used in baking: flours and grains, leaveners, fats, sweeteners, salt, spices and flavorings, eggs, dairy, chocolate, nuts, and fresh and dried fruits. Each category explains the types and techniques associated with the ingredients being discussed.

FLOUR

Flour, made by milling grains such as wheat, rye, and corn, is the baker's most essential, most basic ingredient. It delivers much of the flavor, texture, and structure to whatever is being made.

The type of grain and the way the flour is milled help determine its defining characteristic: how much protein it contains. The protein present in wheat flours, and in very small amounts in rye and oat flours, forms a weblike structure in dough called gluten. It is what makes dough elastic and extensible when kneaded. You can control the amount of gluten by the type of flour you use and how much you manipulate the dough or batter before baking. For example, yeast bread is typically made from a hard-wheat flour, which has a high protein content, and is rigorously kneaded to develop a strong, elastic network of gluten strands. This gluten web traps the gases needed to help the bread rise in the oven. In contrast, quick breads usually call for flours that are relatively low in protein, and ingredients are stirred together rather than kneaded. This produces a mixture with little gluten and a tender crumb.

A variety of flours and other forms of processed grains are used in baking. The most common ones are described here.

Left to right, from top left: ALL-PURPOSE (PLAIN) FLOUR, BREAD FLOUR, WHOLE-WHEAT (WHOLEMEAL) FLOUR, FINE-GRIND CORNMEAL, RYE FLOUR, OLD-FASHIONED ROLLED OATS, CAKE (SOFT-WHEAT) FLOUR, MEDIUM-GRIND CORNMEAL

Wheat Flours

ALL-PURPOSE (PLAIN) FLOUR, a mixture of soft and hard wheats, is the most common flour on the U.S. market. Because it is ground from only the endosperm of the wheat kernel, it remains white. All-purpose flour Is available bleached (chemically treated) and unbleached. Unbleached flour tends to contain more protein and has a more pleasing flavor. It was used to test most of the recipes in this book.

BREAD FLOUR is milled solely from hard wheat and is high in protein. Like all-purpose flour, it is ground from only the endosperm of the wheat kernel.

CAKE (SOFT-WHEAT) FLOUR, made from soft wheat, is milled more finely than other wheat flours and is low in protein and high in starch. It is generally the best choice for delicately crumbed cakes and similar baked goods. As a rule, cake flour is bleached, which makes it whiter. Bleaching also increases the flour's ability to hold sugar and water, which helps cakes keep their loft in the oven, and reduces the amount of protein. Cake flour is often sifted prior to use to aerate it and to remove any lumps.

SEMOLINA FLOUR, made from durum wheat with the bran removed, is used in some Italian breads and desserts and to keep savory breads from sticking to a peel or baking sheet. Look for a fine grind for baking.

WHOLE-WHEAT (WHOLEMEAL) FLOUR is ground from whole wheat berries. It retains all three parts of the grain, the endosperm, the bran, and the germ, and thus contains more vitamins, minerals, starch, and fiber than flours ground from only the endosperm. Because it contains the whole kernel, it is lower in protein than all-purpose flour. Whole-wheat flour yields a dense bread with a nutty, sweet flavor.

Other Flours and Grains

CORN is the source of many different products used in baking. The dried kernels are ground into cornmeal of different textures, from fine (also known as corn flour) to coarse. Stone-ground cornmeal, literally ground between stones, includes the germ of the kernel and has a nuttier flavor than fine- or medium-grind cornmeal. Silky, powdery cornstarch (corn-flour) is ground from the heart—also called the endosperm—of the kernel and used as a gluten-free thickener.

OATS are versatile as well, becoming many different products depending on how the grain is cut and processed. After harvesting, the hull is removed from the whole grain, leaving the

FLOUR SUBSTITUTIONS

If you need	But you have	Substitute
1 cup (5 oz/155 g) all-purpose flour	cake flour	1 cup (4 oz/125g) plus 2 tablespoons cake flour
	self-rising flour	1 cup (5 oz/155 g) self-rising flour; omit salt and baking powder
	bread flour	$^7/_8$ cup (4$^1/_2$ oz/140 g) bread flour
1 cup (4 oz/125g) cake flour	all-purpose flour	$^7/_8$ cup (4$^1/_2$ oz/140 g) all-purpose flour plus 2 tablespoons cornstarch

oat groat behind, which is ground into flour for bread making. When the groats are steamed and flattened, they become old-fashioned rolled oats, a common ingredient in cookie and muffin recipes. Quick-cooking oats, groats that have been cut into pieces before steaming and flattening, are interchangeable with old-fashioned rolled oats in many recipes, although the latter are preferred for their superior texture. Instant oats and steel-cut oats are best for eating as cooked cereal. Oat bran (the husk removed from the groat) is used to add flavor, texture, and nutrients to yeast and quick breads.

RYE FLOUR, milled from rye berries, is low in protein. Dark rye flour includes the germ of the berry, while light rye flour is made with the germ removed. Medium rye flour is a mixture of the two. Rye produces a distinctively flavored, dense, more rustic and earthy bread than wheat flour. Coarse dark rye flour is sometimes labeled pumpernickel flour.

LEAVENERS

Leavening is the creation of gas bubbles in a dough or batter that expand during mixing and baking, lightening the texture of the baked item. Leaveners come in three forms: natural, chemical, and mechanical. Depending on the item you are baking and the result you hope to achieve, you will use one or more of these methods in a recipe.

Natural Leavening

All baked goods containing yeast are considered naturally leavened. Yeast comes in different forms, from the wild yeast naturally present in the environment to commercial yeasts, including active dry, quick-rise, and fresh yeasts.

Regardless of type, yeast is a living organism and is therefore sensitive to certain elements. Temperature is essential. Yeast can live and grow between 65° and 130°F (18° and 54°C) and thrives between 90° and 115°F

(32° and 46°C). It will die in temperatures above 140°F (60°C) or when in direct contact with salt. Recipes often call for proofing the yeast with a small amount of sugar or other sweetener, as yeast likes to eat sugars.

WILD YEASTS are in the air around us, and depending on the climate, they can take on various characteristics and flavors. These yeasts are used to make sourdough starters and naturally fermented sponges, such as those for *pain au levain*, and they yield particularly full-flavored breads. They are unreliable and temperamental, however, and are sometimes used in combination with commercial yeast as a means of stabilizing them.

COMMERCIAL YEAST is most readily available in three forms: quick-rise, also known as rapid rise; active dry; and fresh cake. Quick-rise yeast is granular dehydrated yeast that, unlike active dry and cake yeast, does not need to be rehydrated before using. It raises dough 50 percent faster than active dry yeast. Many bakers believe it works too quickly, however, allowing too little time for the bread to develop flavor. Active dry yeast is also a granular dehydrated yeast, but it must be rehydrated in warm water. It is a highly reliable product and was used for testing the recipes in this book. Fresh cake yeast, which is not dehydrated and has a relatively short shelf life, comes in a compressed block and must be stored in the refrigerator or freezer. It is the preferred yeast of many professional bakers and yields excellent results.

Chemical Leavening

Quick breads, muffins, and many cakes and cookies rely on one or both of two well-known chemical leaveners, baking soda and baking powder. Chemical leaveners are often coupled with mechanical leavening (see below) to achieve a tender product.

BAKING SODA, or bicarbonate of soda, is used if a batter or dough contains an acidic ingredient, such as buttermilk, yogurt, sour cream, molasses, honey, or citrus. When the baking soda comes into contact with the acid, a chemical reaction occurs that produces carbon dioxide. The carbon dioxide bubbles expand when exposed to liquid and heat and produce steam, which is released into the mixture, creating a moist, tender product. Because baking soda reacts immediately, the batter should be baked immediately after mixing.

BAKING POWDER, which combines an acid and an alkaline, is used when there is no additional acidic ingredient in the batter. Most baking powders are "double-acting," meaning that they react twice: once by producing carbon dioxide bubbles in the batter when liquid is added to the dry ingredients, and again in the heat of the oven. If possible, use a nonaluminum-based baking powder to avoid a bitter aftertaste.

Mechanical Leavening

Cakes, cookies, and pastries are all leavened mechanically. This occurs when a physical motion, such as creaming together butter and sugar, or an ingredient, such as butter or eggs,

produces air, steam, or carbon dioxide. Air is physically added to ingredients such as butter and sugar; whole eggs, egg whites, or egg yolks; or heavy (double) cream when those ingredients are beaten. Air is further incorporated when those aerated ingredients are folded into the batter. Steam, used to leaven pastries such as croissants and puff pastry, is created during baking when water is released from the butter, causing the pastries to rise. Carbon dioxide is released when eggs are heated, a reaction that occurs in baked goods such as choux.

FATS

Fat delivers moisture, flavor, and tenderness to baked goods. Each fat contributes its own textural quality, resulting in a light, medium, or dense crumb. Butter and oil are the most widely used fats in baking.

Butter

Most bakers prefer unsalted butter. It tends to be fresher (salt is used as a preservative), is low in moisture, and lends a sweeter, more delicate flavor to the baked item than salted butter. Always purchase good-quality butter, as the better brands have a lower moisture content, making them ideal for baking. All recipes in this book were tested using unsalted butter.

Many recipes call for room-temperature butter, which is most easily achieved by removing butter from the refrigerator about 1 hour before you plan to use it. If it is a particularly hot day, keep an eye on the butter so that it does not oversoften. If it does become too soft, that is, begins looking oily, return it to the refrigerator until it cools off a bit. Room-temperature butter should be slightly cool to the touch but pliable.

TO MAKE CLARIFIED BUTTER

■ Slowly melt at least 1 cup (8 oz/250 g) unsalted butter in a small frying pan over low heat until it is foamy on the surface.

■ Pour the melted butter into a small glass bowl or measuring pitcher and let stand for a minute or two. You should see three distinct layers: milk solids on the bottom, clear, yellow liquid in the middle, and foam on top.

■ Using a tablespoon, carefully remove the foam from the surface. Pour the clear liquid into a clean container, being careful to leave the milk solids behind in the bowl or pitcher. Discard the milk solids. Cover tightly and store in the refrigerator.

TO MAKE BROWN BUTTER

Heat clarified butter in a frying pan over low heat until light brown and fragrant. Immediately remove from the heat.

Oils

Oils come from many sources, including grains, vegetables, nuts, seeds, and even fruits. Choose a mild oil, such as canola, for baking, and store it in a cool, dry, dark place.

Some nut oils—walnut, hazelnut (filbert), almond—are excellent for flavoring baked goods. Nut oils spoil more quickly than other types and should be stored in the refrigerator.

SUGAR AND OTHER SWEETENERS

Sugar, most commonly processed from sugarcane or sugar beets, imparts sweetness, moisture, and flavor to baked goods. It also caramelizes as it cooks, producing a rich brown color. Additionally, it contributes to texture, encourages yeast to grow, helps to aerate ingredients, stabilizes whipped egg whites, and is used for decoration. Bakers rely on a variety of sugars and sweeteners:

GRANULATED SUGAR is the most common sugar used in baking. Its small granules dissolve quickly but still lend enough friction

for aerating ingredients such as butter. It is also used for making syrups and caramel.
SUPERFINE (CASTER) SUGAR is finely ground granulated sugar. It dissolves quickly, making it a good choice for sweetening cold mixtures.
BROWN SUGAR gets its color from molasses, which makes it moist and gives it a rich flavor. It comes in two styles, golden, or light, and the more strongly flavored dark, and is excellent

in earthy baked goods such as gingerbread.
CONFECTIONERS' SUGAR, also known as powdered sugar or icing sugar, is granulated sugar that has been crushed to a powder and mixed with cornstarch (cornflour) to prevent clumping. It dissolves rapidly and is often used to decorate cakes and cookies.
COARSE SUGAR, also known as sparkle sugar or sanding sugar, has large crystals and is typically sprinkled on top of cookies, pastries, and quick breads for texture and decoration.
TURBINADO SUGAR, although often called raw sugar, is actually a partially refined sugar. It has large, light brown crystals. It is typically used as a decoration on baked items and can be used as a replacement for brown sugar.
DEMERARA SUGAR, like its turbinado relative, is partially refined. It is coarse, dry, and brown and is most often used for decorating.
MOLASSES is the sweet, dark syrup that remains after sugar crystals have been extracted from the boiled juice of sugarcane. The resulting liquid, which is pasteurized and filtered, is light molasses. A second boiling yields dark molasses, which is less sweet and more robust. A third boiling yields blackstrap molasses, a strongly flavored, bitter syrup. Molasses is sold both sulfured and unsulfured; the latter has a milder flavor.
HONEY, a natural sweetener, is made when bees extract the syrupy nectar from flowers. Its flavor and color—from off-white to dark brown—depend on the source of the nectar.

SALT

At first glance, you might not think of salt as an essential baking ingredient. But salt, whether used in a savory dish or a sweet dessert, helps enhance and deepen the overall flavors in a dish. Salt is also a key ingredient in yeast breads, working with the yeast and

Left to right, from top left: GRANULATED SUGAR, LIGHT BROWN SUGAR, DARK BROWN SUGAR, CONFECTIONERS' SUGAR, TURBINADO SUGAR, DEMERARA SUGAR.

gluten to produce a better loaf. A few kinds of salt are available. Kosher salt and sea salt are preferred by many professional bakers over the more common iodized table salt. Kosher salt has a medium-coarse grain, and sea salt is sold in various grinds, from fine to coarse. Coarse salts are idea for topping yeast breads such as focaccia and pretzels. The more common iodized table salt contains additives and is usually fortified. It has a "saltier," harsher flavor than kosher salt and sea salt, both of which are processed without iodine.

TO USE A VANILLA BEAN
Vanilla beans impart an incomparable flavor and intoxicating aroma. They are excellent in pastry cream, custards, cakes, and cookies.

■ Using a paring knife, split the vanilla bean lengthwise.

■ Using the tip of the knife, scrape the seeds from the pod. Place the seeds and pod in the item to be flavored.

■ Most of the flavor comes from the pod; if possible, infuse the vanilla in a hot liquid and strain before using.

SPICES, FLAVORINGS, AND EXTRACTS
A whole spectrum of flavors is introduced to baked goods through the addition of spices, flavorings, and extracts. Spices range from cinnamon and nutmeg to allspice and mace. Flavorings include liqueurs, such as Cointreau and framboise, and flower waters, such as orange and rose flower water. Concentrated extracts (essences) cover such flavors as vanilla, almond, peppermint, and citrus.

Freshness is critical. If you do not remember when you purchased the jar of cinnamon on your shelf, or you cannot identify a spice by its aroma, discard it. Whenever possible, use freshly grated whole spices, such as nutmeg, or freshly ground seeds, such as allspice or coriander. If practical, buy spices in bulk in small amounts, and label them with their date of purchase. Use pure extracts, never imitation, and you will be rewarded with richer, more authentic flavors. The flavor of highly aromatic, clear waters distilled from flower petals, such as rose and orange, diminish with age and should be discarded after a year. In general, store spices, extracts, and flavorings in a cool, dark cupboard.

EGGS
Eggs add structure, richness, moisture, and leavening to baked goods. They consist of the yolk, which is high in fat and flavor, and the white, which is a mixture of protein and water and can moisturize or build structure. Eggs come in a variety of sizes and grades. They are graded according to their age and the physical condition of their shell. Most baking recipes, including those in this book, use Grade A large eggs. Store eggs in the refrigerator in their original package away from strong odors and keep only until their sell-by date.

TO SEPARATE AN EGG
Place 2 clean bowls side by side. Crack an egg sharply on its equator on a flat work surface, then hold it upright over one bowl. Gently pull the top half of the shell away from the bottom half, so that the yolk remains in the bottom half. Carefully move the yolk back and forth between the shell halves, allowing the white to fall in the bowl below. Drop the yolk into the second bowl.

For more information about beating whole eggs, whipping egg whites, or beating egg yolks and sugar together, see pages 25–27.

While nowadays the presence of salmonella bacteria in eggs is low, it is a good idea to use caution when working with them. The bacteria can be killed by heating eggs to 140°F (60°C) for 3 minutes or to 160°F (71°C). Children, the elderly, people with compromised immune systems, and pregnant women should avoid eating undercooked or raw eggs. For those concerned about safety, pasteurized eggs can be used as a replacement.

DAIRY

Dairy products add fat, moisture, sugar, richness, and flavor to baked goods. Purchase them fresh and use them by their sell-by date. For information on butter, see the section on Fats (page 17).

Milk

All of the recipes in this book have been tested with whole milk. Its higher fat content makes it a better choice than low-fat or nonfat milk for baking.

Buttermilk

Buttermilk is made by adding live cultures to low-fat or nonfat milk. This thickens the milk and gives it a creamy, tangy flavor. It is an excellent ingredient in baking, adding moisture and flavor, but should not be substituted for regular milk.

Cream

Heavy cream, sometimes labeled heavy whipping cream or whipping cream and also known as double cream, has a high fat content, usually 35 to 40 percent. Nearly all heavy cream sold in the United States is ultra-pasteurized, which helps to extend the life of the cream. It also reduces the cream's natural sweetness and flavor and makes it harder to whip to full volume. Look for pasteurized cream, which is often locally produced, organic, and of better quality.

Sour Cream

Sour cream is cream that has been treated with lactic acid, which thickens it and gives it a slightly sour taste. It is lower in milk fat than heavy cream and, like buttermilk and yogurt, is an excellent addition to many baked items, delivering moisture and flavor.

TO MAKE CRÈME FRAÎCHE

Stir 2 tablespoons buttermilk into 1 cup (8 fl oz/ 250 ml) of heavy (double) cream in a plastic or glass container. Cover with a tight-fitting lid and let stand in a warm spot, shaking once or twice, until thickened, 24 to 48 hours. Refrigerate for up to 3 days.

Crème Fraîche

In France, crème fraîche is made by allowing unpasteurized cream to stand until it sours and thickens naturally. It is similar to, although more deeply flavored than, sour cream. Commercial crème fraîche in the United States, where unpasteurized milk is rare, is made through the addition of cultures. You can make an excellent version of crème fraîche easily at home (see above).

Yogurt

Yogurt is made by adding active cultures to milk, which causes the milk to ferment, thicken, and take on a slightly tangy flavor. It is available in whole milk, low-fat, nonfat, and flavored versions.

Mascarpone Cheese

A thick, soft, and ultracreamy cheese, mascarpone is often used in Italian desserts. It has a consistency reminiscent of sour cream.

CHOCOLATE AND COCOA

Chocolate is made by fermenting, roasting, shelling, and then crushing cocoa beans to produce "nibs," which are about 50 percent cocoa butter. The nibs are then ground and pressed into a paste called chocolate liquor. UNSWEETENED CHOCOLATE is pure chocolate liquor. Depending on the amount of sugar added, the liquor becomes bittersweet (a common European term), semisweet (a common American term, also known as plain chocolate), or sweet chocolate.
MILK CHOCOLATE is a mixture of chocolate liquor, sugar, and milk solids. It has a creamier flavor than bittersweet or semisweet chocolate. WHITE CHOCOLATE, despite its name, is made from cocoa butter, sugar, and milk solids. It is not considered chocolate at all because it lacks the key defining element, chocolate liquor. COCOA POWDER is made by removing most of the cocoa butter from chocolate liquor and then grinding the solid liquor to a powder, which is generally unsweetened. When the powder is treated with an alkali, it is known as Dutch-process cocoa powder and is darker and less acidic that regular cocoa powder. Recipes in this book use Dutch-process cocoa powder.

Always choose the best-quality chocolate you can afford. In general, European chocolate is less sweet and has a deeper, more refined flavor than American-made chocolate. Store chocolate in a cool, dry place away from light and odors. You can wrap it in aluminum foil as a further layer of protection. Never store it in your refrigerator or freezer. If chocolate turns whitish and cloudy, do not despair. Called "bloom," this discoloration occurs when chocolate has been stored in an environment that is humid or too warm, causing the cocoa butter to separate. The bloom will disappear when the chocolate is melted.

TO MELT CHOCOLATE

Place chopped chocolate in the top pan of a double boiler or in a heatproof bowl that will fit snugly in the rim of a heavy saucepan. Fill the bottom pan of the double boiler or the saucepan with water to a depth of about 1 1/2 inches (4 cm) and heat over low heat until it barely simmers. Place the top pan or bowl holding the chocolate over (not touching) the water in the lower pan. Heat, stirring often, until the chocolate melts. Remove the top pan from over the water and set aside to cool slightly before using.

TO MAKE CHOCOLATE SHAVINGS AND CURLS

Using a vegetable peeler, cut thin, flat shavings or long, delicate curls from a large chunk of chocolate that has been warmed slightly, letting the shavings or curls fall onto a piece of parchment (baking) paper or a flat plate.

NUTS

Nuts add their own unique flavors and textures to baked goods. Walnuts, pecans, almonds, hazelnuts (filberts), peanuts, and coconuts are the most common nuts used in baking. Other equally delicious but often forgotten nuts include macadamia nuts, pistachios, cashews, pine nuts, and chestnuts. Different kinds of nuts are often interchangeable in a recipe, creating an entirely new flavor. Buy the freshest nuts you can find, preferably from a market with high turnover, and only what you need, as they go rancid quickly because they are high in oil. Store nuts in an airtight container in the refrigerator or freezer.

To toast nuts and coconut

Most nuts benefit from being toasted before they are used in a recipe. Toasting helps to crisp them, reduce their bitterness, and bring out their flavor. Always toast nuts just before you plan to use them.

Preheat the oven to 325°F (165°C). Spread nuts or shredded dried coconut in a single layer on a half-sheet pan and toast, stirring occasionally for even browning, until fragrant and the color deepens. Watch them carefully, as timing varies depending on the type of nut and the size of the pieces. Most nuts will take between 10 and 20 minutes; shredded coconut will take 5 to 10 minutes.

To skin nuts

To skin hazelnuts, peanuts, or walnuts, first toast the nuts, then pour the still-warm nuts into a kitchen towel and rub the nuts firmly. Using your fingers, peel away any stubborn skins (see photograph on page 222).

To skin almonds or pistachios, place the nuts in a heatproof bowl, pour in boiling water to cover, and let the nuts stand for about 1 minute. Drain, rinse with cold water, and squeeze each nut between two fingers to force it from its skin.

To grind nuts

Nuts are easily ground in a food processor, especially when grinding a large amount. Be careful not to overprocess them, however, or they will turn to a paste. For best results, pulse the machine, rather than run it continuously, and combine the nuts with a small amount of the sugar called for in the recipe. The sugar crystals keep the nutmeats separate. Use a hand-cranked rotary nut mill or a nut grinder for a more even, "drier" grind, especially when replacing wheat flour with nut flour.

FRESH FRUITS

Purchase fruits with freshness and seasonality in mind. Some fruits, such as apples, are available throughout the year because varieties come into season as others go out or because imported fruits fill store bins. Most fruits, however, have limited growing seasons.

Try to buy fruits that are in season, locally grown, and, preferably, organic. You will be rewarded with succulent, juicy, fragrant fruits that are full of flavor and sweetness.

Apples and Pears

Apples and pears, each with scores of varieties, are two of the baker's favorite fruits. Among the best baking apples are Rome Beauty, Baldwin, Gravenstein, Pink Lady, Northern Spy, Winesap, Granny Smith, Royal Gala, and McIntosh. Bartlett (Williams), Anjou, and Bosc are among the best pears for baking. Choose fragrant fruits that are unblemished. Pears should yield slightly to the touch.

Berries

Plump, juicy berries, such as raspberries, blackberries, blueberries, boysenberries, cranberries, strawberries, and more, flourish in summer. When choosing berries, look for fresh, shiny fruits that are dry and free of mold. Quickly rinse berries just before using them. If left in water, they become mushy and will begin to disintegrate.

Citrus

Lemons, limes, oranges, and grapefruits are the primary citrus fruits for baking. Within these broad groups are many more specialized varieties, such as Meyer lemons, Key limes, white grapefruit, and blood oranges. Most parts of the fruits—juice, peel, zest, flesh—are used, but avoid using the bitter white pith just below the fragrant layer of peel. Choose heavy fruits with shiny skins. If a recipe calls for citrus juice, always use freshly squeezed.

Stone Fruits

This family of fruit loves hot summer days. Stone fruits have a single center pit, known as the stone, and include peaches, nectarines, plums, cherries, and apricots. They can be either freestone, meaning the fruit slips easily away from the stone, or cling, meaning the fruit is firmly attached to the pit. The best stone fruits are juicy, fragrant, and sweet. Choose heavy, unblemished fruits that yield slightly to the touch.

SEASONAL FRUITS

The following seasonal categories list fruits according to the season(s) in which they are available. Some are available only in the early or late half of a season, and some year-round.

Year-round

Apples (best late summer and fall), bananas, grapefruits, lemons (best fall to spring), limes (best in spring), oranges (best fall to spring), pineapples (best spring to summer)

TO PEEL AND CORE A PINEAPPLE

■ Using a long, sharp knife, and laying the pineapple on its side, cut off the crown of leaves and cut a slice off the bottom. Stand the pineapple upright and cut off the peel using long, steady strokes. Small, brown "eyes" will remain. (If you cut deeply enough to remove them, you will lose too much flesh.) Using the tip of the knife or a vegetable peeler, cut away the "eyes."

■ Lay the pineapple on its side and cut it crosswise into slices.

■ Using a small cookie or biscuit cutter or a knife, cut out the core from each slice.

Spring

Apricots (available in late spring), blueberries, cherries (available in late spring), plums (available in late spring), raspberries (available in late spring), rhubarb (field rhubarb is not available until late spring), strawberries, tangerines

Summer

Apricots, blueberries, cherries (available in early summer), figs, grapes (available in late summer), mangoes, melons, nectarines (white and yellow), papayas, peaches (white and yellow), pears (some varieties are available in late summer), plums, rhubarb

Fall

Cranberries, figs (available in early fall), grapes, kiwifruits, mangoes (available in early fall), papayas, pears, persimmons, tangerines

Winter

Cranberries, dates, kiwifruits, pears, tangerines

DRIED FRUITS

Dried fruits, such as raisins, currants, cherries, cranberries, and figs, are excellent sources of texture and flavor. Look for moist fruits that feel soft when pressed. To ensure freshness, purchase only as much as you need. Seek out unsulfured, organic fruits for better flavor. Store dried fruits in an airtight container at room temperature for up to 1 month, or in the refrigerator for up to 3 months.

To plump dried fruits

Plumping dried fruits rehydrates and softens them. Pour hot (not boiling) water over the fruits and let them stand until plump, 5 to 20 minutes. The timing depends on the type and size of the fruit and how dry it is. Keep an eye on the fruits so they do not get soggy.

TO ZEST A CITRUS

Holding the cleaned fruit in the palm of one hand, pull the zester from one end of the fruit to the other, removing only the colored portion in fine strips. (The white pith beneath it is bitter.) Use the strips as they are, or chop or mince as directed in the recipe. You can also grate the zest using the fine rasps on a box grater or using a Microplane grater. To form wider strips of zest, pull a vegetable peeler along the contour of the fruit. Use the strips as they are, or finely slice, chop, or mince as directed in the recipe.

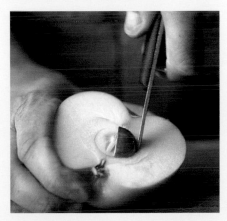

TO CORE APPLES AND PEARS

- If the recipe calls for peeled fruit, using a vegetable peeler, peel the fruit.
- Cut the fruit in half through the stem.
- Using a melon baller, remove the core.
- Using a paring knife, cut out the stem.

TO HULL A STRAWBERRY

Insert a paring knife at a slight angle into the stem end of the berry. Rotate the knife until the stem is free, then lift out the stem and core. You can also use a strawberry huller.

TO PEEL AND PIT A PEACH

Bring a saucepan three-fourths full of water to a boil. Meanwhile, cut a small, shallow X in the blossom end of the peach. Drop the fruit into the boiling water and leave for 30 seconds. Remove the peach with a slotted spoon. When cool enough to handle, starting at the X, peel the skin from the fruit.

Starting at the stem end, use a small, sharp knife to cut the fruit in half lengthwise, cutting around the large, central pit. Grasping each half with a hand, rotate the halves in opposite directions and pull apart. Pluck out the pit with your fingers, use the knife to dislodge it, or cut slices away from the pit.

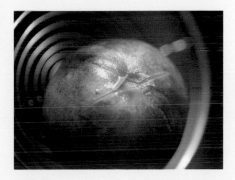

Measuring and Weighing

Much of baking depends on precisely measured ingredients, and problems are common if measurements are faulty. A good grasp of basic measuring techniques is essential.

■ Dry ingredients are measured in cups and spoons specifically designed for the purpose. They are typically metal or plastic and have straight rims. There are two basic methods for measuring. The preferred method is called the spoon-and-sweep method. Use a spoon or scoop to fill the cup or spoon to overflowing, then level it off with the back of a kitchen knife. The second method is the scoop-and-level method. Dip the cup or spoon into the dry ingredient to scoop it up, then level it off with the back of a kitchen knife. Pick one method and use it consistently.

■ Always measure liquid ingredients in a clear glass or plastic measuring pitcher. Place the pitcher on a flat work surface and pour the liquid into the pitcher until it reaches the desired measurement marking on the pitcher. Double check that it lines up perfectly by reading it at eye level.

■ Measure sticky liquid ingredients, such as honey, in a glass measuring pitcher lightly greased with butter or oil. It will glide out easily.

■ The easiest way to measure butter is by using the markings on the butter wrappers. Simply cut off the amount you want to use. You can also measure butter by weighing it (see the Weights and Equivalents chart shown below), or, if the butter is slightly softened, by packing it into a measuring cup or spoon.

■ While most home cooks measure their ingredients in cups, most professional bakers weigh their ingredients. Weighing is more accurate, and less time-consuming if you are working with large amounts. All recipes in this book have been tested with cup measurements; however, you can weigh ingredients by using the Weights and Equivalents chart shown below.

A NOTE ABOUT OVENS

All recipes in this book were tested in conventional gas or electric ovens. These are also known as thermal ovens. Gas ovens use radiant heat from gas flames, and electric ovens use electric elements to cook foods with dry heat. Both types of ovens are mostly interchangeable and can bake equally well, as long as they are of equal quality.

In any oven, hot spots can occur, and large pans and baking sheets can block heat and create noticeable variances in temperature between racks, so be sure to check the food during baking and rotate your pans as needed for even baking.

An oven thermometer is a good idea to make sure that your oven is heating correctly, especially for older models. If not, have a technician adjust the oven thermostat.

Another type of oven is the convection oven, which has a fan that blows heated air throughout the oven. Food cooks much more quickly and evenly in these ovens, so most recipes will have to be adjusted accordingly.

WEIGHTS AND EQUIVALENTS

All-Purpose (Plain) Flour, or Bread Flour, Unsifted		Granulated Sugar		Butter	
1/4 cup	1 1/2 oz/45 g	2 tablespoons	1 oz/30 g	1 tablespoon	1/2 oz/15 g
1/3 cup	2 oz/60 g	3 tablespoons	1 1/2 oz/45 g	2 tablespoons	1 oz/30 g
1/2 cup	2 1/2 oz/75 g	1/4 cup	2 oz/60 g	3 tablespoons	1 1/2 oz/45 g
1 cup	5 oz/155 g	1/3 cup	3 oz/90 g	1/4 cup (4 tablespoons)	2 oz/60 g
		1/2 cup	4 oz/125 g	5 tablespoons	2 1/2 oz/75 g
		1 cup	8 oz/250 g	1/3 cup (6 tablespoons)	3 oz/90 g
All-Purpose (Plain) Flour, Sifted, or Cake Flour, Unsifted		**Brown Sugar, Firmly Packed**		1/2 cup (8 tablespoons)	4 oz/125 g
1/4 cup	1 oz/30 g	1/4 cup	2 oz/60 g	1 cup	8 oz/250 g
1/3 cup	1 1/2 oz/45 g	1/3 cup	2 1/2 oz/75 g	2 cups	1 lb/500 g
1/2 cup	2 oz/60 g	1/2 cup	3 1/2 oz/105 g		
1 cup	4 oz/125 g	1 cup	7 oz/220 g		

Basic Techniques

Here are some general techniques regularly used in baking: preparing pans, creaming butter and sugar, folding ingredients, and whipping whole eggs, egg yolks, egg whites, and cream. Some are simple, and others take a little practice. The easy-to-follow steps will help you master all of them.

TO PREPARE PANS

To prepare a pan for baking so that your baked item does not stick, you can butter, flour, and/or line a pan with parchment (baking) paper.

1 To butter a pan, place a small amount of soft butter on a piece of waxed paper and spread the butter over the bottom and sides of the pan.

2 To flour a pan, add 2 tablespoons flour to the buttered pan and tilt and shake the pan so the flour adheres to the butter. Turn the pan over, tap it on a work surface, and discard the extra flour.

3 To line a pan with parchment, cut a piece of parchment to fit (see page 10). Or grease the pan with butter, then press parchment cut to fit into the bottom of the pan.

TO CREAM BUTTER AND SUGAR

Creaming together butter and sugar creates a light, airy mixture that helps leaven the baked item and creates a more tender texture. The butter should be at cool room temperature: too cold and it is difficult to cream and aerate; too warm and the mixture will be dense and greasy. An electric mixer is easiest, but a wooden spoon can be used.

Put the butter and sugar in a bowl. With the mixer on medium speed, or using firm strokes with the spoon, cream the butter and sugar. The mixture should be pale yellow and fluffy, and the sugar should be dissolved. Use a rubber spatula to scrape down the bowl a few times when mixing.

TO BEAT EGGS UNTIL FOAMY

In a sturdy bowl, using a balloon whisk, beat the whole eggs until they appear foamy and aerated.

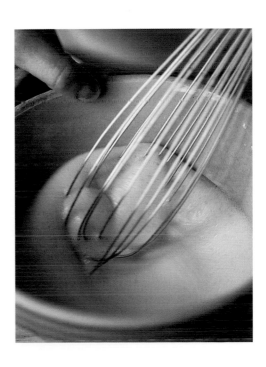

TO CREAM YOLKS AND SUGAR

Creaming together egg yolks and sugar, like creaming butter and sugar, is a way to add air to your baked item. Sugar can "burn" your egg yolks, forming granular lumps, so never add sugar to egg yolks until just before you are ready to use the creamed mixture.

1 In a sturdy bowl, using a regular or balloon whisk, a handheld mixer, or a stand mixer fitted with the whip attachment, whip together the egg yolks and sugar vigorously by hand or on medium-high speed.

2 Continue whipping until the mixture is lighter in color. It is ready when you lift a bit of the mixture with the whisk and it falls back into bowl, forming a ribbon that slowly dissolves on the surface.

TO FOLD INGREDIENTS

Folding a light, aerated mixture, such as whipped egg whites, into a heavier batter is easy with some practice. Use a gentle hand and as few strokes as possible, so as not to deflate the air bubbles you have worked to achieve.

1 Using a large rubber spatula, gently stir in one-fourth of the lighter mixture. This lightens the mixture.

2 Add the rest of the lighter mixture, piling it on top of the batter.

3 Using the spatula, slice down through the center of the mixture to the bottom of the bowl. Then pull the spatula toward the edge of the bowl and, keeping the flat side against the bottom and side of the bowl, pull it up the side and over the top of the lighter mixture, bringing some of the heavier batter with it. Rotate the bowl a quarter turn and repeat. Continue folding in this manner just until the lighter mixture is incorporated into the batter. Do not overfold or you will deflate it. A little streaking is fine.

TO WHIP CREAM

 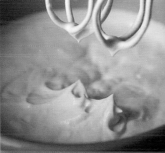 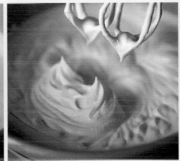 

Soft peak Medium peak Stiff peak Overwhipped and grainy

You will need to whip cream to soft peaks, medium peaks, or stiff peaks, depending on how you will be using it. Look for heavy (double) cream that is not ultrapasteurized, as it is easier to whip to good volume. Cream is also easily overwhipped, turning grainy first and then into butter. Whip cream to soft to medium peaks for serving alongside a dessert. Stiff peaks are usually called for if folding the cream into a heavier mixture. A balloon whisk, a handheld mixer, or a stand mixer fitted with the whip attachment can be used. If using a mixer, start at low speed, gradually increasing the speed to medium-high. For the best results, use a well-chilled bowl and whisk, beaters, or whip.

TO WHIP EGG WHITES

  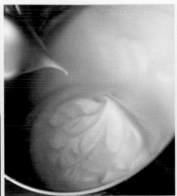 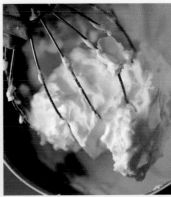

Soft peak Medium peak Stiff peak Overwhipped and grainy

Whipping egg whites can be tricky, unless you follow a few simple rules. Use a clean, large bowl. Any fat or grease, such as butter or even a speck of egg yolk, will impede the fluffiness that you are trying to achieve. Always use room-temperature egg whites. If your eggs are cold, you can still separate them, and then place the bowl of egg whites into a larger bowl filled with hot water to warm them briefly before beating. An unlined copper bowl is the best type to use, but a stainless-steel bowl is a good substitute. If you are adding sugar to the egg whites, start adding it very slowly once the whites are foamy. Use a balloon whisk, a handheld mixer, or a stand mixer fitted with the whip attachment to whip the egg whites. If using a mixer, start on medium speed, increasing the speed to medium-high as the whites thicken. Be careful not to overwhip the egg whites, as they can quickly become grainy and may start to separate.

Yeast Breads

About Yeast Breads

It is hard to think of a more tactile, physical aspect of baking than making bread. Many home cooks feel that making yeast bread is intimidating. But the fearless soon discover that nothing is more rewarding than bread baking in your oven, filling your home with its irresistible aroma.

From brioche to baguette to bagel, yeast breads call for the most basic of ingredients—flour, yeast, salt, and water—yet they boast flavors that range from delicate to robust.

Lean breads, so-named because they call for all-purpose (plain) or bread flour and little or no fat, include baguettes and *ciabatta*. Whole-grain breads, earthy, sturdy, and full flavored, range from honey–whole wheat to traditional pumpernickel to rye. Sourdough-style breads, both *pain au levain* and old-fashioned sourdough, get their character from a fermented starter. Rich breads, dependent on substantial measures of butter or eggs, or a combination, include the crown-topped brioche and the braided challah. Rolls, which can accompany a bowl of soup or a standing rib roast, embrace classic pull-apart dinner rolls and tender potato-buttermilk rolls. And for breakfast, there are delicious cinnamon rolls and chewy bagels.

Bread making involves a series of steps that determines both the structure and flavor of the finished product. Making a sponge, which contributes to the flavor intensity of the baked loaf, is often the first step. The initial mix, during which the rest of the flour is added to the sponge and the resulting mass is kneaded by hand or with a stand mixer, incorporates the dry and liquid ingredients and helps develop the gluten that gives bread its crumb structure and chewiness.

The look of properly kneaded dough varies from bread to bread. One reliable check is the windowpane test, also known as "pulling a gluten window." To do this, pull a small piece of dough until it forms a translucent window. If the dough remains intact as you pull the window, your kneading is complete (page 33).

The first rise happens at room temperature or, for some breads, overnight in the refrigerator. The goal is for the dough to expand, usually to double its bulk, and for flavors to begin to develop. The risen dough is then punched down, evening out the gas bubbles that make up the finished crumb structure, and shaped according to the recipe. Proofing, the rise that the shaped loaf undergoes, varies greatly in duration depending on the individual recipe, the temperature of your kitchen, and the climate.

Many recipes call for slashing the top of the loaf. These slits have a decorative appeal, increase the crust area, and help steam escape as the bread bakes. Some also call for misting the loaves with water, which promotes the formation of a crisp, hard crust during baking.

Baking in a thoroughly heated oven immediately after slashing and misting produces the best results. The dough's initial contact with the hot oven, known as oven spring, creates a jolt of heat that helps deliver a high-rising, well-formed finished loaf.

Most loaf breads are done when they are well browned and emit a hollow sound if tapped on the bottom. Be sure to let your bread brown thoroughly, as browning is what gives the crust its incomparable flavor.

Warm, freshly baked bread is delicious, but cooling a loaf fully before cutting it is essential for trouble-free slicing and the best flavor.

TROUBLESHOOTING YEAST BREADS

What happened	Why it happened
Dough is rising too fast.	Kitchen is too warm; transfer dough to cooler location.
Dough is rising too slowly or is not rising.	Kitchen is too cool, or water in which yeast was proofed was too warm or too cool; transfer dough to warmer location. Or, yeast is too old.
Bread is browning too quickly.	Oven is too hot; cover loosely with aluminum foil and continue baking.
Bread lacks flavor or tastes too yeasty.	Dough was proofed too long.
Bread is dense and too moist.	Dough was not proofed long enough.
Bread looks slack.	Dough was overproofed, or the oven was insufficiently heated.

Stages of Bread Making

This section will take you, step by step, through the process of making and then baking bread, including how to mix and knead the dough; how the dough should look, feel, and smell at each stage; and how to know when your prized loaf is ready to come out of the oven.

TO MAKE A SPONGE

A sponge is typically a mixture of flour, liquid, and commercial yeast or a natural starter, such as sourdough starter, that is allowed to stand for anywhere from a few hours to overnight before being mixed with the balance of the dough ingredients. During this standing time, fermentation is initiated, causing the yeast to begin to multiply and lactic and acetic acids to grow. This early action contributes a deeper flavor and better texture to the finished loaf. Many artisan breads, such as baguettes, *coccodrillo*, and *ciabatta*, benefit from the addition of a sponge.

In a large glass or ceramic bowl, dissolve the yeast in a warm liquid (about 105°–115°F/ 40°–46°C) such as water or milk. Using a wooden spoon, stir in the flour and any additional ingredients indicated in the recipe, mixing until smooth. Cover the bowl with plastic wrap and let stand for at least 3 hours at cool room temperature or for up to overnight in the refrigerator. When the sponge is ready, it will have risen, be bubbly, and have a slightly sour or fermented smell. If the sponge has been refrigerated, bring it to room temperature for 1 hour before finishing the dough.

TO MIX BY HAND

If you are new to baking, start by mixing your dough by hand. It allows you more control and gives you a chance to feel the dough as it changes through the stages of development.

1 Add the flour(s) and other ingredients called for in the recipe to the sponge, if using, or combine the dough ingredients as directed in the recipe. Stir with a wooden spoon or your hands until a rough ball forms. Mix in the salt last; it can kill the yeast if it comes into contact.

2 Using your hand (or a plastic pastry scraper if the dough is wet or sticky), scrape the dough out of the bowl onto a floured surface. The dough should be somewhat shaggy, but hold together in a rough ball. Keep in mind that all doughs are different—some are wetter, some are stickier, some are drier—and the dough you are making may look different than what is shown here. Invert the bowl over the dough and let it rest 10 to 15 minutes before kneading.

TO KNEAD BY HAND

Kneading is crucial to developing the structure of yeast dough. It combines ingredients thoroughly, building gluten at the same time.

1 Remove the bowl covering the dough, and press any loose dough pieces into the mass. Using the heel of one or both hands, push the dough away from you.

2 Pull back the far end of the dough, folding it over on itself. Rotate the dough a quarter turn and repeat the steps, pressing the dough, folding over, and turning. It should become a fluid motion. As you are kneading, add small amounts of flour to prevent the dough from become sticky, allowing the flour to be absorbed into the dough before adding more. Use a bench scraper to lift the dough cleanly from the floured surface. Knead until the dough is smooth and elastic, 8–12 minutes. Use a windowpane test to make sure the dough is fully kneaded (below).

TO MIX AND KNEAD IN A MIXER

A stand mixer fitted with the dough hook mixes and kneads dough faster than by hand, but you miss the chance to feel the dough as it develops.

1 If your recipe calls for a sponge, transfer it to the 5-qt (5-l) bowl of a stand mixer and add the other ingredients called for in the recipe, or combine the dough ingredients in the bowl as directed in the recipe. Place the bowl on the mixer, attach the dough hook, and knead on low speed, stopping the mixer and scraping down the bowl and the hook occasionally with a plastic pastry scraper. The dough is ready when it is smooth and elastic, 5 to 10 minutes.

2 To make sure the dough is fully kneaded, do a windowpane test. Take a piece of dough and, grasping an edge with each hand, gently pull the dough to create a sheer sheet. If the dough looks shaggy and tears, it is not ready. If the dough looks smooth, holds together, and is thin enough to see light through, it is ready.

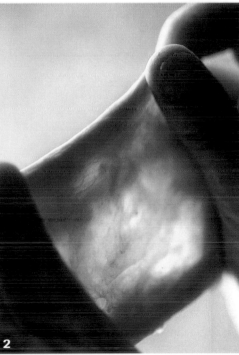

THE FIRST RISE

Once the dough is kneaded, it is ready for its first rise, during which the yeast ferments, giving off carbon dioxide. This action causes the gluten strands to expand and the dough to rise.

1 Form the kneaded dough into a loose ball and place it in a lightly oiled bowl. Turn the ball to coat its surface with oil. Cover the bowl with plastic wrap, and let the dough rise in a warm, draft-free spot until it doubles in bulk. This can take 1 to 2 hours or more, depending on the temperature of the finished dough and the environment in which it is left to rise.

2 The dough is ready if it looks puffy and feels soft when gently poked with a finger. The indentation should remain, but not deflate the mass of dough. If the finger mark fills back in, the dough is not ready; re-cover and test again in 15 minutes.

TO PUNCH DOWN, DIVIDE, AND SHAPE THE DOUGH

Some of the gases that have built up in the dough during rising must be released to ensure an even texture in the finished loaf. This is called "punching down" the dough, an action that also prevents the elastic strands from overstretching and breaking. The dough is then divided, if necessary, and shaped.

1 To punch down the dough, turn the dough out onto a lightly floured work surface and gently press down on it.

2 If a recipe calls for dividing the dough into portions, use a large, sharp knife or bench scraper to cut it. Then shape the dough as directed in the recipe and place on a sheet pan or in a loaf pan.

THE SECOND RISE

Most recipes call for the dough to double in size again during the second rise, or proofing stage. The process can take anywhere from 30 minutes to 3 hours, depending on the conditions of the dough (usually determined by whether commercial yeast or a natural starter has been used) and the temperature of the room (the warmer the conditions, the faster the rise). The longer the dough rises, the more flavor it will develop. If you need to slow down the rising time, place the dough in the refrigerator. Also, to avoid overproofing, remember to preheat your oven at least 15 minutes before the proofing period is completed.

1 Once you have shaped the loaf and placed it on the sheet pan or in the loaf pan, cover the dough loosely with plastic wrap or a damp kitchen towel, and place in a warm spot to proof.

2 When the dough is ready it will be smooth and springy to the touch. To test, poke it with your finger. The indentation should remain, springing back only slightly. If it collapses on itself, it is overproofed. If it does not spring back, it is underproofed.

If the dough is underproofed, re-cover it and check it again in 15 minutes. If the dough is overproofed, you can save it by punching it down, reshaping it, and allowing it to proof again. Never try to bake overproofed dough, or you will end up with a flat, leaden loaf.

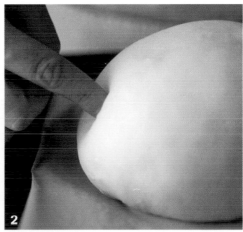

TO SLASH THE DOUGH

Many yeast breads benefit from slashing, or making shallow cuts in the top of a proofed loaf. This allows the bread to open up and expand in the oven. It also gives you the opportunity to leave your own creative mark on the loaf.

Use a sharp serrated knife (pictured); a single-edged razor blade; or, if you have access to one, a baker's *lame*. The last is a double-edged razor blade on a long, thin handle.

Do not be timid about slashing. If you go a little deeper and make your slashes slightly longer, the result will be more beautiful than if you just skim the surface of the dough.

TO SLASH A BAGUETTE

Hold the blade at a shallow (45-degree) angle so that you slit under the surface of the dough, rather than cut too deeply. Starting at the end of the loaf farthest away from you, make 4 or 5 slits the length of the baguette. Each slash should be at a fairly sharp angle, moving from the upper right side down toward the left side of the loaf if you are right-handed, and from the upper left side down toward the right side of the loaf if you are left-handed. Make sure the slashes extend all the way from one side of the loaf to the other.

TO SLASH A BÂTARD OR OVAL LOAF

Hold the blade at a shallow (45-degree) angle so that you slit under the surface of the dough, rather than cut too deeply. Starting at the end of the loaf farthest away from you, make 3 or 4 slits the length of the bâtard. Each slash should be at a fairly sharp angle, moving from the upper right side down toward the left side of the loaf if you are right-handed, and from the upper left side down toward the right side of the loaf if you are left-handed. Make sure the slashes extend all the way from one side of the loaf to the other.

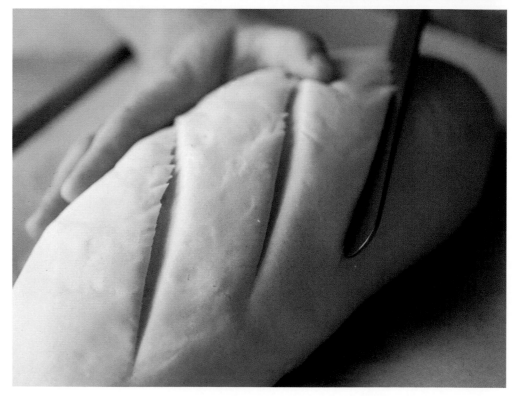

TO SLASH A ROUND LOAF

There are numerous ways to slash a round loaf. Here are three common patterns. Once you have mastered these designs, have fun and create your own.

1 To slash a crescent, hold the blade at a shallow (45-degree) angle so that you slit under the surface of the dough, rather than cut too deeply. Starting at the side of the loaf farthest away from you, slash a slit along the curve of the loaf on the right or the left side, positioning the cut just off-center.

2 To slash a square "top hat," hold the blade at a deep (60-degree) angle so that you slit into and under the surface of the dough. Starting on the right or left side of the round about halfway up the side of the loaf, slash a straight slit from one side of the round to the other. Repeat on each side of the loaf, forming a square.

3 To slash a crisscross, hold the blade straight over the center of the loaf. Starting at the far left side of the loaf, slash a straight slit across the center of the round. Turn the pan so the slit is vertical to you, and slash a perpendicular slit from one side of the loaf to the other.

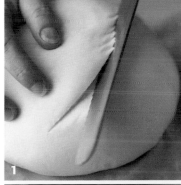

TO MIST THE LOAF

If a recipe calls for it, once you have slashed the loaf, immediately mist it with a fine but generous spray of water using a clean spray bottle. The steam created from misting encourages a better rise in the oven (called "oven spring") and also helps set the crust, brown the bread, and ensure a glossy finish.

TO BAKE THE LOAF

Make sure that your oven is fully preheated, usually a minimum of 15 minutes, before sliding the bread in to bake. Unless the recipe specifies otherwise, place the pan on the center rack for even baking and good heat circulation. If you are using more than one sheet pan to hold the loaves, bake the pans one at a time.

TO TEST FOR DONENESS

There are three ways to judge if your bread is ready: Does it smell like bread? Does it look like bread; that is, has it browned? Does it sound like bread? This last question can be answered by thumping the bottom or top of the baked loaf (see the photograph to the right). If it emits a good hollow sound, it is done.

TO COOL BAKED BREAD

As soon as the bread has finished baking, place it on a cooling rack. The rack allows air to circulate around the loaf, preventing steam from softening the bottom. Make sure the bread is fully cooled before cutting into it. This ensures that the steam created during baking remains inside the loaf and keeps the bread moist.

Olive Bread

Flavorful olives stud this bread, making it moist and rich tasting. The bread is a great accompaniment to a simple green salad. You can change the character of the loaf by using different types of olives, such as Gaeta, or by using a mixture of olives.

BY HAND: In a large bowl, dissolve the yeast in the warm water and let stand until foamy, about 5 minutes. Add the oil, the flours, and the salt and stir in with your hand or a wooden spoon until a rough ball forms. Using a plastic pastry scraper, scrape the dough out of the bowl onto a lightly floured work surface. Knead until it is smooth and elastic, dusting the work surface with flour to keep it from sticking, 5–7 minutes.

BY STAND MIXER: In the 5-qt (5-l) bowl of a stand mixer, dissolve the yeast in the warm water and let stand until foamy, about 5 minutes. Add the oil, the flours, and the salt. Place the bowl on the mixer, attach the dough hook, and knead on low speed. Add a little flour as needed for the dough to come away from the sides of the bowl after a few minutes. Knead until the dough is smooth and elastic, 5–7 minutes. Remove the dough from the bowl.

Sprinkle the olives over the top of the dough and knead them into the dough briefly and gently. Form the dough into a ball and transfer it to a lightly oiled bowl. Cover the bowl with a damp kitchen towel and leave the dough to rise in a warm, draft-free spot until it doubles in bulk, 1–1 1/2 hours.

Punch down the dough and turn it out onto a lightly floured work surface. Knead it briefly and gently to disperse the olives evenly. Using a sharp knife or a bench scraper, cut it in half. Cover with a kitchen towel and let rest for 5 minutes before shaping. Line a half-sheet pan or rimless baking sheet with parchment (baking) paper. Shape each half of the dough into a tight round loaf by rotating the bread in a circular motion on the work surface between your hands. If any olives fall out while shaping, just tuck them back into the underside of the round. Put the loaves on the prepared pan, spacing them generously apart. Cover the loaves loosely with a kitchen towel and let them rise in a warm, draft-free spot until they double in size, 30–40 minutes.

Position a rack in the lower third of the oven, and preheat to 450°F (230°C). Lightly dust the tops of the loaves with flour. Using a serrated knife, slash a half crescent from one end of the loaf to the other, just off-center (page 37). Put the pans into the oven and reduce the heat to 425°F (220°C). Bake the breads until they are golden brown and sound hollow when tapped on the bottom, 35–40 minutes. Transfer to wire racks and let cool for at least 45 minutes.

VARIATIONS

Walnut Bread
Use walnut oil instead of olive oil, and substitute 2 cups (8 oz/250 g) walnut pieces, toasted (page 21), for the olives.

Hazelnut-Fig Bread
Use hazelnut oil instead of olive oil. Plump 1 cup (5 oz/155 g) chopped dried figs in hot water (page 23). Substitute 1 cup (5 oz/155 g) skinned, toasted hazelnut (filbert) pieces (page 21), for the olives. Drain the figs and add them when working the nuts into the dough.

Pine Nut–Asiago Bread
Substitute 1 cup (5 oz/155 g) pine nuts, toasted (page 21), and 1 cup (4 oz/125 g) coarsely shredded Asiago cheese for the olives.

Rosemary-Feta Olive Bread
Add 2 teaspoons finely chopped fresh rosemary and 2 teaspoons coarsely ground pepper with the salt. Reduce the olives to 1 cup (5 oz/155 g) and chop them finer. Add 1 cup (5 oz/155 g) crumbled feta cheese to the dough with the olives.

3 packages (7 1/2 teaspoons) active dry yeast

2 cups (16 fl oz/500 ml) warm water (105°–115°F/ 40°–46°C)

2/3 cup (5 fl oz/160 ml) extra-virgin olive oil

2 cups (10 oz/315 g) bread flour

4 cups (1 1/4 lb/625 g) all-purpose (plain) flour, plus extra for kneading and dusting the loaves

1 tablespoon sea salt

2 cups (10 oz/315 g) Kalamata olives, pitted and coarsely chopped

Baguettes

For the sponge

1 package (2¹/₂ teaspoons) active dry yeast

1¹/₂ cups (12 fl oz/375 ml) warm water (105°–115°F/ 40°–46°C)

1 teaspoon malt syrup or sugar

2 cups (10 oz/315 g) bread flour

For the dough

2 cups (10 oz/315 g) bread flour, plus extra for kneading

1¹/₂ teaspoons sea salt

¹/₄ cup (1¹/₄ oz/40 g) cornmeal or semolina flour

To make the sponge, in a large bowl, dissolve the yeast in the warm water, then add the malt syrup. Let stand until foamy, about 5 minutes. Using a wooden spoon, stir in the flour until the mixture is smooth. Cover the bowl with plastic wrap and let stand for at least 3 hours at cool room temperature or for up to overnight in the refrigerator. If refrigerated, remove from the refrigerator and let warm to room temperature for 1 hour before finishing the dough.

BY HAND: To make the dough, add the flour and salt to the sponge and stir with your hand or a wooden spoon until a rough mass forms. Using a plastic pastry scraper, scrape the dough out of the bowl onto a floured work surface. Invert the bowl over the dough and let the dough rest for 10–15 minutes. Uncover the dough and knead it until it is smooth and elastic, dusting the work surface with flour to keep it from sticking, 5–7 minutes.

BY STAND MIXER: To make the dough, transfer the sponge to the 5-qt (5-l) bowl of a stand mixer. Add the flour and salt. Place the bowl on the mixer, attach the dough hook, and knead on low speed. Add a little more flour as needed for the dough to come away from the sides of the bowl after a few minutes of kneading. Knead until the dough is smooth and elastic, 5–7 minutes. Periodically stop the mixer and scrape down the bowl and the dough hook. Remove the dough from the bowl.

Form the dough into a ball, transfer it to a lightly oiled bowl, and cover the bowl with plastic wrap. Let the dough rise in a warm, draft-free spot until it doubles in bulk, 1¹/₂–2 hours. The dough will look puffy and feel soft when poked gently.

Punch down the dough. Re-cover and let rise again until doubled in bulk, 30–45 minutes.

Turn the dough out onto the work surface and cut it into thirds with a sharp knife or a bench scraper. Shape each third into a loose, round ball. Cover them with a kitchen towel and let rest for 5 minutes before shaping.

Lightly dust a half-sheet pan or rimless baking sheet with the cornmeal.

Working with 1 ball of dough at a time, pick up the ball and slap it hard onto a clean work surface. If the dough feels dry, spritz it with a little water from a mister. Evenly flatten the dough ball with the heel of your hand. Roll the top third down onto itself and seal it by pushing it gently with the heel of your hand.

With so few ingredients, this bread needs lots of time to develop flavor through the magic of fermentation. Spread the rising time out over 2 days, and the resulting deep taste will be worth the wait. The sourdough variation intensifies the flavor even more. A wedge of cheese, some good wine, and a homemade baguette, and your picnic is made.

Continue rolling and sealing the dough until you have an oval loaf. Using your palms, and starting in the center and working outward, elongate the loaf by rolling it gently against the work surface with even pressure until it is as long as as the prepared pan.

Place the loaves on the prepared pan, cover them loosely with a kitchen towel, and let them rise in a warm, draft-free spot until doubled in size, 30–40 minutes. The loaves should feel light and spongy when gently squeezed.

Position a rack in the lower third of the oven, and preheat to 500°F (260°C). Using a single-edged razor blade or a sharp serrated knife, make 4 or 5 slashes, each at a slight angle, down the length of each baguette (page 36). Quickly mist the loaves generously with water.

Immediately put the pan into the oven and reduce the heat to 450°F (230°C). Bake the breads until they are golden brown and sound hollow when tapped on the bottom, 20–25 minutes. Rotate the pan halfway through baking if the loaves are not baking evenly. Let the loaves cool on a wire rack for 20 minutes before serving. These breads are best eaten fresh.

VARIATION

Sourdough Baguettes
Substitute 1/2 cup (4 oz/125 g) sourdough starter (page 54) for the yeast in the sponge. Cover the bowl with plastic wrap and let the sponge stand at room temperature overnight. When making the dough, add 1 1/4 teaspoons active dry yeast with the flour.

Coccodrillo

For the sponge

1 package (2¹/₂ teaspoons) active dry yeast

³/₄ cup (6 fl oz/180 ml) dark beer, at room temperature

3 cups (24 fl oz/750 ml) cool water (78°F/26°C)

1 cup (5 oz/155 g) semolina flour

2¹/₂ cups (12¹/₂ oz/390 g) all-purpose (plain) flour

For the dough

3 cups (15 oz/470 g) all-purpose (plain) flour

1 cup (5 oz/155 g) semolina or whole-wheat (wholemeal) flour

1 tablespoon sea salt

About 1¹/₂ cups (7¹/₂ oz/ 235 g) all-purpose (plain) flour for the work surface and pan

To make the sponge, in a large bowl, combine the yeast, beer, water, and the semolina and all-purpose flours and whisk until well combined. Cover the bowl with plastic wrap and let stand overnight at room temperature.

BY HAND: To make the dough, add the all-purpose and semolina flours and the salt to the sponge and stir with your hand or a wooden spoon until the mixture comes together in a shaggy mass. Using a plastic pastry scraper, scrape the dough out of the bowl onto a floured surface. Knead until it is smooth and elastic, dusting the work surface with only enough flour to keep the dough from sticking, 5–7 minutes. The dough will be soft.

BY STAND MIXER: To make the dough, transfer the sponge to the 5-qt (5-l) bowl of a stand mixer. Add the all-purpose and semolina flours and the salt. Place the bowl on the mixer, attach the dough hook, and knead on low speed. Add a little more flour as needed for the dough to come away from the sides of the bowl after a few minutes of kneading. Knead until the dough is smooth and elastic, 5–7 minutes. The dough will be soft. Remove the dough from the bowl.

Form the dough into a ball, transfer it to a lightly oiled bowl, and cover the bowl with plastic wrap. Let the dough rise in a warm, draft-free spot until it doubles in bulk, 1¹/₂–2 hours.

Dust the work surface with 1 cup (5 oz/155 g) of the all-purpose flour. Heavily dust a half-sheet pan or rimless baking sheet with all-purpose flour. Punch down the dough and, using the pastry scraper, scrape it out onto the floured surface. Bounce the dough around on the flour, shaping it into a large, round loaf. Do not be daunted by the softness of the dough.

Place the round loaf on the prepared pan, cover loosely with a kitchen towel, and let it rise in a warm, draft-free spot until it doubles in size, 30–45 minutes.

Position a rack in the lower third of the oven, and preheat to 400°F (200°C). Liberally sprinkle the top of the loaf with all-purpose flour. Using a sharp knife or a bench scraper, cut straight through the middle of the loaf crosswise, separating it into 2 loaves. Flour your hands and turn the loaves so that they sit cut side up on the pan, spacing them generously apart. Bake the breads until they are brown and sound hollow when tapped on the bottom, 35–45 minutes. Turn off the oven, leave the door closed, and let the breads sit in the oven for 10 minutes to set the crusts. Transfer to wire racks and let cool completely before slicing.

The combination of dark beer and semolina flour gives this special Italian bread a robust flavor. It has a beautiful golden interior and an interesting oval shape. The surface of this loaf is rough, like that of a crocodile, hence the name. One large loaf becomes two, as it is cut in half just before baking. The oven temperature is a bit more gentle than what is used for most other yeast breads, so that the nest of flour in which the loaves sit does not burn.

Ciabatta

For the sponge

1 teaspoon active dry yeast

¹/₂ cup (4 fl oz/125 ml) whole milk, heated to warm (105°–115°F/40°–46°C)

1¹/₄ cups (10 fl oz/310 ml) cool water (78°F/26°C)

1 cup (8 fl oz/250 ml) sourdough starter (page 54)

2 cups (10 oz/315 g) bread flour

For the dough

2 cups (10 oz/315 g) bread flour

1 tablespoon sea salt

1 tablespoon olive oil

¹/₄ cup (1¹/₄ oz/40 g) semolina flour or cornmeal

About ²/₃ cup (3 oz/90 g) all-purpose (plain) flour for the work surface

To make the sponge, in a large bowl, dissolve the yeast in the warm milk and let stand until foamy, about 5 minutes. Using a wooden spoon, stir in the water, sourdough starter, and bread flour. Cover the bowl with plastic wrap and let stand overnight at room temperature.

BY HAND: To make the dough, add the bread flour, salt, and oil to the sponge. Stir with your hand or a wooden spoon until the dough is well mixed and creamy. Knead the dough by cupping your hand under the wet dough and slapping it vigorously in a circular motion against the side of the bowl until it is soft and springy, 5–7 minutes. The dough will be very soft.

BY STAND MIXER: To make the dough, transfer the sponge to the 5-qt (5-l) bowl of a stand mixer. Add the bread flour, salt, and oil. Place the bowl on the mixer, attach the dough hook, and knead on low speed until soft and springy, 5–7 minutes. Periodically stop the mixer and scrape down the sides of the bowl and dough hook with a plastic pastry scraper. Remove the bowl from the mixer and scrape the dough down.

Cover the bowl with plastic wrap and let the dough rise for 3 hours at room temperature or overnight in the refrigerator. It should double in bulk.

If the dough has been refrigerated, shape it while it is cold. If it has been at room temperature, do not be daunted by how loose and wet it is. Sprinkle 2 half-sheet pans or rimless baking sheets with a generous dusting of semolina flour. Generously flour the work surface with ¹/₂ cup (2¹/₂ oz/75 g) of the all-purpose

A classic of northern Italy, *ciabatta* resembles a large, flat but puffy slipper. As a consequence of the wetness of the dough, the bread forms big holes and pockets on the inside of a thin, crusty exterior. The small amount of milk in the recipe gives the bread a touch of sweetness because of the interaction between yeast and lactic acid, or milk sugars. These milk sugars help the yeast with fermentation and create a sweet and flavorful by-product that gives this bread a special flavor. The potato-onion variation is a little more dense, very flavorful, and can almost be a meal by itself. *Ciabatta* is also delicious served as sandwich bread.

VARIATION

Potato-Onion Ciabatta

Bring the 1¹/₄ cups water for the sponge to a boil. Add ¹/₂ large russet potato, peeled and cubed, and cook until tender, 10 minutes. Drain, reserve the water, and let cool before using to make the sponge. Mash the potato with a fork. In a small frying pan over medium heat, warm the 1 tablespoon olive oil called for in the dough. Add ¹/₂ yellow onion, diced, and sauté until soft, 5 minutes. Remove from the heat and let cool completely. Add the potato, onion, and an additional 1 cup (5 oz/155 g) bread flour to the dough with the flour and salt.

flour. Using the pastry scraper, scrape the dough out of the bowl onto the floured surface. Cut the dough in half with a sharp knife or a bench scraper.

Sprinkle more all-purpose flour on top while you gently shape each piece with your hands into a long, flat rectangle about 6 by 16 inches (15 by 40 cm). Carefully pick up the flat loaves and place 1 loaf in the center of each pan.

Dimple the loaves all over with your fingertips. Cover the loaves loosely with a kitchen towel and leave them to rise in a warm, draft-free spot until soft and puffy, 1–2 hours.

Position the oven racks in the middle and lower third of the oven, and preheat to 450°F (230°C).

Mist the loaves generously with water and immediately put the pans into the oven. Bake the breads until they are brown and sound hollow when tapped on the bottom, 20–25 minutes. Transfer to wire racks and let cool completely before slicing or pulling apart to eat.

Honey Whole-Wheat Bread

2 packages (5 teaspoons) active dry yeast

2 cups (16 fl oz/500 ml) whole milk, heated to warm (105°–115°F/40°–46°C)

¹⁄₄ cup (3 oz/90 g) mild honey

2 large eggs

6 cups (30 oz/940 g) whole-wheat (wholemeal) flour, plus extra for kneading and topping the loaves

2 teaspoons sea salt

6 tablespoons (3 oz/90 g) unsalted butter, at room temperature

BY HAND: In a large bowl, dissolve the yeast in the milk and let stand until foamy, about 5 minutes. Using a wire whisk, stir in the honey and eggs. Add the flour, salt, and butter and stir with your hand or a wooden spoon until a rough mass forms. Using a plastic pastry scraper, scrape the dough out of the bowl onto a lightly floured work surface. Knead until it is smooth and elastic, dusting the work surface with only enough flour to keep the dough from sticking, 5–7 minutes.

BY STAND MIXER: In the 5-qt (5-l) bowl of a stand mixer, dissolve the yeast in the milk and let stand until foamy, about 5 minutes. Using a wire whisk, stir in the honey and eggs. Add the flour, salt, and butter. Place the bowl on the mixer, attach the dough hook, and knead on low speed. Add a little more flour as needed for the dough to come away from the sides of the bowl after a few minutes of kneading. Knead until the dough is smooth and elastic, 5–7 minutes. Remove the dough from the bowl.

Form the dough into a ball and transfer it to a lightly oiled bowl. Cover the bowl with plastic wrap and let the dough rise in a warm, draft-free spot until it doubles in bulk, 1¹⁄₂–2 hours.

Butter two 9-by-5-inch (23-by-13-cm) loaf pans.

Punch down the dough and, using the pastry scraper, scrape it out onto a clean work surface. Cut it in half with a sharp knife or a bench scraper. For each half, evenly flatten the dough with the heel of your hand. Roll the bottom third up onto itself and seal it by pushing it gently with the heel of your hand. Continue rolling and sealing the dough until you have an oval log. Place the log, seam side down, in the prepared loaf pans. Press on them to flatten them evenly into the pans.

Cover loosely with a kitchen towel and let the loaves rise in a warm, draft-free spot until they double in size, 45–60 minutes.

Position a rack in the middle of the oven, and preheat to 375°F (190°C).

Dust the tops of the loaves with whole-wheat flour. Bake until they are honey brown and sound hollow when tapped on the top, 35–40 minutes. Be careful not to overbake this bread or it will be dry. Carefully remove the loaves from the pans and let cool completely on wire racks before slicing.

Whole-wheat flour has its own sweetness, which is nicely complemented by honey. Using 100 percent whole-wheat flour makes a hearty loaf, but the honey, eggs, and butter keep the bread tender and not too dense. The soft texture of these loaves makes them especially wonderful for breakfast. Spread a little butter and jam atop a thick, warm slice. If you would like a less sweet sandwich loaf, substitute water for the milk and use only 2 tablespoons honey in the dough.

Oatmeal-Molasses Bread

Sweet and rich, this bread is delicious for breakfast or dinner. For an interesting change, experiment using grain mixtures in place of the oats. Most health-foods stores carry 4-grain or 9-grain cereals that are delicious in this bread. For a crunchy finish, sprinkle a few sunflower seeds on top before baking.

In a small saucepan, bring the water to a boil. Put the oats into a heatproof bowl, and pour the water over the oats. Add the butter and molasses, and let the mixture cool to warm (105°–115°F/40°–46°C).

2¹/₃ cups (19 fl oz/580 ml) water

1 cup (3 oz/90 g) old-fashioned rolled oats, plus extra for topping the loaves

¹/₂ cup (4 oz/125 g) unsalted butter

¹/₃ cup (3¹/₂ oz/105 g) unsulfured molasses

2 packages (5 teaspoons) active dry yeast

5–6 cups (25–30 oz/ 780–940 g) all-purpose (plain) flour, plus extra for kneading

2 teaspoons sea salt

BY HAND: In a large bowl, dissolve the yeast in the warm oat mixture and let stand for 5 minutes. Using a wooden spoon, stir in 3 cups (15 oz/470 g) of the flour and the salt, mixing well. Add the remaining 2–3 cups (10–15 oz/ 315–470 g) flour as needed to make a soft dough. Using a plastic pastry scraper, scrape the dough out of the bowl onto a floured work surface. Knead until it is smooth and elastic, dusting the work surface with only enough flour to keep the dough from sticking, 5–7 minutes.

BY STAND MIXER: In the 5-qt (5-l) bowl of a stand mixer, dissolve the yeast in the warm oat mixture and let stand 5 minutes. Add 3 cups (15 oz/470 g) of the flour and the salt. Place the bowl on the mixer, attach the dough hook, and knead on low speed. Add the remaining 2–3 cups (10–15 oz/315–470 g) flour as needed for the dough to come away from the sides of the bowl after a few minutes of kneading. Knead until the dough is smooth and elastic, 5–7 minutes. Remove the dough from the bowl.

Form the dough into a ball and transfer it to a lightly oiled bowl. Cover the bowl with plastic wrap and let the dough rise in a warm, draft-free spot until it doubles in bulk, about 1 hour.

Butter two 9-by-5-inch (23-by-13-cm) loaf pans. Punch down the dough and, using the pastry scraper, scrape it out onto a clean work surface. Cut it in half with a sharp knife or a bench scraper.

For each half, evenly flatten the dough with the heel of your hand. Roll the top third down onto itself and seal it by pushing it gently with the heel of your hand. Continue rolling and sealing the dough until you have an oval log. Place the logs, seam side down, in the prepared loaf pans. Press on them to flatten them evenly into the pans. Cover loosely with a kitchen towel and let them rise in a warm, draft-free spot until they double in size, 45–60 minutes.

Position a rack in the middle of the oven, and preheat to 375°F (190°C). Mist the tops of the loaves with water. Sprinkle the tops with a generous handful of oats. Bake until they are golden brown and sound hollow when tapped on top, 40–45 minutes. Carefully remove the loaves from the pans and let cool completely on wire racks before slicing.

Light Rye Bread

2 packages (5 teaspoons) active dry yeast

1³/₄ cups (14 fl oz/430 ml) warm water (105°–115°F/ 40°–46°C)

2 tablespoons vegetable oil

1 teaspoon caraway seeds

1 teaspoon fennel seeds

Grated zest of 1 orange

2¹/₂ cups (7¹/₂ oz/235 g) light rye flour, plus extra for dusting the loaf

2 cups (10 oz/300 g) all-purpose (plain) flour, plus extra for kneading

2 teaspoons sea salt

Slightly dense and chewy, this loaf is at once sweet and savory. The hint of orange zest highlights the other flavors in the bread. Make sure to allow the dough two good rises, so that the flavor can develop fully. You can use whole-grain rye in place of the light rye flour for a nuttier bread.

BY HAND: In a large bowl, dissolve the yeast in the warm water and let stand until foamy, about 5 minutes. Add the oil, caraway and fennel seeds, orange zest, flours, and salt and stir with your hand or a wooden spoon until a shaggy mass forms. Using a plastic pastry scraper, scrape the dough out of the bowl onto a lightly floured work surface. Knead the dough, adding up to ¹/₂ cup (2¹/₂ oz/75 g) all-purpose flour if necessary to keep it from sticking, until smooth, elastic, and slightly tacky, 5–7 minutes. Do not knead in too much flour, or the bread will be dry.

BY STAND MIXER: In the 5-qt (5-l) bowl of a stand mixer, dissolve the yeast in the warm water and let stand until foamy, about 5 minutes. Add the oil, caraway and fennel seeds, orange zest, flours, and salt. Place the bowl on the mixer, attach the dough hook, and knead on low speed. Add up to ¹/₂ cup (2¹/₂ oz/ 75 g) all-purpose flour as needed for the dough to come away from the sides of the bowl after a few minutes of kneading. Knead until the dough is smooth, elastic, and slightly tacky, 5–7 minutes. Remove the dough from the bowl.

Form the dough into a ball and transfer it to a lightly oiled bowl. Cover the bowl with plastic wrap, and let the dough rise in a warm, draft-free spot until it doubles in bulk, 1–1¹/₂ hours. Line a half-sheet pan or rimless baking sheet with parchment (baking) paper.

Punch down the dough and turn it out onto a clean work surface. Evenly flatten the dough with the heel of your hand. Roll the top third down onto itself and seal it by pushing it gently with the heel of your hand. Continue rolling and sealing the dough until you have an oval loaf. Place the loaf, seam side down, on the prepared pan. Cover loosely with a kitchen towel and let it rise in a warm, draft-free spot until it doubles in size and feels spongy to the touch, 1¹/₂–2 hours.

Position a rack in the middle of the oven, and preheat to 450°F (230°C). Dust the loaf with rye flour. Using a single-edged razor blade or a serrated knife, make 2 or 3 diagonal slashes, each at a slight angle across the top of the loaf (page 36). Put the pan in the oven and reduce the heat to 400°F (200°C). Bake the bread until it is browned and sounds hollow when tapped on the bottom, 30–40 minutes. Transfer to a wire rack and let cool completely.

VARIATION

Dark Rye Bread

The night before you plan to make the bread, mix 1 cup (8 oz/250 g) sourdough starter (page 54) with ¹/₄ cup (2 fl oz/60 ml) cool water and ¹/₄ cup (³/₄ oz/20 g) light rye flour. Stir well, cover loosely with plastic wrap, and let stand overnight at room temperature.

To make the sponge, mix together 1 cup (8 fl oz/250 ml) water, 1 cup (8 oz/250 g) of the rye sourdough starter, 2 teaspoons active dry yeast, 2 tablespoons dark, unsulfored molasses, and 1 cup (5 oz/155 g) all-purpose (plain) flour in a large bowl. Cover the bowl with plastic wrap and let stand at room temperature until the mixture is foamy and bubbling, 1¹/₂–2 hours.

To finish the dough, stir in 2 tablespoons vegetable oil, 1 teaspoon caraway seeds, 1 teaspoon fennel seeds, the grated zest of 1 orange, 2¹/₂ cups (7¹/₂ oz/235 g) light rye flour, 2 teaspoons salt, 1¹/₂ cups (7¹/₂ oz/235 g) all-purpose (plain) flour, and 2 tablespoons Dutch-process cocoa powder. Knead and finish the dough as directed in the recipe.

Dark Pumpernickel-Raisin Bread

Pumpernickel bread boasts a complex combination of flavors that changes from the first bite to the last. The loaf is rich in color, moist in texture, and bold in personality. It keeps well for several days, the flavors mellowing a bit with time. With its festive lacing of raisins and nuts, it is a perfect addition to a holiday feast.

BY HAND: In a large bowl, dissolve the yeast in the warm water and let stand until foamy, about 5 minutes. Using a wooden spoon, stir in the butter, molasses, espresso powder, caraway and fennel seeds, and cocoa powder. Add the flours, wheat bran, and salt and stir with your hand or the wooden spoon until a rough mass forms. Using a plastic pastry scraper, scrape the dough out of the bowl onto a lightly floured work surface. Knead until it is smooth and elastic, dusting the work surface with only enough flour to keep the dough from sticking, 5–7 minutes.

BY STAND MIXER: In the 5-qt (5-l) bowl of a stand mixer, dissolve the yeast in the warm water and let stand until foamy, about 5 minutes. Using a wooden spoon, stir in the butter, molasses, espresso powder, caraway and fennel seeds, and cocoa powder. Add the flours, wheat bran, and salt. Place the bowl on the mixer, attach the dough hook, and knead on low speed. Add a little more flour as needed for the dough to come away from the sides of the bowl after a few minutes of kneading. Knead until the dough is smooth and elastic, 5–7 minutes. Remove the dough from the bowl.

Form the dough into a ball and transfer it to a lightly oiled bowl. Sprinkle the raisins and the nuts (if using) on top of the dough. Cover the bowl with plastic wrap and let the dough rise in a warm, draft-free spot until it doubles in bulk, 1½–2 hours.

Lightly dust a half-sheet pan or rimless baking sheet with cornmeal, or line it with parchment (baking) paper.

Punch down the dough and turn it out onto a lightly oiled work surface. Knead it briefly and gently to disperse the raisins and nuts evenly. Cut the dough in half with a sharp knife or a bench scraper. Shape each half of the dough into a tight round loaf by rotating the bread in a circular motion on the work surface between your hands. Put the loaves on the prepared pan, spacing them well apart. Cover the loaves loosely with a kitchen towel and let them rise in a warm, draft-free spot until they double in size and feel spongy to the touch, 45–60 minutes.

Position a rack in the lower third of the oven, and preheat to 375°F (190°C). Lightly dust the loaves with rye flour. Bake until they sound hollow when tapped on the bottom, 35–45 minutes. The rye flour will turn a dusky brown when the loaves are done. Transfer to wire racks and let cool completely before slicing.

2 packages (5 teaspoons) active dry yeast

2¼ cups (18 fl oz/560 ml) warm water (105°–115°F/ 40°–46°C)

½ cup (4 oz/125 g) unsalted butter, melted

2 tablespoons unsulfured molasses

2 tablespoons instant espresso powder

1 tablespoon caraway seeds

1 teaspoon fennel seeds

¼ cup (¾ oz/20 g) Dutch-process cocoa powder

3 cups (15 oz/470 g) all-purpose (plain) flour, plus extra for dusting the work surface

2 cups (6 oz/185 g) light rye flour, plus extra for dusting the loaves

½ cup (2½ oz/75 g) whole-wheat (wholemeal) flour

½ cup (1¼ oz/40 g) wheat bran

1 tablespoon sea salt

1 cup (6 oz/185 g) raisins, plumped (page 23) and drained

1 cup (4 oz/125 g) walnut halves, toasted (page 21), optional

Cornmeal for dusting the pan (optional)

Traditional Sourdough Bread

For the sourdough starter

2 cups (10 oz/315 g) unbleached all-purpose (plain) flour

2 cups (16 fl oz/500 ml) cool whole milk (78°F/26°C)

For the sponge

1 cup (8 oz/250 ml) sourdough starter

2 cups (16 fl oz/500 ml) water

2 cups (10 oz/315 g) unbleached all-purpose (plain) flour

For the dough

1 cup (8 fl oz/250 ml) cool water (78°F/26°C)

1 tablespoon sea salt

5–6 cups (25–30 oz/ 780–940 g) all-purpose (plain) flour

All-purpose (plain) flour or semolina flour for shaping and nesting the dough

The best way to understand the miracle of sourdough bread is to bake it regularly. This bread is a paradox. It is both simple and complex. Every loaf has just four basic ingredients, yet it can taste different every time you bake it. The yeast in sourdough bread is airborne and influenced dramatically by its environment. A simple change in weather can affect it, and the same recipe will bake differently from one house to another. More than any other bread, sourdough takes on the personality of the baker. The process of making it is time-consuming, but it is not labor-intensive. In other words, a good sourdough bread requires a little human intervention and a lot of time alone. Once you have successfully made the starter, you will need 3 days to produce a loaf of incomparable depth and flavor.

To make the starter, in a glass or ceramic bowl, combine the flour and water and stir with a wooden spoon until well mixed. Cover the bowl with plastic wrap and let stand at a cool room temperature for 3 to 4 days, stirring the mixture once a day. If it bubbles and has a nice sour smell, you have attracted airborne yeasts and friendly bacteria, which give sourdough its characteristic flavor. If the starter turns moldy or pink or starts to smell bad, throw it away and start again.

To make the sponge, the night before making the bread, combine 1 cup (8 oz/ 250 ml) of the sourdough starter, the water, and the flour in a large bowl and stir with a wooden spoon until well mixed. Cover the bowl with plastic wrap and let stand at room temperature overnight. The next day, scoop out 1 cup (8 oz/ 250 g) of the sponge and mix it back into the original starter to be used for future breads. To maintain your sourdough starter see Care and Feeding of Sourdough Starter (page 56).

To make the dough, add the water, salt, and 3 cups (15 oz/470 g) of the flour to the sponge remaining in the bowl. Stir with a wooden spoon to mix well. Add enough of the remaining 2–3 cups (10–15 oz/315–470 g) flour to make a soft dough. Turn the dough out onto a lightly floured work surface. Knead just until smooth and slightly elastic, 5–7 minutes. Use a bench scraper or plastic pastry scraper when kneading to prevent the dough from sticking.

Return the dough to the bowl, cover the bowl with plastic wrap, and leave the dough to rise at room temperature until it doubles in bulk, 6–8 hours. It is probably most convenient to let the dough rise slowly overnight.

(continued on page 56)

Sourdough starter needs air, so it
is best to store it in a glass jar or
a ceramic, plastic, or metal bowl
covered partially with a lid, a damp
(kitchen) towel, or plastic wrap.
Each time you make a loaf of sourdough, add 1 cup (8 oz/250 g)
of the sponge to your starter to
replenish what you use to make
the sponge. If you do not use the
starter at least every 2 days, store
it in the refrigerator and feed it
once a week: First, pour off any
liquid that has formed on top.
(The liquid is the by-product of
yeast and should be clear, yellow-
ish brown, or gray. If it is pink
or moldy, throw the starter away.)
Then stir 1/2 cup (2 1/2 oz/75 g)
unbleached all-purpose (plain)
flour and 1/4 cup (2 fl oz/ 60 ml)
cool water into the starter. It should
be the consistency of thin pancake
batter. Let the starter stand at
room temperature overnight before
returning it to the refrigerator. If
you use your starter infrequently,
feed it every day for at least 3 days
before using.

Traditional Sourdough Bread continued...

Line an 11-inch (28-cm) basket or bowl at least 3–4 inches (7.5–10 cm) deep with
a kitchen towel, and rub 1/2 cup (2 1/2 oz/75 g) flour evenly onto the towel.

Turn out the dough onto a work surface heavily dusted with flour. The dough
should be quite slack. Shape it into a large ball. Using both hands, tuck and turn
the loaf into a large, loose ball so that one side of its surface is as smooth as
possible. Pick up the ball and gently place it, seam side up, in the towel-lined
basket. Use your fingertips to pinch the seam closed.

Cover the basket loosely with a damp kitchen towel. Let the dough rise slowly at
room temperature until it has again doubled in size and has risen to the top of the
basket. This can take 2–4 hours, depending on the starter's activity and on how
warm the room is. Be sure that the dough does not overproof. It is overproofed if
it has risen above the rim of the basket and is extremely loose and jiggly. If it does
overproof, do not slash it as below.

Position a rack in the lower third of the oven, and preheat to 450°F (230°C).
Have ready a spray bottle filled with water for misting the dough.

Sprinkle the top of the loaf with 1/4 cup (1 1/4 oz/40 g) flour and spread it evenly
over the bread with your hand. Place a heavy 12-inch (30-cm) cake pan or a
heavy-duty half-sheet pan on top of the loaf and, holding the basket and pan,
invert them together. Gently pull the basket and towel off the dough.

Using a single-edged razor blade or a sharp, serrated knife, slash a decorative
crisscross into the top of the loaf (page 37). Each slash should be about 5 inches
(13 cm) long.

Mist the loaf several times with water and immediately put it into the oven. Close
the oven door quickly and do not open it again until you are ready to check the
loaf for doneness. Bake the bread for 30 minutes. Reduce the heat to 400°F
(200°C) and continue baking until the crust is dark and the bread sounds hollow
when tapped on the top, 25–30 minutes. If you baked the loaf in a cake pan, turn
the loaf out of it over a sink, or take it outdoors to tap off the excess flour. Transfer
to a wire rack and let cool completely before slicing.

Pain au Levain

For the first stage starter

1 cup (5 oz/155 g) unbleached all-purpose (plain) flour

¹/₂ cup (4 fl oz/125 ml) cool water (78°F/26°C)

For the second stage starter

1¹/₂ cups (7¹/₂ oz/235 g) unbleached all-purpose (plain) flour

¹/₂ cup (4 fl oz/125 ml) cool water (78°F/26°C)

For the dough

1 cup (8 oz/250 g) starter

3¹/₂ cups (28 fl oz/875 ml) cool water (78°F/26°C)

1 tablespoon sea salt

³/₄ cup (4 oz/125 g) whole-wheat (wholemeal) flour

7–9 cups (2–2³/₄ lb/ 1–1.5 kg) unbleached all-purpose (plain) flour

2 cups (8 oz/250 g) walnut pieces, toasted (page 21), optional

All-purpose (plain) flour or semolina flour for dusting the work surface and the loaf and nesting the dough

In sourdough language, a *levain* is a firm starter, a chef, a mother, or just old dough. Some bakers claim to use a *levain* that has been in their families for hundreds of years. Whether you start it fresh or get a beloved starter from a friend, remember always to pinch off a piece of the dough before you shape the bread. You can then pass it along to your loved ones. You can also experiment with using different quantities of the starter when you make the dough to change the personality of the loaf.

To make the first stage starter (first photograph to the right), in a ceramic or glass bowl, combine the flour with the water. Stir with your fingers or a wooden spoon until well blended. The starter should be soft and sticky. Cover the bowl with plastic wrap and let stand at room temperature for 72 hours. It should rise slightly and take on a fresh, acidic aroma.

To make the second stage starter (second photograph to the right), uncover the starter and, using a plastic pastry scraper, scrape it into a bowl. Stir in the water and the flour, mixing well. The starter should be firm but not too stiff. Cover again with plastic wrap and let stand at room temperature for 24–48 hours. A longer wait will produce a slightly more acidic loaf. When the starter rises and shows signs of life, such as bubbling, it is active, and you are ready to bake.

To make the dough, in a very large bowl, combine the starter, water, and salt. Using your hand or a sturdy wire whisk, stir until the mixture is fairly blended. Begin adding the whole-wheat flour and 5 cups (25 oz/775 g) of the all-purpose flour, 1 cup (5 oz/155 g) at a time, mixing well by hand or with a wooden spoon after each addition. Continue mixing the dough for a few minutes until it is thick and spongy. Add the remaining 2–4 cups (10–25 oz/315–630 g) flour by hand, folding the dough over itself to incorporate air and using only enough flour to form a soft, slightly tacky dough. Cover the bowl with plastic wrap and leave the dough to rise at room temperature until it doubles in bulk, 8–12 hours. It is probably most convenient to let the dough rise overnight.

Line an 11-inch (28-cm) basket or bowl with a dry kitchen towel, and rub ¹/₂ cup (2¹/₂ oz/75 g) all-purpose flour onto the towel.

Turn the dough out onto a work surface heavily dusted with flour. The dough should be quite slack. Cut off a handful of the dough, about 1 cup (8 oz/250 g), and set it aside in a small bowl to use as the starter for future loaves (see Care and Feeding of *Levain*, opposite). Shape the remaining dough into a large, round ball. Gently place it, seam side up, in the towel-lined basket. Pinch the seam

CARE AND FEEDING OF *LEVAIN*

Store the 1 cup (8 oz/250 g) of levain dough that you reserved in a covered plastic, ceramic, or metal container. Let it sit at room temperature and ferment for 6–8 hours before adding it into the dough of a new batch of levain. If you are not going to use it within 2 days, store the levain in the refrigerator and feed it every 5–7 days. Before feeding it, make sure your levain is healthy. Gray or green mold is the result of good bacteria growing, and you simply need to scrape it off. If it turns pinkish and smells bad, throw the levain away. To feed the levain, stir ¹/₂ cup (2¹/₂ oz/ 75 g) all-purpose (plain) flour and 2 tablespoons cool water into it with a fork or spoon. It should form a rough, soft ball. Let the mixture stand at room temperature for a few hours or overnight before returning it to the refrigerator. The less frequently levain is used, the more sour it will be and the slower the dough will rise. If you use your levain infrequently, feed it every day for 3 days before using.

together with your fingertips. Cover the basket loosely with a damp kitchen towel. Let the dough rise slowly at room temperature until it has doubled in size and risen to the top of the basket. This can take 4–6 hours. Be sure that the dough does not overproof. It is overproofed if it has risen above the rim of the basket and is extremely loose and jiggly. If it does overproof, do not slash it as below.

Position a rack in the lower third of the oven, and preheat to 450°F (230°C). Have ready a spray bottle filled with water for misting the dough. Sprinkle the top of the loaf with ¹/₄ cup (1¹/₄ oz/40 g) flour and spread it evenly over the bread with your hand. Place a heavy 12-inch (30-cm) cake pan or a heavy-duty half-sheet pan on top of the loaf and, holding the basket and pan, invert them together. Gently pull the basket and towel off the dough. Using a single-edged razor blade or a sharp, serrated knife, slash a crisscross into the top of the loaf (page 37).

Mist the loaf several times with water, and immediately put it into the oven. Bake the bread for 30 minutes. Reduce the heat to 400°F (200°C) and continue baking until the crust is dark and the bread sounds hollow when tapped on the top, 25–30 minutes. If you baked the loaf in a cake pan, turn the loaf out of it over a sink, or take it outdoors to tap off the excess flour. Transfer to a wire rack and let cool completely before slicing.

Brioche

2 packages (5 teaspoons) active dry yeast

$^1/_4$ cup (2 oz/60 ml) warm water (105°–115°F/ 40°–46°C)

8 large eggs, at room temperature, plus 1 egg, beaten, for glaze

3 tablespoons sugar

4 cups (1$^1/_4$ lb/625 g) all-purpose (plain) flour, plus extra as needed

2 teaspoons salt

$^3/_4$ cup (12 oz/375 g) unsalted butter, at room temperature

In the 5-qt (5-l) bowl of a stand mixer, dissolve the yeast in the warm water and let stand until foamy, about 5 minutes. Beat in the 8 eggs and the sugar with a wire whisk. Add the flour and salt. Place the bowl on the mixer, attach the dough hook, and knead on low speed until smooth and elastic, 5–7 minutes. The dough will be thick and sticky when you start kneading. Periodically stop the mixer and scrape down the sides of the bowl and the dough hook with a plastic pastry scraper. Add the butter and continue kneading on medium-high speed until it is completely incorporated, about 5–10 minutes.

Using the pastry scraper, scrape the dough into a clean, buttered bowl. Cover the bowl with plastic wrap and refrigerate it for at least 6 hours or for up to overnight.

Heavily butter 16 individual brioche molds, two 8-inch (20-cm) brioche molds, or two 9-by-5-inch (23-by-13-cm) loaf pans.

Using the pastry scraper, scrape the chilled dough out of the bowl onto a floured work surface. If using individual molds, cut the dough into 16 pieces with a sharp knife or bench scraper. If using large molds, cut the dough in half. With floured hands, pinch off one-third of the dough from each piece of dough. Then roll each piece of dough, large and small, into a ball. Flour your hands and the work surface only if the dough becomes sticky. Poke a hole in the center of a large ball and open it with your index fingers. Roll a small ball into a cone shape and place the point into the hole, pulling the point through. Place the formed brioche into a prepared mold. Repeat with the remaining large and small balls.

If using loaf pans, cut the dough into 16 pieces with a sharp knife or bench scraper. With floured hands, roll each piece into a ball. Line up 8 balls in a row in each loaf pan.

Cover the shaped breads loosely with a dry kitchen towel and let them rise in a warm, draft-free spot until they almost fill the pans, 1$^1/_2$–2 hours. Alternatively, put them in the refrigerator to proof slowly overnight, and then let the brioche come to room temperature before baking.

Position a rack in the middle of the oven, and preheat to 375°F (190°C). Lightly brush the breads with the beaten egg. Place the molds on a half-sheet pan or rimless baking sheet and bake until a toothpick inserted into the center of a bread comes out clean, 30–40 minutes. If the tops are browning too quickly, cover them with aluminum foil. Transfer to wire racks and let cool in the pans for 5 minutes, then turn out onto the racks and let cool completely before serving.

In addition to being the basis for rich, buttery egg bread, brioche dough can be used in a variety of ways. For example, it can be fashioned into Sticky Buns (page 69) for a decadent breakfast treat. Of course, there's nothing quite as delicious in the morning as a slice of brioche with a little raspberry jam on top. Leftover brioche is also ideal for making French toast or Currant Bread Pudding (page 299). Do not be afraid of this wet, sticky dough. When it is chilled, you can work with it easily. It is best to make this dough in a stand mixer, although you can make it by hand; however, you will probably be huffing and puffing by the time it goes into the refrigerator.

Challah

2 packages (5 teaspoons) active dry yeast

1 cup (8 fl oz/250 ml) warm water (105°–115°F/ 40°–46°C)

¹/₂ cup (4 oz/125 g) sugar

3 large eggs, plus 1 egg, beaten, for glaze

5 cups (25 oz/780 g) all-purpose (plain) flour

2 teaspoons salt

¹/₂ cup (4 oz/125 g) unsalted butter, at room temperature

1 tablespoon poppy seeds or sesame seeds (optional)

The dough used for making the cakelike challah can be formed into a variety of shapes, including braids, rolls, and knots. The ingredients go together easily, and the bread looks beautiful when served. For the dinner table, you can form the dough into a pair of small braids, or into a single large, spectacular one.

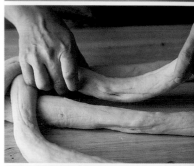

BY HAND: In a large bowl, dissolve the yeast in the warm water and let stand until foamy, about 5 minutes. Using a wooden spoon, stir in the sugar, 3 eggs, 4¹/₂ cups (22¹/₂ oz/ 705 g) of the flour, the salt, and the butter until the dough comes together in a sticky mass. Turn the dough out onto a lightly floured surface and knead, working in the remaining flour as necessary to keep the dough from being too sticky, until the dough is smooth and elastic, 5–7 minutes. Do not be tempted to add too much flour. The dough should stay soft, and will become less sticky with kneading.

BY STAND MIXER: In the 5-qt (5-l) bowl of a stand mixer, dissolve the yeast in the warm water and let stand until foamy, about 5 minutes. Add the sugar, 3 eggs, 4¹/₂ cups (22¹/₂ oz/ 705 g) of the flour, the salt, and the butter. Place the bowl on the mixer, attach the dough hook, and knead on low speed, working in the remaining flour as necessary to keep the dough from being too sticky, until the dough is smooth and elastic, 5–7 minutes. Do not be tempted to add too much flour. The dough should stay soft, and it will become less sticky with kneading. Remove the dough from the bowl.

Form the dough into a ball and transfer it to a lightly oiled bowl. Cover the bowl with a damp kitchen towel and let the dough rise in a warm, draft-free spot until it doubles in bulk, about 2 hours.

Line a half-sheet pan or rimless baking sheet with parchment (baking) paper. Punch down the dough. Using a plastic pastry scraper, scrape the dough out onto a clean work surface.

To make a 4-strand braid, cut the dough into 4 equal pieces with a sharp knife or a bench scraper. Using your palms, and starting in the center and working outward, elongate 1 piece by rolling it gently against the work surface with even pressure until you have formed a rope as long as the prepared pan. Repeat with the remaining 3 pieces.

Line up the 4 strands in front of you horizontally. Cross the strand farthest from you across the other 3 strands so that it is nearest you. Cross the strand that is

VARIATION

Three-Strand Braid

To make one large 3-strand braid, cut the dough into 3 equal pieces with a sharp knife or a bench scraper. Follow the directions for rolling out the ropes for the 4-strand braid. Line the 3 strands up straight so that they are in front of you vertically. Cross the right strand over the middle strand, then cross the left strand over the middle strand. Keep going back and forth crossing left over right, then right over left until you reach the ends of the ropes. Pinch them together at the top and at the bottom, and tuck the strands under at the ends.

now next to it across the other 2 strands away from you. Position the outside strands so that they are away from the center ones, and position the center 2 strands perfectly horizontal. Bring the strand nearest you down between the 2 horizontal strands. Bring the strand farthest from you up and across to the opposite side. Again, bring the strand farthest from you down between the 2 straight strands. Bring the strand nearest you up and across to the opposite side. Starting from the strand nearest you, repeat the braiding until you reach the ends of the ropes. Pinch them together at the top and at the bottom, and tuck the strands under at the ends.

Place the braided loaf on the prepared pan, cover with a dry kitchen towel, and let rise again in a warm, draft-free spot until it doubles in size and is spongy to the touch, 45–60 minutes.

Position a rack in the lower third of the oven, and preheat to 350°F (180°C).

Brush the braid gently with the beaten egg and sprinkle with the seeds, if using. Bake the braid until it is nicely browned and sounds hollow when tapped on the bottom, 30–35 minutes. Transfer to a wire rack and let cool completely.

Classic Dinner Rolls

VARIATIONS

Clover-Leaf Rolls and Pull-Apart Rolls

Cut the completed dough in half as directed. Use one half for clover-leaf rolls, and the other half for pull-apart rolls.

For the clover-leaf rolls, heavily butter a 12-cup muffin pan. Cut the piece of dough into 12 equal pieces, then cut each small piece into thirds. You will have 36 plum-sized pieces. Roll each piece into a small ball. Place 3 balls next to one another in each prepared muffin cup. When all the cups are full, cover the muffin pan loosely with a kitchen towel, then proceed as directed.

For the pull-apart rolls, heavily butter a 9-inch (23-cm) cake pan. Cut the piece of dough into 8 equal pieces. Roll each piece against the work surface into a ball. Put the balls in the cake pan, placing 7 balls around the edge and 1 ball in the center. Cover the cake pan loosely with a kitchen towel, then proceed as directed.

Great dinner rolls should be featherlight, not too sweet, and, above all, a good accompaniment to almost any meal. Despite the name, these breads could be called classic breakfast, lunch, or dinner rolls, as they are perfect for dipping in sauce at supper, for serving alongside a salad at midday, or for spreading with jam first thing in the morning.

BY HAND: In a large bowl, dissolve the yeast in the warm water and let stand until foamy, about 5 minutes. Using a wire whisk, beat in the milk, sugar, 2 eggs, butter, flour, and salt just until mixed, then stir with your hand or a wooden spoon until a rough mass forms. Using a plastic pastry scraper, scrape the dough out of the bowl onto a lightly floured work surface. Knead until it is smooth and elastic, dusting the work surface with flour to keep the dough from sticking, 5–7 minutes. The dough should be soft but not sticky.

BY STAND MIXER: In the 5-qt (5-l) bowl of a stand mixer, dissolve the yeast in the warm water and let stand until foamy, about 5 minutes. Add the milk, sugar, 2 eggs, butter, flour, and salt. Place the bowl on the mixer, attach the dough hook, and knead on low speed. Add a little more flour only if the dough is sticking to the sides of the bowl after a few minutes of kneading. Knead until the dough is smooth and elastic, 5–7 minutes. The dough should be soft but not sticky. Remove the dough from the bowl.

Form the dough into a ball, transfer it to a lightly oiled bowl, and cover the bowl with plastic wrap. Let the dough rise in a warm, draft-free spot until it doubles in bulk, 1 1/2–2 hours.

Line a half-sheet pan or rimless baking sheet with parchment (baking) paper.

Punch down the dough and turn it out onto a clean work surface. Cut it in half with a sharp knife or a bench scraper. Cut each half into 8 equal pieces. Roll each piece against the work surface into a round ball. Place the balls on the prepared pan, spacing them evenly, cover loosely with a kitchen towel, and let them rise until puffy and pillow-soft when gently squeezed, 30–40 minutes.

Position a rack in the lower third of the oven, and preheat to 400°F (200°C).

Brush the rolls lightly with the beaten egg. Bake until puffed and golden brown, 20–25 minutes. Serve immediately.

1 package (2 1/2 teaspoons) active dry yeast

1/4 cup (2 fl oz/60 ml) warm water (105°–115°F/ 40°–46°C)

1 cup (8 fl oz/250 ml) whole milk

2 tablespoons sugar

2 large eggs, at room temperature, plus 1 egg, beaten

6 tablespoons (3 oz/90 g) unsalted butter, at room temperature

4 1/2 cups (22 1/2 oz/705 g) all-purpose (plain) flour, plus extra for kneading

2 teaspoons salt

Potato-Buttermilk Rolls

1 large russet potato, about ¹/₂ lb (250 g), peeled and cubed

1¹/₂ cups (12 fl oz/375 ml) water

1¹/₂ cups (12 fl oz/375 ml) buttermilk

2 packages (5 teaspoons) active dry yeast

6 cups (30 oz/940 g) all-purpose (plain) flour, plus extra for kneading and dusting the rolls

2 tablespoons sugar

1 tablespoon salt

¹/₂ cup (4 oz/125 g) unsalted butter, at room temperature, plus extra if using cake pans

VARIATION
Pull-Apart Rolls
Cut the completed dough in half, then cut each half into 8 equal pieces, as directed. Heavily butter two 10-inch (25-cm) cake pans. Roll each piece against the work surface into a ball. Divide the 16 pieces between the prepared cake pans, placing 7 balls around the edge and 1 ball in the center of each pan. Cover the cake pan loosely with a kitchen towel, then proceed as directed.

In a small saucepan, combine the potato and water, bring to a boil, and cook until the potato is soft and fork-tender, about 10 minutes.

BY HAND: Pour the cooked potato cubes and water into a large bowl and mash the potato cubes with a fork. Stir in the buttermilk and let cool to warm (110°F/43°C). Dissolve the yeast in the potato mixture and let stand 5 minutes. Add the flour, sugar, salt, and butter and stir with your hand or a wooden spoon until a shaggy mass forms. Using a plastic pastry scraper, scrape the dough out onto a floured work surface. Invert the bowl over the dough and let it rest for 5–10 minutes. Uncover the dough and knead until it is smooth and elastic, dusting the work surface with flour to keep the dough from sticking, 5–7 minutes.

BY STAND MIXER: Pour the cooked potato cubes and water into the 5-qt (5-l) bowl of a stand mixer and mash the potato cubes with a fork. Stir in the buttermilk and let cool to warm (110°F/43°C). Dissolve the yeast in the potato mixture and let stand 5 minutes. Add the flour, sugar, salt, and butter. Place the bowl on the mixer, attach the dough hook, and knead on low speed. Add a little more flour as needed for the dough to come away from the sides of the bowl. Knead until the dough is smooth and elastic, 5–7 minutes. Remove the dough from the bowl.

Form the dough into a ball, transfer it to a lightly buttered bowl, and cover the bowl with plastic wrap. Let the dough rise in a warm, draft-free spot until it doubles in bulk, about 1 hour.

Punch down the dough and turn it out onto a clean work surface. Cut it in half with a sharp knife. Cut each half into 8 equal pieces for rolls or 6 equal pieces for sandwich buns. Cover with a kitchen towel and let them rest 5 minutes before shaping. Line a half-sheet pan or rimless baking sheet with parchment (baking) paper. Roll each piece of dough against the work surface into a ball. Place the balls on the prepared sheet pan, spacing them evenly. Cover the rolls with a kitchen towel and let them rise in a warm, draft-free spot until they double in size, 15–30 minutes. If you want a lighter, airier texture for sandwich buns, let the dough rise until spongy and pillow-soft when gently squeezed, 30–45 minutes.

Position a rack in the middle of the oven, and preheat to 375°F (190°C). Lightly dust the tops of the rolls with a little flour. Bake the rolls until they are puffed and lightly browned, 20–25 minutes. Let the rolls cool slightly before serving.

Soft and slightly hearty, these rolls are the perfect accompaniment to a steaming bowl of soup for a midwinter supper. The buttermilk adds a faint tang that contributes to their appeal. Shape them a little bigger and let them rise a little longer, and they make a terrific sandwich roll or burger bun. You can use yams or sweet potatoes instead of russets for a colorful variation.

Cinnamon Rolls

For the dough

2 packages (5 teaspoons) active dry yeast

1 cup (8 fl oz/250 ml) whole milk, heated to warm (105°–115°F/40°–46°C)

1/2 cup (4 oz/125 g) granulated sugar

3 large eggs

5 1/2 cups (27 oz/845 g) all-purpose (plain) flour, plus extra for the work surface

2 teaspoons salt

1 teaspoon ground mace

Grated zest of 1 orange

1/2 cup (4 oz/125 g) unsalted butter, at room temperature

For the filling and egg glaze

6 tablespoons (3 oz/90 g) granulated sugar

2 teaspoons ground cinnamon

About 1/4 cup (2 oz/60 g) unsalted butter, melted, for brushing

1 large egg, beaten

For the vanilla glaze

1/2 cup (2 oz/60 g) confectioners' (icing) sugar, sifted

1/4 cup (2 fl oz/60 ml) heavy (double) cream

1 teaspoon vanilla extract (essence)

You can make the dough for these rolls on a Saturday afternoon, shape them, cover them loosely with a kitchen towel, and put them in the refrigerator until Sunday morning. Let them warm to room temperature while you preheat the oven, then bake them for 20 minutes. The warm, buttery smell will wake up everyone else in the household.

BY HAND: To make the dough, in a large bowl, dissolve the yeast in the warm milk and let stand until foamy, about 5 minutes. Add the granulated sugar, eggs, 5 cups (25 oz/780 g) of the flour, salt, mace, orange zest, and butter and stir with your hand or a wooden spoon until a rough mass forms. Using a plastic pastry scraper, scrape the dough out onto a lightly floured surface. Knead the dough, working in the remaining flour, until it is smooth and elastic, 5–7 minutes. The dough should be soft, but not sticky.

BY STAND MIXER: To make the dough, in the 5-qt (5-l) bowl of a stand mixer, dissolve the yeast in the warm milk and let stand until foamy, about 5 minutes. Add the granulated sugar, eggs, flour, salt, mace, orange zest, and butter. Place the bowl on the mixer, attach the dough hook, and knead on low speed. Add a little more flour as needed for the dough to come away from the sides of the bowl after a few minutes of kneading. Knead until the dough is smooth and elastic, 5–7 minutes. Remove the dough from the bowl.

Form the dough into a ball, transfer it to a lightly oiled bowl, and cover the bowl with plastic wrap. Let the dough rise in a warm, draft-free spot until it doubles in bulk, 1 1/2–2 hours.

To make the filling, in a small bowl, stir together the granulated sugar and cinnamon. Set aside. Line a half-sheet pan or rimless baking sheet with parchment (baking) paper.

Punch down the dough and turn it out onto a lightly floured work surface. Cut it in half with a sharp knife or a bench scraper. Lightly dust the surface of the dough with flour. Roll out one-half of the dough into a 10-by-16-inch (25-by-40-cm) rectangle. Brush the surface of the rectangle with half of the melted butter, then sprinkle evenly with half of the cinnamon-sugar mixture. Starting at the long side farthest from you, roll up the rectangle toward you into a log.

Cut the log crosswise into 8 slices each 2 inches (5 cm) thick. Place the slices, cut side up, in a circle, side by side and barely touching, on half of the prepared pan.

Sticky Buns

Prepare the dough and cut the logs into rolls as directed. Butter the sides of two 9-inch (23 cm) cake pans. To make a smear, in a bowl, combine ³/₄ cup (6 oz/ 185 g) unsalted butter, at room temperature; 1 cup (7 oz/220 g) firmly packed brown sugar; and 1 tablespoon ground cinnamon and mix thoroughly with a wooden spoon. Divide the mixture in half and spread it evenly all over the bottom of each pan. Sprinkle 1¹/₂ cups (6 oz/185 g) pecans, coarsely chopped, on top. Place 8 cinnamon rolls in each pan. Cover the pans with a kitchen towel and let rise as for the

(continued at far right)

Repeat with the remaining half of the dough, melted butter, and cinnamon-sugar mixture, arranging the rolls on the other half of the pan. For crisper rolls, space them evenly on the pan.

Cover the rolls loosely with a kitchen towel and let them rise in a warm, draft-free spot until they have doubled in size and are spongy to the touch, 30–40 minutes. Alternatively, place the rolls in the refrigerator and let them rise slowly overnight.

Position a rack in the middle of the oven, and preheat to 400°F (200°C).

If you have refrigerated the rolls, let them come to room temperature for 30–40 minutes. Brush the rolls lightly with the beaten egg. Bake until golden brown and a toothpick inserted into the center of a roll comes out clean, 20–25 minutes.

Just before the rolls are ready, make the vanilla glaze. In a small bowl, stir together the confectioners' sugar, cream, and vanilla until the sugar dissolves completely and the mixture thickens slightly.

Let the rolls cool slightly in the pan on a wire rack, then brush on the glaze while they are still warm. Pull the buns apart and serve warm.

Sticky Buns continued...

cinnamon rolls, either at room temperature or in the refrigerator.

Position a rack in the lower third of the oven, and preheat to 400°F (200°C). Bake the buns until a toothpick inserted in the center of a bun comes out clean, 25–30 minutes.

Let the buns cool in the pans on a wire rack for 5 minutes. Then, place a serving tray upside down over each pan and, holding the tray and pan, carefully invert them. Pull the cake pan off the buns, leaving them on the serving tray. Be careful not to burn yourself with the hot smear. When the buns are cool, pull them apart.

Egg Bagels

2 large russet potatoes, 6–8 oz (185–250 g) each, peeled and cubed

2¹/₂ cups (20 fl oz/625 ml) water

2 packages (5 teaspoons) active dry yeast

¹/₄ cup (2 fl oz/60 ml) vegetable oil

4 large eggs, at room temperature

7¹/₂ cups (37¹/₂ oz/1.3 kg) all-purpose (plain) flour, plus extra as needed

1¹/₂ tablespoons salt

1 large egg, beaten

Sesame seeds or poppy seeds for sprinkling (optional)

In a saucepan, combine the potatoes and water, bring to a boil, and cook until fork-tender, about 10 minutes. Drain, reserving the water.

BY HAND: Measure 2 cups (16 fl oz/ 500 ml) of the potato water into a large bowl and let cool to warm (110°F/43°C). Dissolve the yeast in the warm water and let stand until foamy, about 5 minutes. Add the oil and eggs and use a wire whisk to combine. Whisk in 2 cups (10 oz/ 315 g) of the flour and the salt until smooth, about 2 minutes. Stir in the remaining flour with a wooden spoon, 1 cup (5 oz/155 g) at a time, using just enough to form a soft dough. Using a plastic pastry scraper, scrape the dough out onto a lightly floured work surface. Knead the dough until smooth and elastic, 5–7 minutes.

BY STAND MIXER: Measure 2 cups (16 fl oz/500 ml) of the potato water into the 5-qt (5-l) bowl of a stand mixer and let cool to warm (110°F/43°C). Dissolve the yeast in the warm water and let stand until foamy, about 5 minutes. Add the oil and eggs and use a wire whisk to combine. Whisk in 2 cups (10 oz/ 315 g) of the flour and the salt until smooth, about 2 minutes. Place the bowl on the mixer, attach the dough hook, and mix in the remaining flour, 1 cup (5 oz/155 g) at a time, using just enough to form a soft dough. Knead the dough on low speed until smooth and elastic, 5–7 minutes. Remove the dough from the bowl.

Unless you are in New York, it's hard to find a good bagel. Soft, tasty, and a little bit chewy, these homemade treats are the most satisfying alternative to what you find in New York. Their distinctive texture comes from the two-step process of first boiling and then baking the bagels. Bagels are extremely versatile. Serve them simply with butter and jam or cream cheese. Or add any number of toppings to the cream cheese, such as lox, capers, and red onion or slices of fresh tomatoes and avocado with basil.

Form the dough into a ball, transfer it to a lightly oiled bowl, and cover the bowl with plastic wrap. Let the dough rise in a warm, draft-free spot until it doubles in bulk, about 1 hour.

TO STORE BAGELS

Bagels store well, so make plenty. Once you have baked the bagels and they have cooled completely, pack them into zippered bags. Store the bagels in the freezer for up to 2 weeks. To refresh the bagels, preheat the oven to 375°F (190°C). Line a half-sheet pan or rimless baking sheet with parchment (baking) paper, place the bagels on it, and heat for about 5 minutes. Slice the bagels in half and toast before serving.

Punch down the dough and turn it out onto a lightly floured work surface. Cut it into quarters with a sharp knife or a bench scraper. Cut each quarter into 3 equal pieces and, using your palms, roll each piece into a rope 10 inches (25 cm) long. Using the heel of your hand, flatten 1 inch (2.5 cm) of one end of each rope. Form each bagel by overlapping the flat end of the rope over 1 inch (2.5 cm) of the round end. Pinch together firmly. As the bagels are formed, set them aside on a lightly floured surface. Cover all the bagels loosely with a kitchen towel and let them rest until they are barely puffy when lifted, about 15 minutes.

Position a rack in the lower third of the oven, and preheat to 425°F (220°C). Line a half-sheet pan or rimless baking sheet with parchment (baking) paper. Lightly brush the parchment with oil, or spray it with nonstick cooking spray.

Fill a large, wide pot three-fourths full of water and bring to a boil over high heat. Reduce the heat to maintain a gentle boil. Using a large slotted spoon, gently lower 3 bagels into the water. Do not crowd them, or they will lose their round shape. Simmer 1 minute, then turn the bagels over and simmer 1 minute longer. Transfer the bagels to the prepared pan, spacing them 1 inch (2.5 cm) apart. Repeat until all the bagels are boiled.

Brush the bagels with the beaten egg and sprinkle with seeds, if using. Bake until golden brown, 25–30 minutes. Transfer to wire racks and let cool completely.

Flatbreads

About Flatbreads

Flatbreads are wonderful canvases for myriad flavors, and although some call for yeast and rising time, they never the reach the heights of their yeasted cousins. Extremely versatile, flatbreads range from crispy crackers to thick, soft focaccia to chewy, cheesy pizza.

Some flatbreads, like crackers, call for no yeast at all—just a rest period for the dough so the gluten can relax and the cracker can be more easily shaped.

Pizza and focaccia, in contrast, are made with yeast and will have a deeper flavor if you give the dough an overnight rise in the refrigerator. The stages for mixing and kneading yeasted flatbread doughs are similar to the techniques outlined in Stages of Bread Making (pages 32–35), but often take less time. The results, however, are no less satisfying.

Toppings for pizza can range from simple to sophisticated, from appetizer to main course. Pizza Margherita, with its traditional crust, is a great destination for a bumper crop of summer tomatoes, while a cornmeal crust crowned with prosciutto, caramelized onion, and sage is the ideal centerpiece for an autumn pizza party. Use these recipes as a starting point to create your own topping combinations. Some ideas include mixed grilled vegetables and basil pesto; goat cheese, roasted red bell peppers (capsicums), and Kalamata olives; sun-dried tomatoes, spinach, and Asiago cheese; or Italian sausage with sautéed red, green, and yellow peppers and onions.

Focaccia takes well to flavoring. It's a showcase for delicate herbs such as basil and tarragon, for stronger-flavored herbs like thyme and rosemary, and for garlic, onions, peppers, and olives, too. A sprinkling of coarse sea salt adds flavor and texture. Plain focaccia also makes a delicious sandwich bread. Try it with layers of fresh mozzarella, roasted red peppers, basil, and a drizzle of fruity olive oil.

Provençal *fougasse* takes similarly well to Mediterranean-style flavorings, and its elegant leaf shape makes for a striking presentation.

Crackers are also an excellent canvas for different herbs, spices, seeds, and toppings. Use the master recipe to make savory mixed-seed crackers, or try adding lemon zest for a refreshing alternative. Because these crackers are not yeasted, you can make the dough, roll it out into sheets, wrap it tightly, and store it in the freezer for up to a month before baking, making it easy to impress your guests at a moment's notice.

All of the flatbreads in this chapter draw on the Mediterranean kitchens of France and Italy. But the tradition of flatbreads—some baked, some not—reaches far beyond the region, to the poori, chapati, and naan of India, the crisp onion cakes of China, the pita and matzoh of the middle east, and the tortillas of Mexico.

The intense, radiant heat of a wood-burning oven is especially good—and traditional—for the short, hot bake that many flatbreads require. You can create similar conditions in your own oven by lining your oven rack with unglazed quarry tiles (available at most hardware stores and tile shops) or by using a pizza stone. A baker's peel, a large, thin rectangular piece of wood with a long handle, works well for transferring the shaped dough to the hot baking surface. If you don't own a baker's peel, you can shape the flatbread on an inverted half-sheet pan and use it to slide the flatbread onto the heated tiles or stone. Always preheat the tiles or stone for a minimum of 20 minutes before baking your flatbread. This will help ensure a crisp, well-baked crust.

TROUBLESHOOTING FLATBREADS	
What happened	Why it happened
Dough is rising too fast.	Kitchen is too warm; transfer dough to cooler location.
Dough is rising too slowly or is not rising.	Kitchen is too cool, or water in which yeast was proofed was too warm or too cool; transfer dough to warmer location. Yeast is old and no longer active; use fresh yeast.
Bread is browning too quickly.	Oven is too hot; cover bread loosely with aluminum foil and continue baking.
Bread is dense and too moist.	Dough was not proofed long enough.
Bread is too hard and chewy.	Bread was overbaked at too low a temperature.

Basic Focaccia

2 packages (5 teaspoons) active dry yeast

1³/₄ cups (14 fl oz/440 ml) warm water (105°–115°F/ 40°–46°C)

1 teaspoon sugar

³/₄ cup (6 fl oz/180 ml) extra-virgin olive oil

5 cups (25 oz/780 g) all-purpose (plain) flour, plus extra for kneading

2 teaspoons fine sea salt

1 teaspoon coarse sea salt (optional)

Focaccia is an all-purpose bread that can be toasted for breakfast, split in half and used for sandwiches for lunch, or tucked into a bread basket on the dinner table. Cut focaccia into cubes and toast them in the oven for adding to a Caesar salad, or grind up a day-old piece of focaccia for bread crumbs.

BY HAND: In a large bowl, dissolve the yeast in the warm water and let stand until foamy, about 5 minutes. Add the sugar, ¹/₂ cup (4 fl oz/120 ml) of the olive oil, the flour, and the fine sea salt and stir with your hand or a wooden spoon until a rough ball forms. Using a plastic pastry scraper, scrape the dough out onto a floured work surface. Knead the dough until smooth and elastic, 5–7 minutes. Add up to ¹/₂ cup (2¹/₂ oz/75 g) flour to the work surface while kneading to prevent the dough from sticking.

BY STAND MIXER: In the 5-qt (5-l) bowl of a stand mixer, dissolve the yeast in the warm water and let stand until foamy, about 5 minutes. Add the sugar, ¹/₂ cup (4 fl oz/ 120 ml) olive oil, the flour, and the fine sea salt. Place the bowl on the mixer, attach the dough hook, and knead on low speed, until the dough is smooth and elastic, 5–7 minutes. Add up to ¹/₂ cup (2¹/₂ oz/75 g) flour while kneading to prevent the dough from sticking. Remove the dough from the bowl.

Form the dough into a ball, transfer it to a lightly oiled bowl, and cover the bowl with plastic wrap. Let the dough rise in a warm, draft-free spot until it doubles in bulk, 1–1¹/₂ hours. For a more flavorful bread, make the dough up to this point, punch it down, cover the bowl with plastic wrap, and refrigerate overnight. Let the dough come to room temperature before shaping.

Pour the remaining ¹/₄ cup (2 fl oz/60 ml) oil evenly into a half-sheet pan. Turn the dough out into the pan. Press the dough evenly into the pan. If it is too elastic to spread without springing back, let it rest for 5 minutes. Cover the pan loosely with a dry kitchen towel. Let the dough rise in a warm, draft-free spot until it doubles in size, about 1 hour.

Position a rack in the lower third of the oven, and preheat to 450°F (230°C). Dimple the dough by pressing your fingertips all the way into it at 1-inch (2.5-cm) intervals over the entire surface. Sprinkle it with the coarse salt, if desired.

Bake the focaccia until golden brown, 20–30 minutes. Transfer to a wire rack and let cool in the pan. Cut it into squares and serve warm or at room temperature. Store tightly wrapped in aluminum foil at room temperature for up to 1 day or freeze for up to 2 weeks. Reheat at 375°F (190°C) for 10 minutes.

VARIATIONS

Herb Focaccia

Add 2 tablespoons chopped fresh herbs, such as thyme, basil, oregano, marjoram, or tarragon, to the dough with the fine salt.

Pepper Focaccia

Seed and thinly slice 3 bell peppers (capsicums), 1 red, 1 green, and 1 yellow. In a frying pan over medium-high heat, warm 2 tablespoons olive oil. Add the sliced peppers and sauté until they soften, about 5 minutes. Let cool. Just before dimpling the dough, spread the peppers on top. Sprinkle with freshly ground black pepper along with the coarse salt.

Onion, Garlic, and Rosemary Focaccia

Thinly slice 2 yellow onions. In a frying pan over high heat, warm 2 tablespoons olive oil. Add the onions and sauté until dark brown and caramelized, about 12 minutes. Add 2 cloves garlic, minced, and 1 tablespoon chopped fresh rosemary to the onions and cook for 2 minutes longer. Just before dimpling the dough, spread the onion mixture on top. Sprinkle with coarse salt.

Olive Focaccia

Midway through baking, sprinkle ¹/₂ cup (2¹/₂ oz/75 g) halved, pitted Kalamata olives and 1 tablespoon chopped fresh rosemary on top of the focaccia.

Provençal Fougasse

This interesting flatbread is as delicious as it is gorgeous. It features the hearty flavors of a wonderful region of southern France where garlic, rosemary, wild oregano, and olives flourish. Serve this bread as an hors d'oeuvre at a summer picnic, as an accompaniment to a niçoise salad, or with an aged goat cheese and some red wine for a light dinner. Make sure to display it whole to your guests before it is eaten.

3 cloves garlic, chopped

1 tablespoon chopped fresh rosemary

1 tablespoon chopped fresh oregano

1 tablespoon chopped fresh thyme

¼ cup (2 fl oz/60 ml) extra-virgin olive oil

1 package (2½ teaspoons) active dry yeast

1¾ cups (14 fl oz/430 ml) warm water (105°–115°F/ 40°–46°C)

4½ cups (22½ oz/705 g) all-purpose (plain) flour

1 tablespoon salt

Semolina flour for dusting

In a small saucepan over medium heat, combine the garlic, rosemary, oregano, thyme, and olive oil. Bring to a simmer and cook just until the garlic is tender, about 1 minute. Remove from the heat and let cool to room temperature.

BY HAND: In a large bowl, dissolve the yeast in the warm water and let stand until foamy, about 5 minutes. Add the oil mixture, flour, and salt and stir with a wooden spoon until a rough ball forms. Using a plastic pastry scraper, scrape the dough out onto a clean, lightly oiled work surface. Knead the dough until elastic and no longer sticky, 5–7 minutes.

BY STAND MIXER: In the 5-qt (5-l) bowl of a stand mixer, dissolve the yeast in the warm water and let stand until foamy, about 5 minutes. Add the oil mixture, flour, and salt. Place the bowl on the mixer, attach the dough hook, and knead on low speed until the dough is smooth and elastic, 5–7 minutes. Remove the dough from the bowl.

Form the dough into a ball, transfer it to a lightly oiled bowl, and cover the bowl with plastic wrap. Let the dough rise in a warm, draft-free spot until it doubles in bulk, 1½–2 hours

Punch down the dough and turn it out onto a clean work surface. Cut the dough in half with a sharp knife or a bench scraper. Shape each piece into a loose ball, cover with a dry kitchen towel, and let rest for 5 minutes.

Liberally dust 2 half-sheet pans or rimless baking sheets with semolina flour. On a lightly floured work surface, roll out each portion of the dough into a rectangle with about the same dimensions as the prepared pan. Transfer each rectangle to the prepared pan, spreading it out with your hands if it shrinks when you pick it up. Facing the narrow end of a rectangle, and eyeing the vertical center of it, use a sharp knife or a pizza wheel to cut 3 slits at an angle down the left side of the center, and 3 slits down the right side of the center. Gently pull on the dough to open the slits up slightly so that they widen into ovals.

Cover the dough loosely with a dry kitchen towel and let the breads rise again until they double in size, 20–30 minutes.

Position a rack in the lower third of the oven, and preheat to 425°F (220°C). Bake the breads until they are lightly browned and sound hollow when tapped on the bottom, 15–20 minutes. Transfer to wire racks and let cool completely in the pans. Store tightly wrapped in aluminum foil at room temperature for up to 1 day or freeze for up to 2 weeks. Reheat at 375°F (190°C) for 10 minutes.

Seeded Crackers

2 cups (10 oz/315 g) all-purpose (plain) flour, plus extra for the work surface

2 teaspoons sugar

2 teaspoons salt

1 teaspoon coarsely ground pepper

1 teaspoon poppy seeds

1 teaspoon sesame seeds

1 teaspoon mustard seeds

1 tablespoon solid vegetable shortening (vegetable lard), at room temperature

1 tablespoon cold unsalted butter

$1/2$ cup (4 fl oz/125 ml) heavy (double) cream, plus extra if needed

These crisp, homemade crackers can be completely altered by using different spices and herbs. Once you make the dough, you can roll it out, wrap it tightly with plastic wrap, and freeze the sheets for up to 1 month. When you are ready for fresh crackers, just bake the frozen sheet for 20 minutes. They are excellent served as part of a cheese course with a variety of different cheeses or alongside a steaming bowl of homemade soup.

BY HAND: In a small bowl, stir together the flour, sugar, salt, pepper, and poppy, sesame, and mustard seeds. Using a pastry blender or 2 knives, cut in the shortening and butter until the mixture forms large, coarse crumbs the size of peas. Pour in the cream and mix with a fork until a rough mass forms.

BY FOOD PROCESSOR: Combine the flour, sugar, salt, pepper, and poppy, sesame, and mustard seeds and pulse 1 or 2 times to mix. Add the shortening and butter and pulse 7–10 times until the mixture forms large, coarse crumbs the size of peas. Pour in the cream and pulse a few times until the dough comes together in a rough mass.

Using a plastic pastry scraper, scrape the dough out onto a clean work surface and gently squeeze it together. Add a few more drops of cream if the dough will not hold a soft shape. Gently press the dough into a disk, wrap it in plastic wrap, and let rest at room temperature for at least 20 minutes or for up to 1 hour.

Position a rack in the middle of the oven, and preheat to 350°F (180°C). Line 2 half-sheet pans or rimless baking sheets with parchment (baking) paper.

Unwrap the dough disk and place on a lightly floured work surface. Cut the dough in half with a sharp knife or a bench scraper. Roll out one-half of the dough into a rectangular sheet as thin as possible without tearing, dusting it with flour as needed to prevent sticking to either the work surface or the rolling pin. Trim the edges of the dough to fit the prepared pan, then carefully transfer the sheet to the pan. Repeat with the second half of the dough. Alternatively, using a pizza wheel or a sharp knife, cut the dough sheets into shapes and place on the pans.

Bake 1 sheet of crackers at a time until they are crisp and brown, 12–15 minutes. Transfer to wire racks and let cool completely until crisp. If you have baked the dough in sheets, break each sheet into shards. The crackers are best when eaten fresh, but they may be stored in an airtight container for up to 5 days.

VARIATIONS

Lemon-Thyme Crackers
Omit the poppy, sesame, and mustard seeds. Add the finely grated zest of 1 lemon and 1 tablespoon chopped fresh thyme with the pepper.

Oregano-Parmesan Crackers
Omit the poppy, sesame, and mustard seeds. Add 1 tablespoon chopped fresh oregano and 2 tablespoons grated Parmesan cheese with the pepper.

Spicy Jack Cheese Crackers
Omit the pepper, poppy, and sesame seeds. Add 1 teaspoon ground cayenne pepper, 1 teaspoon paprika, and 2 tablespoons grated dry jack cheese with the mustard seeds.

Pizza Margherita

For the crust

2 packages (5 teaspoons) active dry yeast

2¹⁄₄ cups (18 fl oz/560 ml) warm water (105°–115°F/ 40°–46°C)

2 teaspoons malt syrup or sugar

¹⁄₄ cup (2 fl oz/60 ml) olive oil

5 cups (25 oz/780 g) bread flour, plus extra as needed

1 tablespoon sea salt

All-purpose (plain) flour and semolina flour for rolling and shaping

For the topping

1 cup (4 oz/125 g) grated Parmesan cheese

1 cup (2 oz/60 g) loosely packed fresh basil, finely shredded

6 tomatoes, about 2 lb (1 kg) total weight, peeled (page 23), seeded, and diced

Sea salt and freshly ground pepper

1 lb (500 g) fresh mozzarella cheese, sliced ¹⁄₄-inch (6-mm) thick

2 tablespoons olive oil

BY HAND: To make the crust, in a large bowl, dissolve the yeast in the warm water and let stand until foamy, about 5 minutes. Add the malt syrup, oil, flour, and salt and stir with your hand or a wooden spoon until a rough ball forms. Using a plastic pastry scraper, scrape the dough out onto a floured work surface. Knead the dough until soft, smooth, and elastic, 8–10 minutes. Add up to 1 cup (5 oz/155 g) flour to the work surface while kneading to prevent the dough from sticking.

BY STAND MIXER: To make the crust, in the 5-qt (5-l) bowl of a stand mixer, dissolve the yeast in the warm water and let stand until foamy, about 5 minutes. Add the malt syrup, oil, flour, and salt. Place the bowl on the mixer, attach the dough hook, and knead on low speed until soft, smooth, and elastic, about 8–10 minutes. Add up to 1 cup (5 oz/155 g) flour while kneading so the dough will pull away from the sides of the bowl. Remove the dough from the bowl.

Form the dough into a ball, transfer it to a lightly oiled bowl, and cover the bowl with plastic wrap. Let the dough rise in a warm, draft-free spot until it doubles in bulk, 1¹⁄₂–2 hours. For a more flavorful crust, make the dough up to this point, punch it down, cover the bowl with plastic wrap, and refrigerate overnight. Let the dough come to room temperature before shaping.

Place a pizza or baking stone (page 12) on a rack in the lower third of the oven, and preheat to 500°F (260°C) for at least 30 minutes before baking. Turn the dough out of the bowl onto a lightly oiled work surface. Cut it in half with a sharp knife or a bench scraper. Gently shape each half into a loose ball. Cover loosely with a kitchen towel and let rest for 10 minutes. Lightly dust 1 dough ball with all-purpose flour. Roll it out into a round 12–14 inches (30–35 cm) in diameter. Spread ¹⁄₄ cup (1¹⁄₂ oz/45 g) semolina flour on a baker's peel or on the top of an inverted half-sheet pan. Transfer the dough round to the peel or pan.

To top the round, sprinkle half of the Parmesan cheese and then half of the basil over the surface. Scatter half the tomatoes evenly over the surface. Lightly sprinkle with salt and pepper. Nestle half of the mozzarella slices around the tomatoes and drizzle the top evenly with 1 tablespoon of the olive oil.

Slide the pizza off the peel or pan onto the hot stone. Bake the pizza until the crust is crisp and brown, 10–15 minutes. Using the baker's peel or a wide metal spatula, carefully transfer the pizza to a cutting board. Repeat with the remaining dough and topping ingredients. Serve the pizza hot, cut into wedges.

This is the perfect summer-time pizza, made when the traditional flavors of fresh basil and tomatoes are at their peak. To peel the tomatoes, follow the same directions for peeling peaches (page 23). If tomatoes out of season, spread a thin layer of a good-quality (preferably homemade) marinara sauce over the crust before adding the cheese. Use the best-quality ingredients you can find, since this pizza relies on few flavors for its perfection.

Prosciutto, Caramelized Onion, and Sage Pizza

For the crust

1 package (2¹/₂ teaspoons) active dry yeast

3 cups (24 fl oz/750 ml) warm water (105°–115°F/ 40° to 46°C)

¹/₂ teaspoon sugar

2 tablespoons olive oil

¹/₂ cup (2¹/₂ oz/75 g) medium- or fine-grind cornmeal or corn flour

2 cups (10 oz/315 g) bread flour

3 cups (15 oz/470 g) all-purpose (plain) flour, plus extra for kneading

1 tablespoon sea salt

Olive oil for shaping

All purpose (plain) flour and semolina flour for rolling and the baker's peel

BY HAND: To make the crust, in a large bowl, dissolve the yeast in the warm water and let stand until foamy, about 5 minutes. Add the sugar, oil, cornmeal, bread flour, all-purpose flour, and salt and stir with your hand or a wooden spoon until a rough ball forms. Using a plastic pastry scraper, scrape the dough out onto a floured work surface. Knead the dough until it is soft, smooth, and elastic, 8–10 minutes. Add up to 1 cup (5 oz/160 g) all-purpose flour to the work surface while kneading to prevent the dough from sticking.

BY STAND MIXER: To make the crust, in the 5-qt (5-l) bowl of a stand mixer, dissolve the yeast in the warm water and let stand until foamy, about 5 minutes. Add the sugar, oil, cornmeal, bread flour, all-purpose flour, and salt. Place the bowl on the mixer, attach the dough hook, and knead on low speed until soft, smooth, and elastic, about 8 minutes. Add up to 1 cup (5 oz/160 g) all-purpose flour while kneading so the dough will pull away from the sides of the bowl. Remove the dough from the bowl.

For the topping

¹/₄ cup (2 fl oz/60 ml) extra-virgin olive oil, plus 2 tablespoons for drizzling

2 yellow onions, thinly sliced

Sea salt and freshly ground pepper

¹/₄ cup (¹/₄ oz/7 g) fresh sage leaves, coarsely chopped

¹/₄ cup (1 oz/30 g) grated Parmesan cheese

8–12 paper-thin slices prosciutto di Parma

Form the dough into a ball, transfer it to a lightly oiled bowl, and cover the bowl with plastic wrap. Let the dough rise in a warm, draft-free spot until it doubles in bulk, 1¹/₂–2 hours. For a more flavorful crust, make the dough up to this point, punch it down, cover the bowl with plastic wrap, and refrigerate overnight. Let the dough come to room temperature before shaping.

Meanwhile, make the topping. In a large frying pan over high heat, warm the ¹/₄ cup extra-virgin olive oil. Add the onions and sauté until caramelized and deep brown, about 12 minutes. Season to taste with salt and pepper. Remove from the heat and let cool completely.

Place a pizza or baking stone (page 12) on a rack in the lower third of the oven, and preheat to 500°F (260°C) for at least 30 minutes before baking.

Turn the dough out of the bowl onto a lightly oiled work surface. Cut it in half with a sharp knife or bench scraper. Gently shape each piece of dough into a loose ball. Cover loosely with a dry kitchen towel and let rest for 10 minutes.

Silky prosciutto, sweet caramelized onions, and smoky sage come together flawlessly in a pizza that is sophisticated enough for a dinner party. Choose the best-quality prosciutto that you can find, preferably one from Parma. The cornmeal in the crust adds wonderful texture and crunch, but make sure to use medium- or fine-grind cornmeal, as coarse cornmeal is too heavily textured for a crust. You can also make a simple snack with the dough: Bake a round of it unadorned, then slather it with butter while it is still hot.

Lightly dust 1 dough ball with all-purpose flour. Roll it out into a round about 12–14 inches (30–35 cm) in diameter, depending on how thick you like your crust. Spread $1/4$ cup ($1^{1}/_2$ oz/45 g) semolina flour on a baker's peel or on the top of an inverted half-sheet pan. Transfer the dough round to the peel or pan.

To top the round, using your fingers, spread half of the cooled onion mixture evenly over the surface. Sprinkle on half of the sage and then half of the Parmesan cheese. Drizzle the top evenly with 1 tablespoon of the extra-virgin olive oil.

Slide the pizza off the peel or pan onto the hot stone. Bake until the crust is crisp and brown, 10–15 minutes. Using the peel or a wide metal spatula, carefully transfer the pizza to a cutting board. Arrange half of the prosciutto slices on top of the melted cheese. Repeat with the remaining dough and topping ingredients. Serve the pizza hot, cut into wedges.

Quick Breads

About Quick Breads

From loaves to muffins to biscuits, quick breads are a snap to assemble, usually requiring little more than stirring together a handful of everyday ingredients and slipping the mixture into a hot oven. They are a great way for the novice baker to get started in baking.

Quick breads refer to most types of loaf and pan breads, muffins, biscuits, scones, or baked oven "pancakes" that are not yeasted. While yeast breads get their lift from yeast, quick breads rely on baking powder and/or baking soda for leavening. Many quick breads, in fact, are more like cake than they are like bread. Yeast breads require at least 5–10 minutes of kneading to develop their distinctive texture and strong structure, but quick breads generally need none at all because the aim is for a tender, rather than a chewy, product.

Most quick breads go together rapidly and are mixed according to one of two different techniques, quick mixing or creaming. In quick mixing, sometimes called the muffin method, the wet and dry ingredients are first whisked or stirred together separately, and then gently combined just before the mixture goes into the oven.

The creaming method is less frequently used for making quick breads. It calls for first creaming together butter and sugar, the common beginning for many cake recipes as well. Creaming (the action of sugar granules scraping against the butter) develops little air pockets that set the stage for the leaveners to work and give the finished bread its structure. Eggs are typically beaten into the lightened butter mixture before being mixed with the dry ingredients, which have been stirred together separately.

The moment you combine the wet ingredients with the dry ones, go easy on the mixing and observe all recipe directions to stir just until combined. Whether you are whipping up corn bread, muffins, shortcakes, or biscuits, with quick breads it is important not to develop gluten (unlike yeast breads). If you are new to baking, you will find that quick breads are excellent practice before moving on to more difficult cakes.

Quick breads also usually contain more fat, such as butter or oil, and more sugar than yeast breads. These ingredients, along with gentle and limited mixing, are what give quick breads their tender crumb.

As with most baking recipes, it is important to use the correct pan type and size. Pans that are too full will cause the batter to drip over the sides as it rises in the heat of the oven, while pans that are not full enough will result in homely flat-topped muffins and breads. Yet there is some versatility. For example, muffin pans come in three sizes: 12-cup pans for standard muffins; 6-cup pans for jumbo muffins, which turn out muffins at least twice the standard size; and 24-cup pans for minia-ture muffins no bigger than bite-size. The same batter can be used in all sizes, plus the standard pan can be used for baking cupcakes, cinnamon rolls, and popovers. Or the same coffee cake batter can go into a 9- or 10-inch (23- or 25-cm) round springform pan or an 8- or 9-inch square cake pan.

Most bakers love quick breads not only because they are typically fast and easy, but also because they offer so many flavor possibilities. Loaf-type breads can be enriched with fresh fruits, such as bananas or berries; dried fruits, such as cranberries or cherries; purées, such as pumpkin; or even shredded vegetables, such as carrots or zucchini.

Muffins take well to combinations of sweet flavorings, such as chocolate and cherry or pear and ginger, and savory flavorings, such as cheddar cheese and chiles, herbs and yogurt. You can also make your own flavor choices, such as trading pecans or almonds for walnuts, dried currants or cranberries for raisins, or apples for pears.

TROUBLESHOOTING QUICK BREADS

What happened	Why it happened
Bread caved in.	Rose too fast because of too much leavening.
Bread is too dry.	Baked too long; not enough fat or liquid.
Bread is underbaked in spots.	Oven was not hot enough; oven heats unevenly.
Bread is too dense.	Batter or dough was overmixed.
Bread is tough.	Batter or dough was overmixed.

Mixing Techniques for Quick Breads

Quick breads rely on two basic mixing techniques for combining wet and dry ingredients, quick mixing and creaming. The quick-mixing method is shown here, both by hand and by mixer. For more information on the creaming method, see page 208.

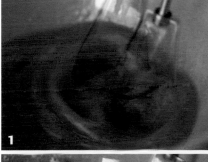

BY HAND

1 In a medium bowl, using a sturdy wire whisk, whisk together the wet ingredients until blended and smooth. In a separate large bowl, using a wooden spoon, stir together the dry ingredients.

2 Add the dry ingredients to the wet ingredients and stir together gently with the wooden spoon.

3 Stir just until the mixture comes together and the dry ingredients are moistened, being careful not to overmix. The batter may be lumpy, but the lumps will vanish during baking. Then, if adding fruits or nuts, stir in just until evenly distributed.

BY MIXER

1 In the large bowl of a stand mixer fitted with the paddle attachment or with a handheld mixer, beat together the wet ingredients on medium speed just until blended. In a separate bowl, using a wooden spoon, stir together the dry ingredients.

2 Reduce the speed to low and slowly add the dry ingredients to the wet ingredients.

3 Beat just until mixed, being careful not to overmix. Then, if adding fruits or nuts, stir in just until evenly distributed. Mix on low speed only briefly.

Baking Powder Biscuits

To make tender, flaky biscuits, it is important to have a light touch. Biscuits, and quick breads in general, benefit from minimal stirring. These old-fashioned biscuits can be rolled and cut out into any shape. Round is the classic, but if you roll out the dough into a rectangle and cut out squares, there are no scraps to reroll (biscuits made from dough rolled a second time are never as tender as first-cut ones). You can make drop biscuits by dropping the dough by tablespoons onto the pan. For a more flavorful biscuit, replace the milk with buttermilk, reduce the baking powder to 2 teaspoons, and add ½ teaspoon baking soda (bicarbonate of soda).

Position a rack in the middle of the oven, and preheat to 425°F (220°C). Line a half-sheet pan with parchment (baking) paper or butter lightly.

BY HAND: In a bowl, stir together the flour, baking powder, and salt. Add the butter. Using a pastry blender or 2 knives, cut in the butter just until the mixture forms large, coarse crumbs the size of small peas. Pour in the milk and mix with a fork or rubber spatula just until the dry ingredients are moistened.

BY FOOD PROCESSOR: Combine the flour, baking powder, and salt and pulse 2 or 3 times to mix. Add the butter and pulse 3 or 4 times or just until the mixture forms large, coarse crumbs the size of small peas. Pour in the milk and pulse for a few seconds just until the dry ingredients are moistened.

Turn the dough out onto a lightly floured work surface and knead gently a few times until it clings together. Roll or pat out the dough into a round about ¾ inch (2 cm) thick.

Using a 3-inch (7.5-cm) round biscuit cutter, cut out biscuits, pressing straight down and lifting straight up. Place the biscuits on the prepared pan, spacing them 1 inch (2.5 cm) apart. Gather up the scraps, roll or pat out again, and cut out more biscuits.

Bake the biscuits until lightly browned, 15–18 minutes. Serve immediately or let cool on a wire rack. Store in an airtight container or plastic bag at room temperature for up to 2 days. Reheat in a 375°F (190°C) oven for 3–5 minutes.

2 cups (10 oz/315 g) all-purpose (plain) flour

2½ teaspoons baking powder

½ teaspoon salt

6 tablespoons (3 oz/90 g) cold unsalted butter, cut into ½-inch (12-mm) pieces

¾ cup (6 fl oz/180 ml) whole milk

Strawberry Shortcakes

For the dough

2 cups (8 oz/250 g) cake (soft-wheat) flour, or 1³/₄ cups (9 oz/280 g) all-purpose (plain) flour

¹/₄ cup (2 oz/60 g) granulated sugar

1 tablespoon baking powder

¹/₂ teaspoon salt

¹/₂ cup (4 oz/125 g) cold unsalted butter, cut into ¹/₂-inch (12-mm) pieces

1 large egg

¹/₃ cup (3 fl oz/80 ml) heavy (double) cream, plus extra cream if making drop biscuits and for brushing

2 tablespoons Demerara or turbinado sugar

For the filling

4 cups (1 lb/500 g) straw-berries, hulled and sliced

3 tablespoons granulated sugar

Whipped Cream (page 306)

Position a rack in the middle of the oven, and preheat to 425°F (220°C). Line a half-sheet pan or rimless baking sheet with parchment (baking) paper.

BY HAND: In a bowl, stir together the flour, granulated sugar, baking powder, and salt. Using a pastry blender or 2 knives, cut in the butter until the mixture forms large, coarse crumbs the size of small peas. In a small bowl, whisk together the egg and the ¹/₃ cup cream until blended. Pour the egg mixture over the dry ingredients and mix with a rubber spatula just until moistened.

BY FOOD PROCESSOR: Combine the flour, granulated sugar, baking powder, and salt and pulse 2 or 3 times to mix. Add the butter and pulse 3 or 4 times, or just until the mixture forms large, coarse crumbs the size of small peas. In a bowl, whisk together the egg and the ¹/₃ cup cream until blended. Pour over the dry ingredients and pulse 2 or 3 times just until moistened.

For drop-biscuit shortcakes, the dough must be soft. Add additional cream, 1 tablespoon at a time, as needed. Spoon out the dough onto the prepared pan in mounds 3 inches (7.5 cm) wide and about ³/₄ inch (2 cm) high, spacing them 1 inch (2.5 cm) apart.

For rolled and cut shortcakes, turn the dough out onto a lightly floured work surface and knead gently a few times until it clings together. Roll or pat out into a round about ³/₄ inch (2 cm) thick. Using a 3-inch (7.5-cm) round biscuit cutter, cut out rounds, pressing straight down and lifting straight up. Place the shortcakes on the prepared pan, spacing them 1 inch (2.5 cm) apart. Gather up the scraps, roll or pat out again, and cut out more shortcakes.

Brush the tops of the shortcakes with 1–2 tablespoons cream and sprinkle with the Demerara sugar. Bake until lightly browned, 12–15 minutes.

While the shortcakes are baking, prepare the berry filling. In a bowl, using a fork, crush 1 cup (4 oz/125 g) of the berries. Add the remaining berries and the granulated sugar, mix well, and refrigerate for up to 30 minutes to macerate.

Transfer the shortcakes to a wire rack and let cool for 15 minutes. Meanwhile, prepare the whipped cream. To serve, split the warm shortcakes horizontally and place the bottom half of each, cut side up, on a plate. Spoon the berries on top, dividing them evenly. Top with the whipped cream. Cover with the shortcake tops. Serve immediately.

Fresh, warm shortcakes, split and filled with whipped cream and sugared straw-berries, are an old-fashioned American tradition. These golden, fluffy cream biscuits can be dropped from a spoon or rolled and cut into neat rounds. Coarse sugar crystals give the biscuits a crunchy finish. Raspberries, blackberries, or sliced peaches or nectarines can replace the strawberries.

Banana-Nut Bread

2 large bananas

1¹/₂ cups (7¹/₂ oz/235 g) all-purpose (plain) flour

¹/₂ cup (2¹/₂ oz/75 g) whole-wheat (wholemeal) flour

2 teaspoons baking powder

¹/₂ teaspoon baking soda (bicarbonate of soda)

¹/₄ teaspoon salt

¹/₄ teaspoon grated nutmeg

1 tablespoon grated orange zest

¹/₂ cup (2 oz/60 g) chopped walnuts, toasted (page 21)

2 large eggs

³/₄ cup (6 oz/185 g) firmly packed golden brown sugar

6 tablespoons (3 oz/90 g) unsalted butter, melted

¹/₂ cup (4 fl oz/125 ml) whole milk

Position a rack in the middle of the oven, and preheat to 350°F (180°C). Butter and flour a 9-by-5-inch (23-by-13-cm) loaf pan.

In a small bowl, using a fork, mash the bananas. You should have 1¹/₃ cups (10 oz/315 g). In a separate bowl, stir together the all-purpose and whole-wheat flours, baking powder, baking soda, salt, nutmeg, orange zest, and nuts. Set aside.

BY HAND: In a large bowl, whisk the eggs until blended and stir in the brown sugar, butter, and milk. Add the dry ingredients in 3 batches alternately with the bananas and stir with a rubber spatula just until the batter is moistened.

BY MIXER: In a large bowl, combine the eggs, brown sugar, butter, and milk. Beat on medium-low speed just until blended. Add the dry ingredients in 3 batches alternately with the bananas and mix on low speed just until mixed. Do not overmix.

Pour the batter into the prepared pan and smooth the top with the rubber spatula. Bake until a toothpick inserted into the center comes out clean, 55–60 minutes. If the surface starts to brown too much, cover with a sheet of aluminum foil the last 15 minutes of baking.

Transfer to a wire rack and let cool in the pan for 5 minutes, then turn out onto the rack and cool completely. Store in an airtight container at room temperature for 2–3 days or freeze for up to 1 month.

The addition of whole-wheat flour lends a wholesome goodness to this moist quick bread. Let your bananas fully ripen with some brown spots for extra sweetness. For a handsome topping, pour the batter into the pan, smooth the top, and then stud it with a row of walnut halves lined up down the center. Sprinkle lightly with Demerara sugar, which will caramelize during baking. You can also substitute pecans for the walnuts in the batter and on top.

MAKES 1 LOAF

Classic Corn Bread

MAKES 1 LOAF

VARIATIONS

Corn Bread with Red Pepper and Jack Cheese

Sauté 1 red bell pepper (capsicum), seeded and chopped, in 1 tablespoon olive oil until glazed, about 3 minutes. Add the sautéed peppers and 1/2 teaspoon ground cumin to the dry ingredients. Sprinkle the top with 1/2 cup (2 oz/60 g) shredded Monterey jack cheese after 15 minutes of baking.

Corn Bread with Sun-Dried Tomatoes and Pistachios

Add 1/2 cup (4 oz/125 g) chopped oil-packed or moist, dry-packed sun-dried tomatoes; 1/3 cup (1 1/2 oz/45 g) grated Parmesan cheese; and 1/2 cup (2 oz/60 g) pistachios or pine nuts, toasted (page 21), to the dry ingredients.

Cornmeal is available in various grinds, from fine to medium to coarse. The standard medium grind yields a relatively light bread, while stone-ground meal produces a more rustic result. This versatile recipe offers a wide range of flavoring choices. Experiment with ingredients such as chiles, roasted pumpkin seeds, or diced prosciutto. For a crusty exterior, bake the bread in a cast-iron frying pan.

Position a rack in the middle of the oven, and preheat to 425°F (220°C). Butter an 8-inch (20-cm) cast-iron frying pan or an 8-inch square baking pan or dish.

In a bowl, whisk together the cornmeal, flour, baking powder, baking soda, salt, and the corn kernels, if using. Set aside.

BY HAND: In a large bowl, whisk the eggs until blended. Add the honey, buttermilk, and butter and whisk until blended. Add the dry ingredients and stir until evenly moistened.

BY MIXER: In a large bowl, beat the eggs on medium speed until blended. Add the honey, buttermilk, and butter and beat until blended. Add the dry ingredients and mix on low speed just until mixed.

Pour the batter into the prepared pan and smooth the top with a rubber spatula. Bake until a toothpick inserted into the center comes out clean, 20–25 minutes. Let the bread cool slightly in the pan on a wire rack. Serve warm. Store in an airtight container at room temperature for 2–3 days or freeze for up to 1 month.

1 cup (5 oz/155 g) cornmeal

1 cup (5 oz/155 g) all-purpose (plain) flour

1 1/2 teaspoons baking powder

1/2 teaspoon baking soda (bicarbonate of soda)

1/2 teaspoon salt

2 cups (12 oz/375 g) fresh corn kernels (about 3 ears), optional

2 large eggs

3 tablespoons honey or firmly packed golden brown sugar

1 1/3 cups (11 fl oz/340 ml) buttermilk

3 tablespoons unsalted butter, melted, or canola oil or olive oil

Cinnamon Streusel Coffee Cake

Crumbly cinnamon streusel ribbons the center and crowns the top of this fine-textured cake. It is ideal to set out for a gathering of friends invited over for coffee, for a weekend brunch, or for a dinnertime buffet. A Bundt pan makes a decorative design, but the cake may also be baked in a tube pan.

Position a rack in the middle of the oven, and preheat to 350°F (180°C). Butter and flour a 10-inch (25-cm) tube pan or Bundt pan.

To make the streusel filling, in a small bowl, combine the butter, flour, brown sugar, nuts, and cinnamon. Using a pastry blender or fork, mix until crumbly. Set the streusel aside.

To make the batter, in a bowl, stir together the flour, baking powder, baking soda, and salt. Set aside.

BY HAND: In a large bowl, using a wooden spoon, beat together the butter and granulated sugar until light and creamy. Mix in the eggs and vanilla, beating until smooth. Add the dry ingredients in 3 batches alternately with the sour cream and stir with a rubber spatula just until the batter is almost smooth.

BY MIXER: In a large bowl, beat together the butter and granulated sugar on medium-low speed until creamy. Beat in the eggs, one at a time. Stir in the vanilla. Add the dry ingredients in 3 batches alternately with the sour cream and mix on low speed just until the batter is blended and almost smooth.

Pour half of the batter into the prepared pan and smooth the surface with the rubber spatula. Sprinkle evenly with half the streusel filling. Cover with the remaining batter and sprinkle with the remaining streusel.

Bake until a toothpick inserted into the center comes out clean, 40–45 minutes. Transfer to a wire rack and let cool in the pan for 10 minutes, then turn out of the pan and let cool completely. Store in an airtight container at room temperature for up to 3 days or freeze for up to 1 month.

For the streusel filling

2 tablespoons unsalted butter, at room temperature

3 tablespoons all-purpose (plain) flour

$1/3$ cup ($2^1/2$ oz/75 g) firmly packed golden brown sugar

$3/4$ cup (3 oz/90 g) chopped pecans or walnuts, toasted (page 21)

$1^1/2$ teaspoons ground cinnamon

For the batter

$2^1/2$ cups ($12^1/2$ oz/390 g) all-purpose (plain) flour

2 teaspoons baking powder

$1/2$ teaspoon baking soda (bicarbonate of soda)

$1/4$ teaspoon salt

$3/4$ cup (6 oz/185 g) unsalted butter, at room temperature

$1^1/4$ cups (10 oz/315 g) granulated sugar

4 large eggs

1 teaspoon vanilla extract (essence)

$1^1/2$ cups (12 oz/375 g) sour cream

Lavender-Polenta Coffee Cake

For the coffee cake

³/₄ cup (4¹/₂ oz/140 g) golden raisins (sultanas)

2 tablespoons brandy or sweet Marsala

³/₄ cup (4 oz/125 g) fine-grind polenta or cornmeal

1³/₄ cups (9 oz/280 g) all-purpose (plain) flour

1¹/₂ teaspoons baking powder

¹/₂ teaspoon baking soda (bicarbonate of soda)

¹/₄ teaspoon salt

1 tablespoon grated lemon zest

3 large eggs

¹/₂ cup (4 fl oz/125 ml) olive oil

¹/₄ cup (3 oz/90 g) honey

³/₄ cup (6 oz/185 g) plain yogurt or ³/₄ cup (6 fl oz/ 180 ml) buttermilk

³/₄ cup (3 oz/90 g) pine nuts, toasted (page 21)

For the glaze

¹/₄ cup (3 oz/90 g) honey

¹/₃ cup (3 fl oz/80 ml) fresh lemon juice, strained

1 tablespoon dried lavender flowers

Position a rack in the middle of the oven, and preheat to 350°F (180°C). Butter and flour a 9-inch (23-cm) springform pan.

In a small bowl, toss the raisins with the brandy and let stand for 10 minutes to plump. In another bowl, stir together the polenta, flour, baking powder, baking soda, salt, and lemon zest. Set aside.

BY HAND: In a large bowl, whisk the eggs until blended. Stir in the olive oil, honey, and yogurt. Set aside 3 tablespoons of the pine nuts for topping. Add the dry ingredients, raisins, and the remaining nuts to the egg mixture and stir with a wooden spoon just until the batter is almost smooth.

BY MIXER: In a large bowl, combine the eggs, olive oil, honey, and yogurt and beat on medium-low speed just until blended. Set aside 3 tablespoons of the pine nuts for topping. Add the dry ingredients, raisins, and the remaining nuts to the egg mixture and mix on low speed just until the batter is almost smooth.

Pour the batter into the prepared pan and smooth the top with a rubber spatula. Sprinkle the reserved nuts evenly over the top. Bake until a toothpick inserted into the center comes out clean, 25–30 minutes.

While the cake is baking, make the glaze. In a small saucepan, combine the honey, lemon juice, and lavender flowers. Bring to a boil over medium heat, stirring until the sugar is dissolved, then remove from the heat. Let cool.

Transfer the cake to a wire rack. Immediately poke the top all over with a thin wooden skewer, and brush the top with half of the glaze. Let the cake cool in the pan on the rack for 10 minutes, then release and lift off the pan sides. Invert the cake onto the rack and lift off the pan bottom. Poke the bottom of the cake all over with the skewer. Brush with the remaining glaze. Invert the cake again so that it is right side up. Let the cake cool completely on the rack before serving.

A lemon-honey glaze gilds this golden cake laced with bits of sweet golden raisins and crunchy pine nuts. The delicate flavor of lavender adds a fragrant note to the cake. Dried flowers or buds, especially those from Provence, are preferable to fresh ones. If you cannot find dried lavender at your market, you can dry your own fresh lavender bunches. Most farmers' markets or gourmet supermarkets carry lavender in the summer. Make sure to use only pesticide-free flowers. To dry, hang the bunches upside down in a dark room for a few days, then strip or shake the buds from the stalks; they should release easily. If you have only coarse-grind polenta, place it in a food processor and pulse several seconds until finely ground.

Popovers

1 cup (5 oz/155 g) all-purpose (plain) flour

¹/₄ teaspoon salt

2 large eggs

1 tablespoon unsalted butter, melted, or vegetable oil

1¹/₄ cups (10 fl oz/310 ml) whole milk

Position a rack in the middle of the oven, and preheat to 425°F (220°C).

If you are using a steel popover pan, muffin-pan cups, or custard cups, butter and flour them lightly. This will help the popovers cling to the sides as they rise. If using custard cups, place on a baking sheet. If you are using a cast-iron popover pan, leave the cups ungreased.

BY HAND: In a bowl, stir together the flour and salt. In another bowl, whisk together the eggs, butter, and milk until blended. Pour the egg mixture over the dry ingredients and stir just until blended.

BY FOOD PROCESSOR: Combine the flour, salt, eggs, butter, and milk. Process for a few seconds, just barely to combine. Scrape down the sides of the bowl and process again briefly to incorporate any loose flour.

Pour the batter into the prepared cups, filling them half full. Bake for 30 minutes. Reduce the heat to 375°F (190°C) and continue baking until well browned, 15–20 minutes longer. Remove from the oven, immediately unmold onto a wire rack, and puncture the sides with a toothpick or the tip of a sharp knife to let steam escape. Serve immediately.

These dramatic-looking, fragile puffs are show-offs at the table. Despite their impressive appearance, they are surprisingly easy to make. Bake them in a traditional cast-iron popover pan, a metal muffin pan, or individual custard cups. To ensure the maximum rise, the batter must be the consistency of heavy (double) cream and not overbeaten. Although some recipes specify putting the popovers in a cold oven at the start of baking, a preheated oven works best for this recipe.

Apple Oven Pancake

Sautéed apple pieces are a delicious addition to this classic Dutch baby, a simple oven pancake that billows like a popover. It reportedly got its name in the early twentieth century when the owner of a Seattle restaurant baked miniatures of the giant German pancake, and his children dubbed them "Dutch babies." Preheating the baking dish before adding the fruit and batter gives the pancake a head start. Anjou or Red Bartlett (Williams) pears can be substituted for the apples. Serve plain, or with pure maple syrup or warm lavender honey.

Position a rack in the lower third of the oven, and preheat to 425°F (220°C).

In a large frying pan over medium-high heat, melt 2 tablespoons of the butter. Add the apples and sauté, turning as needed, just until tender, 5–7 minutes. Sprinkle with the brown sugar, lemon juice, and cinnamon and stir to combine. Remove from the heat.

Place a baking dish 12 inches (30 cm) in diameter or 9 by 13 inches (23 by 33 cm) in the oven to heat for 5 minutes. Remove the baking dish from the oven, add the remaining 2 tablespoons butter to it, and tilt the dish to coat the bottom and sides with the butter. Spoon the sautéed apples over the bottom of the dish to make an even layer.

BY HAND: In a bowl, whisk together the eggs, milk, flour, vanilla, and salt and until blended.

BY FOOD PROCESSOR: Combine the eggs, milk, flour, vanilla, and salt. Pulse 2 or 3 times, just until blended.

Carefully pour the batter over the hot fruit. Bake until puffed and golden brown, 20–25 minutes. Remove from the oven and, using a fine-mesh sieve, dust the top with confectioners' sugar. Serve immediately.

4 tablespoons (2 oz/60 g) unsalted butter

4 cups (1 lb/500 g) diced peeled tart apples, such as Granny Smith (3 medium)

2 tablespoons firmly packed golden brown sugar

Juice of 1/2 lemon, strained

1/2 teaspoon ground cinnamon

4 large eggs, lightly beaten

1 cup (8 fl oz/250 ml) whole milk

1 cup (5 oz/155 g) all-purpose (plain) flour

1 teaspoon vanilla extract (essence)

1/8 teaspoon salt

Confectioners' (icing) sugar for dusting

Cheddar Herb Muffins

VARIATION

Green Chile Muffins

Omit the rosemary and chives. Add 1 can (4 oz/125 g) diced green chiles, drained, to the batter with the buttermilk.

This hearty, golden muffin is a great addition to a soup or salad meal. An extra sharp cheddar lends zesty flavor, and a mixture of fresh herbs delivers fragrance to each bite. To put a different flavor spin on these savory muffins, replace the rosemary with chopped fresh dill.

Position a rack in the middle of the oven, and preheat to 400°F (200°C). Butter 12 standard muffin-pan cups or line them with paper liners.

In a bowl, stir together the all-purpose and whole-wheat flours, baking powder, baking soda, salt, chives, rosemary, and $1^{1}/_{4}$ cups (5 oz/155 g) of the cheese.

BY HAND: In a bowl, whisk the eggs until blended, then stir in the buttermilk, honey, and oil. Pour over the dry ingredients and stir with a rubber spatula just until moistened.

BY MIXER: In a large bowl, beat the eggs on low speed until blended. Add the buttermilk, honey, and oil and beat until blended. Add the dry ingredients and mix just until moistened.

Spoon the batter into the prepared muffin cups, filling each cup about three-fourths full. Sprinkle the remaining $^{1}/_{4}$ cup (1 oz/30 g) cheese evenly over the tops. Bake until a toothpick inserted in the center of a muffin comes out clean, 15–18 minutes. Let cool in the pan on a wire rack for 2 minutes, then turn out onto the rack. Serve warm. Store in an airtight container at room temperature for up to 2 days.

$1^{1}/_{4}$ cups ($6^{1}/_{2}$ oz/200 g) all-purpose (plain) flour

$^{1}/_{2}$ cup ($2^{1}/_{2}$ oz/75 g) whole-wheat (wholemeal) flour

2 teaspoons baking powder

$^{1}/_{2}$ teaspoon baking soda (bicarbonate of soda)

$^{1}/_{2}$ teaspoon salt

3 tablespoons chopped fresh chives

1 tablespoon chopped fresh rosemary

$1^{1}/_{2}$ cups (6 oz/185 g) finely shredded extra-sharp cheddar cheese

2 large eggs

1 cup (8 fl oz/250 ml) buttermilk

2 tablespoons honey

$^{1}/_{3}$ cup (3 fl oz/80 ml) olive oil or canola oil

Blueberry-Cornmeal Muffins

1¹/₂ cups (7¹/₂ oz/235 g) all-purpose (plain) flour

¹/₂ cup (2¹/₂ oz/75 g) fine-grind cornmeal

2 teaspoons baking powder

¹/₂ teaspoon baking soda (bicarbonate of soda)

¹/₄ teaspoon salt

¹/₄ teaspoon grated nutmeg

²/₃ cup (5 oz/155 g) firmly packed golden brown sugar

2 large eggs

1 cup (8 fl oz/250 ml) whole milk

6 tablespoons (3 oz/90 g) unsalted butter, melted

1 cup (4 oz/125 g) fresh or frozen blueberries

2 tablespoons granulated sugar mixed with 1 teaspoon ground cinnamon

Position a rack in the middle of the oven, and preheat to 400°F (200°C). Butter 12 standard muffin-pan cups or line them with paper liners.

In a bowl, stir together the flour, cornmeal, baking powder, baking soda, salt, nutmeg, and brown sugar. Set aside.

BY HAND: In a large bowl, whisk the eggs until blended. Whisk in the milk and butter. Pour the egg mixture over the dry ingredients and stir with a rubber spatula just until moistened. Fold in the berries.

BY MIXER: In a large bowl, combine the eggs, milk, and butter and beat on low speed just until blended. Add the dry ingredients to the egg mixture and mix on low speed just until moistened. Fold in the berries.

Spoon the batter into the prepared muffin cups, filling each cup about three-fourths full. Sprinkle the cinnamon-sugar evenly over the tops. Bake until a toothpick inserted into the center of a muffin comes out clean, 15–18 minutes. Let cool in the pan on a wire rack for 2 minutes, then turn out onto the rack. Serve warm. Store in an airtight container at room temperature for up to 2 days, or freeze for up to 1 month.

The crunch of cornmeal is a nice counterpoint to the juicy burst of blueberries in these tender muffins. If organic wild blueberries or huckleberries are available fresh or frozen in your market, they are a wonderful stand-in for cultivated blueberries. These wild fruits are smaller and have thinner skins than their domestic kin. To keep the berries from sinking to the bottom of the muffins, toss them in a sieve with 1 tablespoon flour before adding them to the batter. If using frozen berries, add them without thawing or they will exude a lot of juice.

Pear-Ginger Muffins

Chunks of fresh pear punctuate these flavorful muffins enlivened with the spicy zing of fresh, ground, and crystallized ginger. You can use pears that are still slightly firm, as they will keep their shape nicely. Use a firm variety such as Bartlett (Williams), Bosc, or Anjou. It is easy to remove the skin of fresh ginger with a vegetable peeler, and then grate the flesh on the fine rasps of a grater.

Position a rack in the middle of the oven, and preheat to 425°F (220°C). Butter 12 standard muffin-pan cups or line them with paper liners.

In a bowl, stir together the flour, baking powder, baking soda, salt, sugar, ground ginger, fresh ginger, and $1/3$ cup (2 oz/60 g) of the crystallized ginger. Set aside.

BY HAND: In a bowl, whisk the eggs until blended. Stir in the milk and butter. Pour over the dry ingredients and stir with a rubber spatula just until moistened. Fold in the pear. Do not overmix.

BY MIXER: In a large bowl, combine the eggs, milk, and butter and beat on low speed just until blended. Add the dry ingredients and mix just until moistened. Fold in the pear. Do not overmix.

Spoon the batter into prepared muffin cups, filling each cup about three-fourths full. Sprinkle the remaining crystallized ginger evenly over the tops. Bake until a toothpick inserted into the center of a muffin comes out clean, 15–18 minutes. Let cool in the pan on a wire rack for 2 minutes, then turn out onto the rack. Serve warm. Store in an airtight container at room temperature for up to 2 days, or freeze for up to 1 month.

$1^3/4$ cups (9 oz/280 g) all-purpose (plain) flour

2 teaspoons baking powder

$1/2$ teaspoon baking soda (bicarbonate of soda)

$1/4$ teaspoon salt

$2/3$ cup (5 oz/155 g) firmly packed golden brown sugar

1 teaspoon ground ginger

1 tablespoon peeled and grated fresh ginger

$2/3$ cup (4 oz/120 g) finely chopped crystallized ginger

2 large eggs

1 cup (8 fl oz/250 ml) whole milk

6 tablespoons (3 oz/90 g) unsalted butter, melted

$1^1/4$ cups (5 oz/155 g) chopped, peeled pear (about 1 large)

Carrot-Apple-Nut Muffins

1 cup (5 oz/155 g)
all-purpose (plain) flour

1 cup (5 oz/155 g) whole-
wheat (wholemeal) flour

1/4 cup (2/3 oz/20 g) oat bran
or wheat bran

2 teaspoons baking powder

1/2 teaspoon baking soda
(bicarbonate of soda)

1/4 teaspoon salt

1 teaspoon ground cinnamon

2/3 cup (5 oz/155 g) firmly
packed dark brown sugar

2 large eggs

1 1/2 cups (12 oz/375 g) plain
yogurt or 1 1/2 cups (12 fl oz/
375 ml) buttermilk

1/4 cup (2 oz/60 g) unsalted
butter, melted

1 1/4 cups (5 oz/155 g)
grated, peeled tart apple
(about 1 large)

1 1/4 cups (6 oz/185 g)
finely grated, peeled carrots
(about 2 medium)

1/2 cup (2 oz/60 g) chopped
walnuts or pecans, toasted
(page 21)

1/2 cup (3 oz/90 g) golden
raisins (sultanas)

2 tablespoons granulated
sugar mixed with 1 teaspoon
ground cinnamon

These moist and fruity muffins get raves for being a great breakfast bread to eat on the run. They offer many options for flavor variations with nuts and dried fruits; play with different combinations to find your personal favorite. Dried cranberries or cherries are an excellent alternative to raisins. Oat or wheat bran and the fruits and carrots add a nice boost of fiber. Because this recipe yields sixteen muffins, you will need two standard muffin pans. Always fill any empty muffin cups with water to prevent scorching in the oven.

Position a rack in the middle of the oven, and preheat to 400°F (200°C). Butter 16 standard muffin-pan cups or line with paper liners.

In a large bowl, stir together the flours, bran, baking powder, baking soda, salt, cinnamon, and brown sugar. Set aside.

BY HAND: In a large bowl, whisk the eggs until blended. Stir in the yogurt and butter. Pour over the dry ingredients and stir with a rubber spatula just until half moistened, 8–10 strokes. Add the apple, carrots, nuts, and raisins and stir just until evenly distributed. Do not overmix.

BY MIXER: In a large bowl, beat the eggs on low speed until blended, then beat in the yogurt and butter. Add the dry ingredients and mix on low speed just until half moistened. Add the apple, carrots, nuts, and raisins and stir just until evenly distributed. Do not overmix.

Spoon the batter into the prepared muffin cups, filling each cup about three-fourths full. Sprinkle the cinnamon sugar evenly over the tops. Bake until a toothpick inserted into the center of a muffin comes out clean, 15–18 minutes. Let cool in the pan on a wire rack for 2 minutes, then turn out onto the rack. Serve warm. Store in an airtight container at room temperature for up to 2 days, or freeze for up to 1 month.

Dried Cherry–Chocolate Muffins

2 oz (60 g) unsweetened chocolate, chopped

1³/₄ cups (9 oz/280 g) all-purpose (plain) flour

1 teaspoon baking soda (bicarbonate of soda)

¹/₄ teaspoon salt

¹/₂ cup (4 oz/125 g) unsalted butter, at room temperature

1 cup (7 oz/220 g) firmly packed golden brown sugar

1 large egg

1 teaspoon vanilla extract (essence)

1 cup (8 fl oz/250 ml) buttermilk

³/₄ cup (3 oz/90 g) dried cherries

¹/₂ cup (2 oz/60 g) toasted, skinned, and chopped hazelnuts (filberts), page 21

Position a rack in the middle of the oven, and preheat to 375°F (190°C). Butter 12 standard muffin-pan cups.

Place the chocolate in the top of a double boiler placed over (not touching) barely simmering water. Heat, stirring often, until the chocolate melts. Remove it from over the water and set aside to cool slightly. In a bowl, stir together the flour, baking soda, and salt. Set aside.

BY HAND: In a large bowl, using a wooden spoon, beat the butter until creamy. Gradually beat in the brown sugar until dissolved. Stir in the egg, vanilla, and chocolate. Add the dry ingredients in 3 batches alternately with the buttermilk and mix just until smooth.

BY MIXER: In a large bowl, beat the butter on low speed until creamy. Gradually beat in the brown sugar until dissolved. Beat in the egg, vanilla, and chocolate. Add the dry ingredients in 3 batches alternately with the buttermilk and mix on low speed just until smooth.

Fold in the cherries and nuts. Spoon the batter into the prepared muffin cups, filling each cup about three-fourths full. Bake until a toothpick inserted into the center of a muffin comes out clean, 20–25 minutes. Let cool in the pan on a wire rack for 2 minutes, then turn out onto the rack. Serve warm. Store in an airtight container at room temperature for up to 2 days.

Sweet, tangy cherries flavor these dark chocolate muffins for a regal treat at brunch or coffee time or for dessert. For the best results, have all the ingredients at room temperature. The muffins have an excellent crusty exterior, so you will want to butter the muffin cups rather than use paper liners, which may come away with the crust. For a decorative touch, top each filled muffin cup with either a whole or half nut before baking.

Orange–Poppy Seed Mini-Muffins

With their lively crunch, poppy seeds make a festive addition to quick breads. To enhance and deepen their subtle flavor, steep the seeds in milk before adding to the batter. Like nuts, poppy seeds are rich in oils, and they should be stored in the refrigerator or freezer if kept for more than a few months. You can also bake these muffins in 12 standard muffin cups. Fill them three-fourths full, and increase the baking time to 15–18 minutes. For a simpler topping, omit the glaze and sprinkle with Demerara sugar before baking.

Position a rack in the middle of the oven, and preheat to 400°F (200°C). Butter 24 mini-muffin-pan cups or line them with paper liners. In a small bowl, combine the poppy seeds and milk and let stand for 20 minutes. In a bowl, stir together the flour, baking powder, baking soda, salt, and orange zest. Set aside.

BY HAND: In a bowl, whisk the eggs until blended. Stir in the granulated sugar, butter, the 1/4 cup orange juice, and milk–poppy seed mixture, stirring until smooth. Add to the dry ingredients and stir with a rubber spatula just until moistened.

BY MIXER: In a large bowl, beat the eggs on low speed until blended. Add the granulated sugar, butter, the 1/4 cup orange juice, and milk–poppy seed mixture and beat on low speed just to combine. Add the dry ingredients and mix just until moistened.

Spoon the batter into the prepared muffin cups, filling each cup about three-fourths full. Bake until a toothpick inserted into the center of a muffin comes out clean, 12–14 minutes. Let cool in the pan on a wire rack for 2 minutes, then turn out onto the rack.

To make the glaze, in a small bowl, stir together the orange juice and confectioners' sugar until smooth. Drizzle over the tops of the warm muffins in a zigzag pattern. Store in an airtight container at room temperature for up to 2 days.

3 tablespoons poppy seeds

1/2 cup (4 fl oz/125 ml) whole milk

1 3/4 cups (9 oz/280 g) all-purpose (plain) flour

2 teaspoons baking powder

1/2 teaspoon baking soda (bicarbonate of soda)

1/4 teaspoon salt

1 tablespoon grated orange zest

2 large eggs

3/4 cup (6 oz/185 g) granulated sugar

6 tablespoons (3 oz/90 g) unsalted butter, melted

1/2 cup (4 fl oz/125 ml) plus 1 tablespoon orange juice

1/2 cup (2 oz/60 g) confectioners' (icing) sugar

Currant Cream Scones

For the dough

2 cups (10 oz/315 g) all-purpose (plain) flour

1/4 cup (2 oz/60 g) granulated sugar

1 tablespoon baking powder

1/2 teaspoon salt

2 teaspoons grated lemon zest

6 tablespoons (3 oz/90 g) cold unsalted butter, cut into 1/2-inch (12-mm) pieces

1/2 cup (3 oz/90 g) dried currants

3/4 cup (6 fl oz/180 ml) heavy (double) cream

For the topping

1 tablespoon granulated, Demerara, or turbinado sugar

1 teaspoon ground cinnamon

2 teaspoons whole milk or heavy (double) cream

Cream scones—rich British tea biscuits—have a flaky, slightly cakelike texture. The secret to making tender scones is to use a very light touch, work quickly, and put them into the oven immediately after cutting. Glaze them with cream and a sprinkle of cinnamon sugar or Demerara sugar for the finishing touch just before they go into the oven. Scones are traditionally served warm, split open, and topped with chunky fruit preserves, clotted cream, or Lemon Curd (page 309).

Position a rack in the middle of the oven, and preheat to 425°F (220°C). Line a half-sheet pan or rimless baking sheet with parchment (baking) paper.

BY HAND: In a bowl, stir together the flour, granulated sugar, baking powder, salt, and lemon zest. Using a pastry blender or 2 knives, cut in the butter until the mixture forms large, coarse crumbs the size of small peas. Stir in the currants. Pour the cream over the dry ingredients and mix with a fork or rubber spatula just until the dry ingredients are moistened.
BY MIXER: Combine the flour, granulated sugar, baking powder, salt, and lemon zest and beat on low speed for a few seconds to mix. Add the butter and mix on medium-low speed just until the mixture forms large, coarse crumbs the size of small peas. Scatter the currants over the dough. Pour in the cream and mix for a few seconds just until moistened.
BY FOOD PROCESSOR: Combine the flour, granulated sugar, baking powder, salt, and lemon zest and pulse 2 or 3 times to mix. Add the butter and pulse 7 or 8 times just until the mixture forms large, coarse crumbs the size of small peas. Scatter the currants over the dough. Pour in the cream and pulse just until moistened.

Turn the dough out onto a lightly floured work surface and press together gently until the dough clings together in a ball. Pat out into a round about 1/2 inch (12 mm) thick and 6 1/2 inches (16.5 cm) in diameter. Cut the round into 6 wedges, or use a 3-inch (7.5-cm) biscuit cutter to cut out rounds. Place the wedges 1 inch (2.5 cm) apart on the prepared pan.

To make the topping, in a small bowl, stir together the sugar and cinnamon. Brush the wedges with the milk and sprinkle evenly with the cinnamon sugar.

Bake until golden brown, 13–17 minutes. Transfer to a wire rack to cool slightly. Serve warm. Store in an airtight container at room temperature for up to 2 days.

VARIATION

Ginger Scones
Omit the currants. Add 1/3 cup (2 oz/60 g) diced crystallized ginger to the dry ingredients.

Oat Scones

Both rolled oats and oat bran lend a traditional Scottish flavor to these rich scones. Choose freshly milled organic oats for the best flavor. Serve the scones with crème fraîche and raspberries for an elegant teatime or brunch treat.

Position a rack in the middle of the oven, and preheat to 425°F (220°C). Line a half-sheet pan or rimless baking sheet with parchment (baking) paper.

BY HAND: In a bowl, stir together the flour, rolled oats, oat bran, brown sugar, baking powder, and salt. Using a pastry blender or 2 knives, cut in the butter until the mixture forms large, coarse crumbs the size of small peas. Pour the half-and-half over the dry ingredients and mix with a fork or rubber spatula until the dry ingredients are moistened.

BY MIXER: Combine the flour, rolled oats, oat bran, brown sugar, baking powder, and salt and beat on low speed for a few seconds to mix. Add the butter and mix on medium-low speed just until the mixture forms large, coarse crumbs the size of small peas. Pour in the half-and-half and mix just until moistened.

BY FOOD PROCESSOR: Combine the flour, rolled oats, oat bran, brown sugar, baking powder, and salt and pulse 2 or 3 times to mix. Add the butter and pulse 7 or 8 times just until the mixture forms large, coarse crumbs the size of small peas. Pour in the half-and-half and pulse 5 or 6 times until moistened.

Turn the dough out onto a lightly floured work surface and press together gently until the dough clings together in a ball. Pat out into a round about 1/2 inch (12 mm) thick and 6 1/2 inches (16.5 cm) in diameter. Cut the round into 6 wedges. Place the wedges 1 inch (2.5 cm) apart on the prepared pan.

To top the wedges, brush them with the milk and sprinkle evenly with the rolled oats and the cinnamon sugar.

Bake until golden brown, 13–17 minutes. Transfer to a rack to cool slightly. Serve warm. Store in an airtight container at room temperature for up to 2 days.

For the dough

1 cup (5 oz/155 g) all-purpose (plain) flour

3/4 cup (2 1/2 oz/75 g) old-fashioned rolled oats

1/3 cup (2/3 oz/20 g) oat bran

1/4 cup (2 oz/60 g) firmly packed golden brown sugar

1 tablespoon baking powder

1/2 teaspoon salt

6 tablespoons (3 oz/90 g) cold unsalted butter, cut into 1/2-inch (12-mm) pieces

2/3 cup (5 fl oz/160 ml) half-and-half (half cream) or whole milk

For the topping

2 teaspoons whole milk or half-and-half (half cream)

2 tablespoons rolled oats

1 tablespoon Demerara or turbinado sugar mixed with 1/2 teaspoon ground cinnamon

Cookies, Bars, and Brownies

About Cookies, Bars, and Brownies

From macaroon sandwiches to shortbread wedges, fudgy brownies to vanilla wafers, cookies are a welcome treat anytime. Come holiday season, home-baked cookies are a memorable gift when packaged in decorative bags and boxes, or even vintage metal molds.

Most cookies, bars, and brownies are simple mixtures of butter, flour, sugar, and a flavoring or two. How you shape them is the best way to categorize them.

Dropped cookies, such as chocolate chip, gingersnap, and oatmeal, are formed by dropping spoonfuls of dough onto a prepared baking sheet. Piped cookies, such as almond or hazelnut (filbert) macaroons, are formed by spooning the cookie batter into a piping bag and then piping mounds onto a baking sheet. Rolled cookies, including Russian tea cakes and chocolate crinkles, are fashioned into balls between your palms before being baked. Pressed cookies, also known as spritz cookies, are pushed through a cookie press, while delicate French madeleines are baked in a mold.

Tuiles, made by spreading a thin batter onto a nonstick baking liner, are baked free-form and then shaped while still warm. Sugar cookies are cut out from a sheet of dough, and refrigerator cookies, such as wafers and pinwheels and checkerboards, are neatly sliced from a chilled log of dough. Filled cookies, including rugelach and pretty heart-shaped sandwiches, are lined with delicious jams. Bars and brownies of countless flavors are made either by spreading a soft cookielike batter into a pan, or by layering a crumbly crust with a jam or curd before baking.

Despite the great variety in form and flavor, a handful of simple, helpful baking tips apply to nearly every cookie recipe. Start out with all of your ingredients at room temperature, unless the recipe instructs otherwise.

Use heavy-duty rimless baking sheets, or stack a pair of thinner sheets. Whenever possible, line your baking sheets with parchment (baking) paper to make transferring the cookies from the pan to the cooling rack more efficient and to speed cleanup. For even browning, rotate the sheets from back to front halfway through the baking time. If baking more than one sheet of cookies at a time, place one on the top oven rack and one on the middle rack; then, halfway during the baking time, reverse their positions on the racks and rotate them. Start checking for doneness a couple of minutes before the recipe indicates. Depending on your oven, you may need to pull the sheets at different times.

Cooling instructions for cookies vary among recipes. Some cookies need to cool only briefly on the pan, while others must cool completely. Always try to let a baking sheet cool completely before loading it with another batch. Finally, do not store cookies until they are fully cooled, and pack each type separately to avoid mingling the flavors.

Cookies are always welcome gifts and can be packaged in a variety of ways. Arrange them on a sturdy paper plate and then wrap in colorful cellophane and tie with ribbon, or tuck them into a vintage tin or lidded box.

When sending cookies through the mail, pack them close together—less space to move and break—in a cookie tin or other hard-sided container, separating the layers with parchment or waxed paper. Again, keep different types of cookies separated to preserve their true flavors. Slip the cookie tin into a mailing box lined with bubble wrap or other packing material, then fill in any spaces with additional packing material. Finally, send them off, loading them up with first-class postage so they don't age in the post office.

TROUBLESHOOTING COOKIES, BARS, AND BROWNIES

What happened	Why it happened
Cookies spread too much during baking.	Butter was too soft when added, or dough was placed on hot baking sheet.
Cookies are burned on bottom.	Cookies were too thin, oven was too hot, pan was too thin or too low in the oven, or pan was not rotated during baking.
Cookies did not bake evenly.	Pan was not rotated during baking.
Cookies fell apart when removed from pan.	Cookies were removed too soon.
Cookies stuck to the pan.	Cookies were not baked long enough or were left too long on pan.

Triple Chocolate Chip Cookies

1¹/₄ cups (6¹/₂ oz/200 g) all-purpose (plain) flour

1 teaspoon baking soda (bicarbonate of soda)

¹/₂ teaspoon salt

¹/₂ cup (4 oz/125 g) unsalted butter, at room temperature

¹/₂ cup (3¹/₂ oz/105 g) firmly packed golden brown sugar

6 tablespoons (3 oz/90 g) granulated sugar

1 large egg

1 teaspoon vanilla extract (essence)

1 cup (6 oz/185 g) semisweet (plain) chocolate chips

³/₄ cup (4¹/₂ oz/140 g) white chocolate chips

³/₄ cup (4¹/₂ oz/140 g) milk chocolate chips

Cookie history was made in the early 1930s when Ruth Wakefield, the owner of the Toll House Inn in Massachusetts, cut up a chocolate bar, added it to her cookie dough, and created the first chocolate chip cookie. In 1939, Nestlé began selling the first chocolate morsels that held their shape during baking, and Wakefield's recipe was printed on every package. Chocolate chip cookies soon swept the country. In addition to semisweet chips, these cookies include white chocolate and milk chocolate chips, making a great American cookie even better. For the best flavor, look for white chocolate chips that contain cocoa butter.

Position a rack in the middle of the oven, and preheat to 350°F (180°C). Line 2 rimless baking sheets with parchment (baking) paper.

In a bowl, sift together the flour, baking soda, and salt. Set aside.

BY HAND: In a large bowl, combine the butter, brown sugar, and granulated sugar. Beat with a wooden spoon until smooth. Add the egg and vanilla and beat until well blended. Slowly add the dry ingredients and stir just until incorporated. Stir in the chocolate chips.

BY MIXER: In a large bowl, combine the butter, brown sugar, and granulated sugar. Beat on medium speed until smooth. Add the egg and vanilla and beat on low speed until well blended. Slowly add the dry ingredients and beat on low speed just until incorporated. Mix in the chocolate chips.

Drop the dough by heaping tablespoons onto the prepared baking sheets, spacing the cookies 2 inches (5 cm) apart. Bake the cookies, 1 sheet at a time, until the bottoms and edges are lightly browned and the tops feel firm when lightly touched, 10–13 minutes. Let the cookies cool on the baking sheets for 5 minutes, then transfer them to wire racks to cool completely. Store in an airtight container at room temperature for up to 3 days.

Old-Fashioned Oatmeal Cookies

1¹/₂ cups (7¹/₂ oz/235 g) all-purpose (plain) flour

1 teaspoon baking powder

1 tablespoon ground cinnamon

¹/₄ teaspoon salt

¹/₂ cup (4 oz/125 g) unsalted butter, at room temperature

1 cup (7 oz/220 g) firmly packed dark brown sugar

¹/₂ cup (4 oz/125 g) granulated sugar

2 large eggs

2 teaspoons vanilla extract (essence)

1¹/₂ cups (4¹/₂ oz/140 g) old-fashioned rolled oats

2 cups (12 oz/375 g) raisins

Position a rack in the middle of the oven, and preheat to 350°F (180°C). Line 2 rimless baking sheets with parchment (baking) paper.

In a bowl, sift together the flour, baking powder, cinnamon, and salt. Set aside.

BY HAND: In a large bowl, combine the butter, brown sugar, and granulated sugar. Beat with a wooden spoon until smooth. Add the eggs and vanilla and beat until well blended. Add the dry ingredients and rolled oats and stir until incorporated. Stir in the raisins.

BY MIXER: In a large bowl, combine the butter, brown sugar, and granulated sugar. Beat on medium speed until smooth. Add the eggs and vanilla and beat on low speed until well blended. Add the dry ingredients and rolled oats and beat until incorporated. Mix in the raisins.

Drop the dough by heaping tablespoons onto the prepared baking sheets, spacing the cookies 3 inches (7.5 cm) apart. Bake the cookies, 1 sheet at a time, until they are evenly light brown and the tops feel firm when lightly touched, 15–20 minutes. Let the cookies cool on the baking sheets for 5 minutes, then transfer them to wire racks to cool completely. Store in an airtight container at room temperature for up to 3 days.

These are the oatmeal cookies that you remember from childhood—crisp on the outside and thick, chewy, and full of raisins on the inside. Dark brown sugar gives them their appealing color. At 3 inches (7.5 cm) across, these two-fisted treats are the perfect addition to lunch boxes and picnic baskets, and make delicious after-school snacks.

Gingery Gingersnaps

Chopped crystallized ginger plus ground ginger add a robust flavor to these spicy cookies, which are crispy on the outside and chewy in the middle. Measure the oil in a measuring cup, then use the same cup to measure the molasses, and the molasses will flow freely from the cup.

Position a rack in the middle of the oven, and preheat to 350°F (180°C). Line 3 rimless baking sheets with parchment (baking) paper.

In a bowl, sift together the flour, baking soda, salt, cinnamon, ground ginger, and cloves. Set aside.

BY HAND: In a large bowl, combine the vegetable oil, molasses, brown sugar, egg, and crystallized ginger. Beat with a wooden spoon until well blended. Add the dry ingredients and stir until incorporated.

BY MIXER: In a large bowl, combine the vegetable oil, molasses, brown sugar, egg, and crystallized ginger. Beat on low speed until well blended. Add the dry ingredients and beat until incorporated.

Drop the dough by level tablespoons onto the prepared baking sheets, spacing the cookies 2 inches (5 cm) apart. Bake the cookies, 1 sheet at a time, until the tops are crinkled and feel firm when lightly touched, 10–13 minutes. Let the cookies cool on the baking sheets for 5 minutes, then transfer them to wire racks to cool completely. Store in an airtight container at room temperature for up to 3 days.

2 cups (10 oz/315 g) all-purpose (plain) flour

1 1/2 teaspoons baking soda (bicarbonate of soda)

1/4 teaspoon salt

1 teaspoon ground cinnamon

1 teaspoon ground ginger

1/2 teaspoon ground cloves

3/4 cup (6 fl oz/180 ml) vegetable oil

1/2 cup (5 1/2 oz/170 g) light molasses

1 cup (7 oz/220 g) firmly packed golden brown sugar

1 large egg

1/2 cup (3 oz/90 g) chopped crystallized ginger

Hazelnut Macaroon Sandwiches

A visitor to Paris today can look into almost any *pâtisserie* window and see perfect rows of these addictive macaroon cookie sandwiches in different flavors and colors lined up on trays. Before they are baked, the cookies rest at room temperature, which produces their characteristic crusty exterior and soft, moist interior. Ground blanched almonds can be used in place of the hazelnuts, and apricot jam can be substituted for the ganache.

Line 2 rimless baking sheets with parchment (baking) paper. Have ready a third rimless baking sheet, unlined.

In a large, clean bowl, combine the egg whites and cream of tartar. Using a stand mixer fitted with the whip attachment or a hand mixer, beat on medium speed until the whites begin to thicken. Increase the speed to medium-high and beat just until soft peaks form. Slowly add the superfine sugar and continue to beat until stiff, shiny peaks form (page 27). Beat in the vanilla until blended. Using a rubber spatula, fold in the hazelnuts and confectioners' sugar until incorporated.

Scoop the mixture into a pastry (piping) bag fitted with a $^1/_2$-inch (12-mm) plain tip. Pipe mounds $1^1/_2$ inches (4 cm) in diameter onto the prepared baking sheets, spacing the mounds 1 inch (2.5 cm) apart (page 213). With a damp fingertip, gently smooth any pointy tips. Let the cookies sit, uncovered, at room temperature for 35–45 minutes.

Position a rack in the middle of the oven, and preheat to 350°F (180°C). Bake the cookies, 1 sheet at a time, putting the cookie-filled baking sheet on top of the unlined baking sheet. (This insulates the top baking sheet so that the cookie bottoms do not darken too much.) Bake until the tops and bottoms are firm and golden, 10–13 minutes.

Remove the baking sheet from the oven, carefully lift the parchment, one end at a time, and sprinkle about 2 tablespoons water under the paper. Be careful that the steam does not burn you and that water does not splash on the cookies. (The steam loosens the cookies from the paper.) After 3 minutes, slide the parchment paper off the baking sheet, peel the cookies from the paper, and transfer them to wire racks to cool completely.

Make the ganache filling and refrigerate until cooled and thickened enough to spread. Turn half of the cookies bottom side up. Spread a thin layer of the ganache (about 1 rounded teaspoon) over the cookie bottoms. Press a plain cookie, bottom side down, onto the ganache. Store the cookies in an airtight container at room temperature for up to 3 days.

4 large egg whites, at room temperature

$^1/_4$ teaspoon cream of tartar

$^1/_4$ cup (2 oz/60 g) superfine (caster) sugar

1 teaspoon vanilla extract (essence)

1 cup (4 oz/125 g) toasted, skinned, and ground hazelnuts (filberts), page 21

2 cups (8 oz/250 g) confectioners' (icing) sugar, sifted

About $^2/_3$ cup (5 fl oz/ 160 ml) Ganache Filling (page 309)

Vanilla and Chocolate Spritz Cookies

1 cup (8 oz/250 g) unsalted butter, at room temperature

1/2 cup (4 oz/125 g) sugar

1/4 teaspoon salt

1 teaspoon vanilla extract (essence)

1 teaspoon almond extract (essence)

1 large egg, at room temperature

2 cups (10 oz/315 g) all-purpose (plain) flour, sifted

Ganache Filling (page 309)

A cookie press lets you turn out fancy cookies quickly. By simply changing the disk, you can make cookies shaped like wreaths, flowers, stars, or candy canes. These spritz cookies have a swirl of fudge added after they bake, but a scattering of colored crystal sugars or nonpareils can be sprinkled on before the cookies go in the oven. Or drizzle melted dark or white chocolate in thin lines over the cooled cookies.

Position a rack in the middle of the oven, and preheat to 350°F (180°C). Line 3 half-sheet pans or rimless baking sheets with parchment (baking) paper.

BY HAND: In a large bowl, combine the butter, sugar, and salt. Beat with a wooden spoon until smooth. Add the vanilla and almond extracts and the egg and beat until blended. Stir in the flour just until incorporated.

BY MIXER: In a large bowl, combine the butter, sugar, and salt. Beat on medium speed until smooth. Add the vanilla and almond extracts and the egg and beat until blended. Mix in the flour on low speed just until incorporated.

Divide the dough into 4 equal portions. Roll each portion into a log that fits into your cookie press. Pack 1 log into the press, then fit the press with the disk of your choice. Choose a disk that produces a cookie with a solid center that can hold the fudge topping.

Holding the press upright and resting it on a baking sheet, grasp the handle securely and apply even pressure to release 1 cookie. Move the press and repeat, spacing the cookies 1 inch (2.5 cm) apart. Continue until you have filled the baking sheet, refilling the press as necessary.

Bake the cookies, 1 sheet at a time, until the bottoms and edges are light brown, 12–17 minutes. Let the cookies cool on the baking sheets for 5 minutes, then transfer them to wire racks to cool completely.

Make the ganache gilling and refrigerate until thickened enough to pipe, about 1 hour. Fit a pastry bag with a small star tip and fill the bag with the ganache. Pipe a small chocolate swirl in the center of each cooled cookie (page 213). Refrigerate the cookies until the ganache is firm. Store the cookies in a single layer in an airtight container for up to 3 days in the refrigerator.

VARIATION

Chocolate Spritz Cookies
Increase the sugar to 3/4 cup (6 oz/185 g). Substitute 1 2/3 cups (8 1/2 oz/265 g) all-purpose (plain) flour sifted with 1/3 cup (1 oz/ 30 g) Dutch-process cocoa powder for the 2 cups (10 oz/ 315 g) flour. Bake the cookies until the tops are firm and look dull, not shiny, about 12 minutes. Omit the Ganache Filling, if desired. Store in an airtight container at room temperature for up to 3 days.

Russian Tea Cakes

The name may change, but whether they are called Mexican wedding cookies, Austrian *Kipferln*, or Russian tea cakes, these cookies have a lot in common. They all carry a good measure of chopped or ground nuts, a small amount of granulated sugar, plenty of butter, a coating of confectioners' sugar, and an appealing "melt-away" texture.

Position a rack in the middle of the oven, and preheat to 325°F (165°C). Line a rimless baking sheet with parchment (baking) paper.

In a bowl, sift together the flour and salt. Set aside.

BY HAND: In a large bowl, combine the butter, granulated sugar, and vanilla. Beat with a wooden spoon until smooth, about 1 minute. Add the hazelnuts and stir until blended. Add the dry ingredients and mix until the soft dough comes together in large clumps.

BY MIXER: In a large bowl, combine the butter, granulated sugar, and vanilla. Beat on medium speed until smooth, about 1 minute. Add the hazelnuts and beat on low speed until blended. Add the dry ingredients and beat until the soft dough comes together in large clumps.

To form each cookie, roll a level tablespoon of dough between your palms into a 1-inch (2.5-cm) ball. Place the balls 1 inch (2.5 cm) apart on the prepared baking sheet. Make sure to set them firmly onto the baking sheet so they stay in place.

Bake the cookies until the bottoms are light brown and the tops are lightly colored, 20–25 minutes. Let the cookies cool on the baking sheet for 5 minutes, then transfer them to a wire rack to cool completely.

Sift the confectioners' sugar into a bowl. Gently roll the cookies in the sugar to coat them evenly. You will not use all of the confectioners' sugar. Store in an airtight container at room temperature for up to 3 days.

1 cup (5 oz/155 g) all-purpose (plain) flour

1/4 teaspoon salt

1/2 cup (4 oz/125 g) unsalted butter, at room temperature

1/3 cup (3 oz/90 g) granulated sugar

1 teaspoon vanilla extract (essence)

3/4 cup (3 oz/90 g) toasted, skinned, and ground hazelnuts (filberts), page 21

1/2 cup (2 oz/60 g) confectioners' (icing) sugar

Classic Shortbread

1¹/₂ cups (7¹/₂ oz/235 g)
all-purpose (plain) flour

¹/₄ cup (1 oz/30 g)
cornstarch (cornflour)

¹/₈ teaspoon salt

³/₄ cup (6 oz/185 g) unsalted
butter, at room temperature

¹/₃ cup (3 oz/90 g) sugar

1 teaspoon vanilla extract
(essence)

VARIATIONS

Nut or Citrus Shortbread
Add ¹/₂ cup (2 oz/60 g) chopped,
toasted nuts (page 21) or
1 tablespoon grated lemon or
orange zest to the dry ingredients.

Chocolate Shortbread
Replace ¹/₄ cup (1¹/₂ oz/45 g)
flour with ¹/₄ cup (³/₄ oz/20 g)
Dutch-process cocoa powder.
Increase the sugar to ¹/₄ cup
(4 oz/125 g).

Position a rack in the middle of the oven, and preheat to 300°F (150°C).

In a bowl, sift together the flour, cornstarch, and salt. Set aside.

BY HAND: In a large bowl, combine the butter and sugar. Using a wooden spoon, beat until smooth and light in color, about 3 minutes. Mix in the vanilla. Add the dry ingredients and stir until the dough comes together and pulls away from the sides of the bowl.

BY MIXER: In a large bowl, combine the butter and sugar. Beat on medium speed until smooth and light in color, about 3 minutes. Mix in the vanilla. Add the dry ingredients and beat on low speed, mixing until the dough comes together and pulls away from the sides of the bowl.

Using an offset spatula, spread the dough evenly into a 9¹/₂-inch (24-cm) tart pan with a removable bottom. Smooth the top with the spatula. Prick lightly all over with a fork, and use a knife to make shallow cuts to mark 12 equal wedges.

Bake until the top is evenly golden, 55–65 minutes. Remove from the oven and cut the warm shortbread into 12 wedges, using the marks as a guideline. Let the shortbread cool completely in the pan on a wire rack. Remove the sides of the pan and slide the cookies off the bottom. Store in an airtight container at room temperature for up to 5 days.

Good shortbread has two basic requirements: butter should be the dominant flavor, and the texture should be tender and crumbly. Because there are so few ingredients, be sure to use the freshest available. Cut the shortbread while it is still warm, or it may crumble. The fluted sides of a tart pan with a removable bottom give an attractive edge to the cookie wedges, but a 9-inch (23-cm) round cake pan lined with parchment (baking) paper (page 10) can be used as well.

Orange Madeleines

Madeleines are tender, spongy cookie-cakes that bake in a special shell-shaped pan. The intricate indentations of the pan must be carefully and generously buttered and floured to prevent the delicate cookies from sticking to the pan. These ingredients can be doubled to make twenty-four madeleines, but make sure the pan is cool before baking a second batch. Since they are best eaten fresh and slightly warm, serve madeleines soon after baking, or reheat them for a few minutes in a low oven until warm.

Position a rack in the middle of the oven, and preheat to 375°F (190°C). Using a pastry brush, heavily brush room-temperature butter over each of the 12 molds in a madeleine pan, carefully buttering every ridge. Dust the molds with flour, tilting the pan to coat the surfaces evenly. Turn the pan upside down, tap it gently, and discard the excess flour.

BY HAND: In a large bowl, combine the eggs, granulated sugar, and salt. Using a wire whisk, beat vigorously until pale, thick, and fluffy, about 5 minutes. Beat in the vanilla and almond extracts. Sprinkle the sifted flour over the egg mixture and stir to incorporate.

BY MIXER: In a large bowl, combine the eggs, granulated sugar, and salt. Beat on medium-high speed until pale, thick, and fluffy, about 5 minutes. Beat in the vanilla and almond extracts. Sprinkle the sifted flour over the egg mixture and mix on low speed to incorporate.

Using a rubber spatula, gently fold in the orange zest and half of the melted butter just until blended. Fold in the remaining melted butter.

Divide the batter among the 12 prepared molds, using a heaping tablespoon of batter for each mold. Bake the cookies until the top springs back when lightly touched, 8–12 minutes.

Remove the pan from the oven and invert it over a wire rack, then rap it on the rack to release the madeleines. If any should stick, use your fingers to loosen the edges, being careful not to touch the hot pan, and invert and rap again.

Let cool on the rack for 10 minutes. Using a fine-mesh sieve, dust the tops with confectioners' sugar and serve. Alternatively, cover with plastic wrap and store at room temperature for up to 3 days. Before serving, heat the cookies in a 250°F (120°C) oven until warm, then dust with the confectioners' sugar.

2 large eggs

$1/3$ cup (3 oz/90 g) granulated sugar

$1/4$ teaspoon salt

$1/2$ teaspoon vanilla extract (essence)

$1/4$ teaspoon almond extract (essence)

$1/2$ cup ($2^1/2$ oz/75 g) all-purpose (plain) flour, sifted

1 teaspoon grated orange zest

$1/4$ cup (2 oz/60 g) unsalted butter, melted and cooled

Confectioners' (icing) sugar for dusting

Chocolate Crinkle Cookies

4 oz (125 g) unsweetened chocolate, chopped

1/4 cup (2 oz/60 g) unsalted butter

1 1/2 cups (7 1/2 oz/235 g) all-purpose (plain) flour

1/2 cup (1 1/2 oz/45 g) Dutch-process cocoa powder

2 teaspoons baking powder

1/4 teaspoon salt

4 large eggs

2 cups (1 lb/500 g) granulated sugar

1 teaspoon vanilla extract (essence)

1 1/2 cups (9 oz/280 g) miniature semisweet (plain) chocolate chips

1/2 cup (2 oz/60 g) confectioners' (icing) sugar

Place the chocolate and butter in the top of a double boiler placed over (not touching) barely simmering water. Heat, stirring often, until the butter and chocolate melt. Remove from over the water and set aside to cool slightly. In a bowl, stir together the flour, cocoa powder, baking powder, and salt. Set aside.

BY HAND: In a large bowl, combine the eggs, granulated sugar, and vanilla. Using a wire whisk, beat until light in color and thick, about 3 minutes. Stir in the melted chocolate mixture with a wooden spoon until blended. Add the dry ingredients and beat until incorporated. Stir in the chocolate chips.

BY MIXER: In a large bowl, combine the eggs, granulated sugar, and vanilla. Beat on medium speed until light in color and thick, about 3 minutes. Beat in the melted chocolate mixture on low speed until blended. Add the dry ingredients and beat until incorporated. Mix in the chocolate chips.

Cover the bowl with plastic wrap and refrigerate until the dough is firm enough to roll into balls, about 2 hours.

Position a rack in the middle of the oven, and preheat to 325°F (165°C). Line 2 rimless baking sheets with parchment (baking) paper. Sift the confectioners' sugar into a small bowl.

To form each cookie, roll a rounded tablespoon of dough between your palms into a 1 1/2-inch (4-cm) ball, and roll the ball in the confectioners' sugar. Place the cookies 3 inches (7.5 cm) apart on the prepared baking sheets. Make sure to set them firmly onto the baking sheet so they stay in place.

Bake the cookies, 1 sheet at a time, until the tops are puffed and crinkled and feel firm when lightly touched, 13–17 minutes. Let the cookies cool on the baking sheets for 5 minutes, then transfer the cookies to wire racks to cool completely. Store in an airtight container at room temperature for up to 3 days.

With a crispy, crackled exterior and a chewy, fudgy interior, these crinkle cookies satisfy multiple chocolate cravings. They are perfect with a tall glass of ice-cold milk. Make sure to refrigerate the batter until it is firm enough to form into balls.

Cranberry-Pistachio Biscotti

VARIATION

Chocolate-Dipped Biscotti

Bake and cool the biscotti. Line a half-sheet pan with parchment (baking) paper and place a wire rack on it. Place 8 oz (250 g) semisweet (plain) chocolate, chopped, in the top of a double boiler placed over (not touching) barely simmering water. Heat, stirring often, until the chocolate melts. Remove from over the water and set aside to cool slightly. One at a time, dip the tips of the cooled cookies in the melted chocolate. Place on the rack and let stand until the chocolate is firm.

Dried cranberries and toasted pistachios make these cookies a colorful choice for the holidays or any festive occasion. Biscotti are twice-baked: first in a log shape and then in slices to make them crisp. This makes them exceptionally good keepers, and, if stored in a tightly sealed tin, they will stay fresh for up to two weeks. Experiment with other dried fruits and nuts, such as dried cherries and almonds.

Position a rack in the middle of the oven, and preheat to 350°F (180°C). Line a rimless baking sheet with parchment (baking) paper.

In a bowl, sift together the flour, baking powder, and salt. Set aside.

BY HAND: In a large bowl, combine the eggs and sugar. Using a wire whisk, beat until light in color and thick, about 3 minutes. Beat in the melted butter, orange zest, and vanilla and almond extracts with a wooden spoon until blended. Add the dry ingredients and beat until incorporated. Stir in the pistachio nuts and cranberries. The dough will be soft and sticky.

BY MIXER: In a large bowl, combine the eggs and sugar. Beat on medium speed until light in color and thick, about 3 minutes. Beat in the melted butter, orange zest, and vanilla and almond extracts on low speed until blended. Add the dry ingredients and beat until incorporated. Using a wooden spoon, stir in the pistachio nuts and cranberries. The dough will be soft and sticky.

Scoop out half of the dough onto one half of the prepared baking sheet, and form it into a log 10 inches (25 cm) long. Repeat with the remaining dough, spacing the logs 3 inches (7.5 cm) apart. Press the logs gently to make them 3 inches (7.5 cm) wide. With damp fingertips, gently smooth the surface of the logs.

Bake the logs until they are crisp and golden on the outside, 20–25 minutes. The centers will be soft. Remove from the oven. Reduce the oven temperature to 300°F (150°C). Let the logs cool on the baking sheet for 10 minutes.

With a wide spatula, transfer the logs to a cutting board and, using a serrated knife, cut each log crosswise on the diagonal into slices 3/4 inch (2 cm) thick. Arrange the slices, cut side down and at least 1/2 inch (12 mm) apart, on the baking sheet. Return to the oven and bake until the cookies are crisp and brown on the outside, 17–22 minutes. Let the cookies cool on the baking sheet for 5 minutes, then transfer them to wire racks to cool completely. The interiors of the cookies become crisp as they cool. Store in an airtight container at room temperature for up to 2 weeks.

2 cups (10 oz/315 g) all-purpose (plain) flour

1 1/2 teaspoons baking powder

1/2 teaspoon salt

2 large eggs

3/4 cup (6 oz/185 g) sugar

1/2 cup (4 oz/125 g) unsalted butter, melted and cooled

1 1/2 teaspoons grated orange zest

1 teaspoon vanilla extract (essence)

1 teaspoon pure almond extract (essence)

1 cup (4 oz/125 g) coarsely chopped pistachio nuts, toasted (page 21)

1/2 cup (2 oz/60 g) dried cranberries

Almond Tuiles

¹/₂ cup (2 oz/60 g) cake (soft-wheat) flour

²/₃ cup (2¹/₂ oz/75 g) confectioners' (icing) sugar

2 large egg whites

1 teaspoon vanilla extract (essence)

¹/₂ teaspoon almond extract (essence)

¹/₄ cup (2 oz/60 g) unsalted butter, melted and cooled

³/₄ cup (3 oz/90 g) sliced (flaked) almonds

Tuiles are ultrathin, crisp curved cookies that imitate the shape of a French roof tile (*tuile* means "tile" in French). In addition to the classic arch shape, the versatile batter can be spread into large rounds for molding into cups to hold ice cream, berries, or mousse, or into long strips that can be twisted into corkscrews for a fanciful garnish. These delicate cookies are most successful when baked on silicone-coated nonstick liners (see note).

Position a rack in the middle of the oven, and preheat to 350°F (180°C). Line 3 rimless baking sheets with silicone-coated nonstick liners or parchment (baking) paper, or use 3 nonstick baking sheets.

In a large bowl, using a wire whisk, stir together the flour and confectioners' sugar. Add the egg whites and vanilla and almond extracts and whisk until smooth, about 2 minutes. Whisk in the melted butter until blended and the batter is smooth and shiny.

Using 1 tablespoon of batter for each cookie, form six 4-inch (10-cm) rounds on a prepared baking sheet, spreading them with a narrow, thin offset metal spatula and spacing them about 3 inches (7.5 cm) apart. The batter will look translucent, and in some spots the baking liner may show though. Scatter about 2 teaspoons sliced almonds over the top of each cookie.

Bake the cookies until they have a border that is evenly brown, but the center remains light gold, 6–8 minutes.

Remove the cookies from the oven. Using the offset metal spatula, immediately lift the warm cookies one at a time, working quickly but carefully, from the baking sheet. Drape them over a rolling pin, a clean bottle, or a clean, small can, making sure they do not touch.

When the cookies are firm and have cooled slightly, after about 1 minute, carefully transfer them to a wire rack to cool completely. Prepare the other baking sheets while the first sheet bakes. If you are reusing a baking sheet, let it cool before spreading batter on it. Store the cookies carefully—they break easily—in an airtight container at room temperature for up to 2 days.

SILICONE-COATED NONSTICK LINERS

Developed for pastry chefs, these flexible nonstick pan liners let you remove baked goods without breakage and keep cleanup to a minimum. They can be used any time a recipe calls for a buttered or lined pan, and they are ideal for delicate cookies, meringues, and sheet cakes, as well as being an excellent surface for rolling out pastry dough. The liners also promote uniform browning, come in a range of sizes, and can withstand oven temperatures of up to 500°F (260°C). They are reusable, too; to clean them, simple wipe with a soft, clean cloth.

Vanilla Wafers

1 cup (8 oz/250 g) unsalted butter, at room temperature

¹/₂ cup (4 oz/125 g) sugar

¹/₄ teaspoon salt

2 large egg yolks

1 tablespoon vanilla extract (essence)

2 cups (10 oz/315 g) all-purpose (plain) flour

BY HAND: In a large bowl, combine the butter, sugar, and salt. Beat with a wooden spoon until smooth. Add the egg yolks and vanilla and stir until blended. Add the flour and mix until incorporated and a smooth dough forms.

BY MIXER: In a large bowl, combine the butter, sugar, and salt. Beat on medium speed until smooth. Add the egg yolks and vanilla and beat on low speed until blended. Add the flour and mix until incorporated and a smooth dough forms.

Divide the dough into 4 equal portions. Roll each portion into a log 7 inches (18 cm) long and about 1¹/₂ inches (4 cm) in diameter. Wrap the logs in plastic wrap and refrigerate until firm, at least 2 hours.

Position a rack in the middle of the oven, and preheat to 350°F (180°C). Line 3 rimless baking sheets with parchment (baking) paper.

Using a sharp knife, cut each unwrapped log crosswise into slices ¹/₄ inch (6 mm) thick. Place the cookies 1 inch (2.5 cm) apart on the prepared baking sheets.

Bake the cookies, 1 sheet at a time, until the edges and bottoms are golden, 12–15 minutes. Let the cookies cool on the baking sheets for 5 minutes, then transfer them to wire racks to cool completely. Store in an airtight container at room temperature for up to 5 days.

Once these logs of vanilla dough have been chilled, they can be quickly and easily sliced into perfectly shaped, thin, round wafers. You can also tightly wrap the logs and freeze them for up to 2 months, then thaw them, still wrapped, in the refrigerator overnight, and slice and bake them the next morning. Crystal sugar, toasted nuts (page 21), or chocolate chips can be pressed onto the tops of the cookies before they are baked. Serve these classic wafers with your favorite ice cream.

Peanut Butter Wafers

This slice-and-bake icebox version of peanut butter cookies produces wafers that are crisp, yet have a soft, crumbly texture. The logs of dough are rolled in ground peanuts, to give the cookies crunchy and flavorful edges. Using salted rather than unsalted peanuts for the coating intensifies the peanut flavor of the cookies. Store the cookies in an airtight container at room temperature for up to 5 days.

In a bowl, sift together the flour, baking soda, and salt. Set aside.

BY HAND: In a large bowl, combine the butter and sugars. Beat with a wooden spoon until smooth. Stir in the egg and vanilla, then add the dry ingredients and mix until incorporated. Add the peanut butter and mix until blended.

BY MIXER: In a large bowl, combine the butter and sugars. Beat on medium speed until smooth. Add the egg and vanilla and beat on low speed until blended. Mix in the dry ingredients. Add the peanut butter and mix until blended.

Wrap the dough in plastic wrap and refrigerate for 15 minutes to firm slightly. Divide the dough in half, and form each half into a log 5 inches (13 cm) long and about 2 inches (5 cm) in diameter. Spread the ground peanuts on a piece of waxed paper and roll each log in the peanuts, pressing them gently into the dough. Wrap the logs in plastic wrap and refrigerate until firm, at least 2 hours.

Position a rack in the middle of the oven, and preheat to 325°F (165°C). Line 2 rimless baking sheets with parchment (baking) paper. Cut each unwrapped log crosswise into slices 1/3 inch (9 mm) thick. Place the cookies 1 inch (2.5 cm) apart on the baking sheets. Bake the cookies, 1 sheet at a time, until the edges and bottoms are lightly colored, 12–15 minutes. Let the cookies cool on the baking sheets for 5 minutes, then transfer them to wire racks to cool completely.

1 1/4 cups (6 1/2 oz/200 g) all-purpose (plain) flour

1 teaspoon baking soda (bicarbonate of soda)

1/4 teaspoon salt

1/2 cup (4 oz/125 g) unsalted butter, at room temperature

1/2 cup (4 oz/125 g) granulated sugar

1/2 cup (3 1/2 oz/105 g) firmly packed golden brown sugar

1 large egg

1 teaspoon vanilla extract (essence)

3/4 cup (7 1/2 oz/235 g) smooth peanut butter, at room temperature

1/2 cup (2 oz/60 g) coarsely ground salted peanuts

Chocolate-Orange Pinwheels and Checkerboards

**1 cup (5 oz/155 g)
all-purpose (plain) flour**

¹/₄ teaspoon baking powder

¹/₈ teaspoon salt

**1 oz (30 g) semisweet (plain)
chocolate, chopped**

**¹/₂ cup (4 oz/125 g) unsalted
butter, at room temperature**

¹/₂ cup (4 oz/125 g) sugar

1 large egg, separated

**1 teaspoon vanilla extract
(essence)**

1 teaspoon grated orange zest

**2 teaspoons Dutch-process
cocoa powder**

Despite their whimsical names, these are not children's toys and games, although they are child's play to make. These slice-and-bake cookies use two differently colored—and flavored—doughs to form a pinwheel or a checkerboard design.

In a bowl, sift together the flour, baking powder, and salt. Set aside. Place the chocolate in the top of a double boiler placed over (not touching) barely simmering water. Heat, stirring often, until the chocolate melts (page 21). Remove from over the water and set aside to cool slightly.

BY HAND: In a large bowl, combine the butter and sugar. Beat with a wooden spoon until smooth, about 3 minutes. Add the egg yolk and vanilla and beat until blended. Add the dry ingredients and mix until incorporated and the dough is smooth.

BY MIXER: In a large bowl, combine the butter and sugar. Beat on medium speed until smooth, about 3 minutes. Add the egg yolk and vanilla and beat on low speed until blended. Add the dry ingredients and mix until incorporated and the dough is smooth.

Divide the dough in half. Put one-half of the dough in a separate bowl and stir in the orange zest. Add the melted chocolate and cocoa powder to the dough

VARIATIONS

Chocolate-Raspberry
Omit the orange zest from the light-colored dough. Add 5 teaspoons raspberry purée and 2 additional tablespoons flour to the light-colored dough.

Chocolate-Coffee
Omit the orange zest from the light-colored dough. Add 1 teaspoon instant espresso powder to 1 teaspoon hot water and stir to dissolve. Add to the light-colored dough.

Chocolate-Vanilla
Omit the orange zest from the light-colored dough. Add 1 teaspoon vanilla extract (essence) to the light-colored dough.

remaining in the large bowl and mix on low speed or with a wooden spoon until blended completely into the dough. Gather up each portion of dough, form each into a 5-inch (13-cm) square, and wrap separately in plastic wrap. Refrigerate until firm, about 45 minutes.

To make pinwheels (see photographs to the left): Remove the dough from the refrigerator. One at a time, place each dough portion between 2 sheets of waxed paper and roll out into a rectangle 10 by 5 inches (25 by 13 cm) and about $^1/_8$ inch (3 mm) thick. Remove the top piece of waxed paper from each rectangle. In a small bowl, using a fork, beat the egg white until foamy. Brush it lightly over the top surface of the chocolate dough. Using the waxed paper, flip the chocolate dough onto the orange dough and press the doughs together. Peel off and discard the top piece of waxed paper. Trim the dough edges evenly. Roll up the 2 layers of dough into a tight log, removing the remaining piece of waxed paper as you roll. Gently press the seam along the length of the roll to seal it. Trim the ends evenly. The roll should be about 9 inches (23 cm) long. Wrap in plastic wrap and refrigerate until firm, at least 1 hour or overnight.

To make checkerboards (see photographs to the right): Remove the dough from the refrigerator. Cut each piece of dough into 6 strips. One at a time, roll each strip between your palms into a rope $7^1/_2$ inches (19 cm) long, flouring your hands lightly, if necessary. In a small bowl, using a fork, beat the egg white until foamy. On a work surface, lay 3 ropes parallel to one another, alternating the colors—chocolate, orange, chocolate—and press the ropes together. Brush the egg white lightly on the top. Place a second set of 3 ropes of alternating colors—orange, chocolate, orange—on top of the first set of 3, press them together, and brush with egg white. Press the layers gently to seal them together. Repeat until you have a stack of 4 rows, always alternating the colors so that a checkerboard pattern is visible when the stack is viewed from the end. Do not brush the top row with egg white. Trim the ends evenly. The 4-sided strip will be about 7 inches (18 cm) long. Wrap in plastic wrap and refrigerate until firm, at least 1 hour or overnight.

Position a rack in the middle of the oven, and preheat to 350°F (180°C) oven. Line 2 rimless baking sheets with parchment (baking) paper. Unwrap the pinwheel or checkerboard log on a cutting board. Using a large, sharp knife, cut the dough crosswise into slices $^1/_4$ inch (6 mm) thick. Place them 1 inch (2.5 cm) apart on the prepared baking sheets.

Bake the cookies, 1 sheet at a time, until the edges just begin to turn lightly golden, 8–12 minutes. Let the cookies cool on the baking sheets for 5 minutes, then transfer them to wire racks to cool completely. Store in an airtight container at room temperature for up to 5 days.

Apricot-Pecan Rugelach

The origins of rugelach are eastern European, but their popularity has spread around the world. Rugelach are traditionally served on the Hanukkah table. They are made with a rich butter-and-cream-cheese dough that is cut into wedges, rolled up with a filling of fruit and nuts, and then shaped into crescents. Fillings can be varied by using different combinations (in the same proportions listed in the recipe) of jam, dried fruit, and nuts, or by substituting miniature chocolate chips.

BY HAND: To make the dough, in a large bowl, combine the flour, sugar, and salt. Stir with a wooden spoon to mix. While continuing to stir, add the cream cheese and butter and mix until large clumps of dough form. Add the sour cream and vanilla and mix just until blended.

BY MIXER: To make the dough, in a large bowl, combine the flour, sugar, and salt. Beat on low speed until blended. With the mixer running, add the cream cheese and butter and mix until large clumps of dough form. Add the sour cream and vanilla and mix just until blended.

Divide the soft, sticky dough into 4 equal portions. Gather each portion into a ball and flatten into a disk 4 inches (10 cm) in diameter. Wrap each disk in plastic wrap and refrigerate until firm, at least 1½ hours or for up to overnight.

Position a rack in the middle of the oven, and preheat to 375°F (190°C). Line 2 rimless baking sheets with parchment (baking) paper.

Remove 1 disk of dough from the refrigerator. Lightly dust a work surface and a rolling pin with flour. Roll out the dough into a 10-inch (25-cm) round. To add the filling, using a narrow offset metal spatula, spread 2 tablespoons of the preserves evenly over the dough, leaving a ¾-inch (2-cm) border. Sprinkle with 2 tablespoons of the raisins and ¼ cup of the pecans, and press them gently into the dough.

Using a large, sharp knife, cut the dough round into 12 equal wedges. Starting from the wide end, roll up each wedge tightly to the pointed end. Place point side down and 1 inch (2.5 cm) apart on a prepared baking sheet. Bend the edges slightly to curve inward, forming a crescent. When all the crescents are formed, brush the top of each one lightly with cream. Sprinkle the tops lightly with the cinnamon-sugar. Repeat with the 3 remaining dough portions and filling and topping ingredients, filling both baking sheets.

Bake the cookies, 1 sheet at a time, until the bottoms are light brown and the edges are golden, 22–25 minutes. Let the cookies cool on the baking sheets for 5 minutes, then transfer them to wire racks to cool completely. Store in an airtight container at room temperature for up to 4 days.

For the dough

2¼ cups (11½ oz/360 g) all-purpose (plain) flour

3 tablespoons sugar

¼ teaspoon salt

8 oz (250 g) cream cheese, at room temperature, cut into ¾-inch (2-cm) pieces

1 cup (8 oz/250 g) unsalted butter, cut into ¾-inch (2-cm) pieces

¼ cup (2 oz/60 g) sour cream

1 tablespoon vanilla extract (essence)

For the filling and topping

8 tablespoons (5 oz/155 g) apricot preserves

8 tablespoons (3 oz/90 g) golden raisins (sultanas)

1 cup (4 oz/125 g) coarsely chopped pecans, toasted (page 21)

1 tablespoon heavy (double) cream

4 teaspoons sugar mixed with ½ teaspoon ground cinnamon

Raspberry Jam Sandwich Hearts

2 cups (10 oz/315 g) all-purpose (plain) flour

$1/2$ teaspoon salt

1 cup (8 oz/250 g) unsalted butter, at room temperature

$3/4$ cup (3 oz/90 g) confectioners' (icing) sugar, plus extra for dusting

$1 1/2$ teaspoons vanilla extract (essence)

$1/2$ teaspoon almond extract (essence)

6 tablespoons seedless raspberry jam

In a small bowl, sift together the flour and salt. Set aside.

BY HAND: In a large bowl, combine the butter and confectioners' sugar. Beat with a wooden spoon until smooth. Add the vanilla and almond extracts and stir until well blended. Add the dry ingredients and mix until the dough comes together in large clumps.

BY MIXER: In a large bowl, combine the butter and confectioners' sugar. Beat on medium speed until smooth. Add the vanilla and almond extracts and beat on low speed until well blended. Add the dry ingredients and beat until the dough comes together in large clumps.

Press the dough together into a ball, then divide it in half. Gather each half into a ball, flatten each ball into a disk 5 inches (13 cm) in diameter, wrap in plastic wrap, and refrigerate until firm, about 40 minutes.

Position a rack in the middle of the oven, and preheat to 325°F (165°C). Line 2 rimless baking sheets with parchment (baking) paper.

Remove 1 dough disk from the refrigerator. Lightly dust a work surface and a rolling pin with flour. Roll out the dough $1/4$ inch (6 mm) thick. Slide a thin metal spatula under the dough to loosen it from the rolling surface. Using a $2 1/2$-inch (6-cm) heart-shaped cookie cutter, cut out cookies. Using a 1-inch (2.5 cm) heart-shaped cookie cutter, cut out the center of half of the cookies. Place the larger hearts $1 1/2$ inches (4 cm) apart on a prepared baking sheet. Place the smaller hearts about 1 inch (2.5 cm) apart on a prepared baking sheet. Repeat with the second dough disk. Press the dough scraps together and repeat the rolling and cutting process.

Bake the cookies, 1 sheet at a time, until the edges are light brown, 12–15 minutes. Let the cookies cool on the baking sheets for 5 minutes, then transfer them to wire racks to cool completely.

Leaving a $1/4$-inch (6-mm) border uncovered, spread about 1 teaspoon of the raspberry jam over each cookie without a cutout. Using a fine-mesh sieve, dust the cutout cookies with confectioners' sugar. Place the cutout cookies on top of the jam-covered cookies. Dust the miniature heart cookies with confectioners' sugar. Store in an airtight container at room temperature for up to 4 days.

Hearts are always in season, but this easy-to-roll dough can be cut into other shapes, such as stars, trees, leaves, or shamrocks, to adapt this recipe to any occasion. Although the buttery dough makes a cookie that pairs well with any flavor jam, it is best to use a seedless one. The small centers that are cut out from half the cookies can be baked along with the cookies, dusted with confectioners' sugar, and served as miniature heart cookies.

Maple Pecan Squares

In early spring, the warm days and cold nights start the sap flowing in sugar maple trees. It takes 40 gallons (160 l) of sap to produce only 1 gallon (4 l) of pure maple syrup, and just a small amount of the concentrated syrup to give these toffeelike pecan bars their distinctive maple flavor. The bars will be set but soft when warm, and become crisp and brittle when cool.

Position a rack in the middle of the oven, and preheat to 350°F (180°C). Carefully line a 9-inch (23-cm) square baking pan with heavy-duty aluminum foil, letting the foil extend up the sides and over the edges of the pan. Butter the foil liner.

BY HAND: To make the crust, in a large bowl, stir together the flour, brown sugar, and salt until blended. Using a pastry blender or 2 knives, cut the butter into the dry ingredients until the mixture forms large, coarse crumbs the size of small peas.

BY FOOD PROCESSOR: To make the crust, combine the flour, brown sugar, and salt and pulse 2 or 3 times to blend. Add the butter and pulse 8–10 times until the mixture forms large, coarse crumbs the size of small peas.

Press the crumb mixture into the bottom of the prepared pan. Bake the crust until the edges are lightly browned and the top feels firm when lightly touched, 12–17 minutes. Set aside.

To make the filling, in a saucepan over medium heat, combine the butter, maple syrup, and brown sugar and stir together until the butter melts and the brown sugar dissolves. Bring to a boil and boil for 1 minute. Remove from the heat and immediately stir in the cream. Then stir in the pecans. Pour the hot filling over the partially baked crust, spreading it evenly to the edges with an icing spatula.

Bake until the filling is set when you give the pan a gentle shake, 22–25 minutes. During baking, the filling will bubble vigorously, then the bubbles will subside and become smaller toward the end of baking. Transfer to a wire rack to let cool until firm, about 1 1/2 hours.

Using the ends of the foil liner, carefully lift the maple-pecan square in its liner from the baking pan. Run a small knife around the edges of the square to loosen it from the foil. Using a large, sharp knife, cut into 25 small squares. The squares will slide easily off the foil. Store in an airtight container at room temperature for up to 3 days.

For the crust

1 1/4 cups (6 1/2 oz/200 g) all-purpose (plain) flour

1/3 cup (2 1/2 oz/75 g) firmly packed golden brown sugar

1/4 teaspoon salt

1/2 cup (4 oz/125 g) cold unsalted butter, cut into 3/4-inch (2-cm) pieces

For the filling

6 tablespoons (3 oz/90 g) unsalted butter

1/3 cup (3 1/2 oz/105 g) pure maple syrup

2/3 cup (5 oz/155 g) firmly packed golden brown sugar

1/3 cup (3 fl oz/80 ml) heavy (double) cream

2 cups (8 oz/250 g) coarsely chopped pecans

Black Cherry–Oatmeal Crunch Squares

1³/₄ cups (9 oz/280 g) all-purpose (plain) flour

1¹/₂ cups (4¹/₂ oz/140 g) old-fashioned rolled oats

1 cup (7 oz/220 g) firmly packed golden brown sugar

1¹/₂ teaspoons ground cinnamon

1 cup (8 oz/250 g) cold unsalted butter, cut into ³/₄-inch (2-cm) pieces

1 cup (10 oz/315 g) black cherry jam

Position a rack in the middle of the oven, and preheat to 325°F (165°C). Butter a 9-inch (23-cm) square baking pan.

BY HAND: In a large bowl, stir together the flour, rolled oats, brown sugar, and cinnamon until blended. Using a pastry blender or 2 knives, cut in the butter until the mixture forms large, coarse crumbs the size of small peas.

BY FOOD PROCESSOR: Combine the flour, rolled oats, and brown sugar and pulse 2 or 3 times until blended. Add the butter and pulse 8–10 times until the mixture forms large, coarse crumbs the size of small peas.

Remove 2 cups (10 oz/315 g) of the crumb mixture and set aside. Press the remaining crumb mixture into the bottom and 1 inch (2.5 cm) up the sides of the prepared pan.

Drop teaspoons of the jam evenly over the crust, then spread it gently with the back of the spoon to cover the crust. If a few spaces remain, they will be covered by jam as it melts during baking. Sprinkle the reserved crumbs evenly over the jam layer.

Bake until the top is lightly browned, 50–55 minutes. Transfer to a rack and let cool until firm, about 2 hours. Using a large, sharp knife, cut into 25 small squares. Store in an airtight container at room temperature for up to 3 days.

A single oatmeal crumb mixture serves as both the press-in crust and the crisp topping for these jam-filled squares. Use a good-quality black cherry jam that includes some pieces of fruit. Strawberry, raspberry, blueberry, and apricot jam are other excellent filling choices. Transform the squares from snack fare to dessert by serving them warm with a scoop of vanilla or black cherry ice cream.

Meyer Lemon Squares

The filling for these squares is a homemade lemon curd, a thick, smooth lemon-butter sauce that originated in England, where it is often spread on muffins, cakes, or even bread. Meyer lemons, which are appreciated for their sweet flavor and flowery fragrance, are used here, but common lemons, such as Eureka, may be substituted. Although the lemon filling remains soft even when cold, it holds its shape when the squares are cut.

Position a rack in the middle of the oven, and preheat to 350°F (180°C). Butter an 8-inch (20-cm) square baking pan.

BY HAND: To make the crust, in a large bowl, stir together the flour, confectioners' sugar, and salt until blended. Using a pastry blender or 2 knives, cut in the butter until the mixture forms large, coarse crumbs the size of small peas.

BY FOOD PROCESSOR: To make the crust, combine the flour, confectioners' sugar, and salt and pulse 2 or 3 times until blended. Add the butter and pulse 6–8 times until the mixture forms large, coarse crumbs the size of small peas.

Press the crumb mixture into the bottom and 1 inch (2.5 cm) up the sides of the prepared pan. Bake the crust until golden and the top feels firm when lightly touched, 15–20 minutes. Set aside. Reduce the heat to 325°F (165°C).

To make the lemon filling, in the top of a double boiler, whisk together the whole eggs, egg yolks, lemon juice, and granulated sugar until the sugar dissolves. Place over (not touching) barely simmering water and add the butter pieces. Using a large spoon, stir constantly until the butter melts and the mixture is thick enough to coat the back of the spoon and registers 160°F (71°C) on an instant-read thermometer, about 12 minutes. Remove from over the water and strain the lemon curd through a medium-mesh sieve placed over a bowl. Stir in the lemon zest. Let cool for 10 minutes. Pour the lemon curd into the baked crust.

Bake until the center is just set, 13–17 minutes. Transfer to a wire rack and let cool for 20 minutes, then cover and refrigerate until well chilled, at least 3 hours or for up to overnight. The filling will thicken further as it cools.

If desired, just before serving, using a fine-mesh sieve, sift a thick layer of confectioners' sugar over the top of the squares. Using a large, sharp knife, cut into 16 squares and serve. Store in a covered container in the refrigerator for up to 3 days. The confectioners' sugar tends to melt if stored, however, so it is best not to use it if you will not be serving the squares the same day.

For the crust

³/₄ cup (4 oz/125 g) all-purpose (plain) flour

¹/₄ cup (1 oz/30 g) confectioners' (icing) sugar

¹/₈ teaspoon salt

6 tablespoons (3 oz/90 g) cold unsalted butter, cut into ³/₄-inch (2-cm) pieces

For the filling

3 large whole eggs, plus 3 large egg yolks

³/₄ cup (6 fl oz/180 ml) fresh Meyer lemon juice, strained (about 5 lemons)

1 cup (8 oz/250 g) granulated sugar

6 tablespoons (3 oz/90 g) unsalted butter, cut into ³/₄-inch (2-cm) cubes

1 teaspoon grated Meyer lemon zest

Confectioners' (icing) sugar, for dusting (optional)

Blueberry Cheesecake Squares with Hazelnut Crust

For the crust

1¹/₄ cups (6¹/₂ oz/200 g) all-purpose (plain) flour

¹/₃ cup (3 oz/90 g) sugar

³/₄ cup (3 oz/90 g) toasted, skinned, and finely chopped hazelnuts (filberts), page 21

¹/₈ teaspoon salt

¹/₂ cup (4 oz/125 g) cold unsalted butter, cut into ³/₄-inch (2-cm) pieces

For the filling

1 pound (500 g) cream cheese, at room temperature

³/₄ cup (6 oz/185 g) sugar

2 tablespoons all-purpose (plain) flour

3 large eggs, at room temperature

¹/₄ cup (2 fl oz/60 ml) heavy (double) cream

1 teaspoon vanilla extract (essence)

1 teaspoon almond extract (essence)

1¹/₂ cups (6 oz/185 g) blueberries

Position a rack in the middle of the oven, and preheat to 325°F (165°C). Butter a 9-inch (23-cm) square baking pan.

BY HAND: To make the crust, in a large bowl, stir together the flour, sugar, hazelnuts, and salt until blended. Using a pastry blender or 2 knives, cut in the butter until the mixture forms large, coarse crumbs the size of small peas.

BY FOOD PROCESSOR: To make the crust, combine the flour, sugar, hazelnuts, and salt and pulse 2 or 3 times to mix. Add the butter and pulse 8–10 times until the mixture forms large, coarse crumbs the size of small peas.

Press the crust mixture into the bottom and 1 inch (2.5 cm) up the sides of the prepared pan. Bake the crust until golden and the top looks dry and firm, 15–20 minutes. Set aside.

To make the filling, in a large bowl, combine the cream cheese and sugar and beat together with a wooden spoon or a mixer until blended and smooth. Stir in the flour until blended. Add the eggs one at a time, beating well after each addition until the batter is smooth. Stir in the cream and vanilla and almond extracts and stir until incorporated. Gently fold in the blueberries. Pour the batter into the prepared crust.

Bake until the center is set when you give the pan a gentle shake, 30–35 minutes. Remove from the oven and, using a small knife, loosen the warm cheesecake square from the sides of the pan. Let cool on a wire rack for 1 hour. Cover with plastic wrap and refrigerate until chilled, at least 3 hours or overnight.

Using a large, sharp knife, cut into 16 squares. Serve cold. Store tightly covered in the refrigerator for up to 3 days.

Hazelnuts, which have a rich, buttery texture, lend their pleasingly assertive flavor to the press-in crust for these rich cheesecake squares. Blueberries add the perfect amount of juicy sweetness to complement the creamy cheese and nutty crust. Raspberries or blackberries can be substituted. You can also use frozen berries if fresh are not available; add them frozen directly to the filling.

Brown Butter Blondies

1¹/₂ cups (7¹/₂ oz/235 g) all-purpose (plain) flour

1 teaspoon baking powder

¹/₂ teaspoon salt

²/₃ cup (5 oz/155 g) clarified unsalted butter (page 17)

1 cup (7 oz/220 g) firmly packed golden brown sugar

¹/₂ cup (4 oz/125 g) granulated sugar

2 large eggs

2 teaspoons vanilla extract (essence)

1 tablespoon fresh lemon juice, strained

Confectioners' (icing) sugar for dusting

Position a rack in the middle of the oven, and preheat to 325°F (165°C). Butter an 8-inch (20-cm) square baking pan.

In a bowl, sift together the flour, baking powder, and salt. Set aside.

In a frying pan over low heat, heat the clarified butter until light brown and fragrant, about 6 minutes (page 17). Remove the pan from the heat and pour into a small bowl to cool slightly.

In a large bowl, combine the brown butter, brown sugar, and granulated sugar and stir with a wooden spoon until blended. Mix in the eggs, vanilla, and lemon juice until smooth. Stir in the dry ingredients just until incorporated. Pour the batter into the prepared pan, spreading it evenly with a rubber spatula.

Bake until a toothpick inserted into the center comes out almost clean or with a few moist crumbs clinging to it, 35–45 minutes. Transfer to a wire rack and let cool completely.

If desired, using a fine-mesh sieve, dust the top with confectioners' sugar. Using a large, sharp knife, cut into 2-inch (5-cm) squares. Store in an airtight container at room temperature for up to 3 days.

Cooking butter until it is a deep, rich brown, before it darkens and burns, produces a nutty-flavored butter that enhances the traditional blondie. French chefs call this brown butter *beurre noisette* (hazelnut butter) because of its nut-brown color and taste. These blondies go well with an ice cream made with nuts, such as butter pecan or toasted almond.

Classic Dark Chocolate Brownies

Brownie history is sketchy at best, but legend has it that the first brownie was probably a chocolate cake that failed to rise. The name of the baker is lost, but there is no question that it was a clever way to turn a baking failure into a delicious baking success. In order to achieve their dense, moist fudge texture, these brownies have a high proportion of sugar and butter to flour and include a generous quantity of chocolate. Be sure to use good-quality chocolate.

Position a rack in the middle of the oven, and preheat to 350°F (180°C). Butter an 8-inch (20-cm) square baking pan.

Place the chocolate and butter in the top of a double boiler placed over (not touching) barely simmering water. Heat, stirring often, until the butter and chocolate melt (page 21). Remove from over the water and set aside to cool slightly.

In a large bowl, whisk together the eggs, sugar, salt, and vanilla until blended. Whisk in the chocolate mixture until blended. Sprinkle all of the flour over the mixture and whisk slowly just until blended. Pour the batter into the prepared pan, spreading it evenly with a rubber spatula.

Bake until a toothpick inserted into the center comes out almost clean or with a few moist crumbs clinging to it, 35–40 minutes. Be careful not to overbake. Transfer to a wire rack and let cool completely.

Using a large, sharp knife, cut into 2-inch (5-cm) squares. Store in an airtight container at room temperature for up to 3 days.

6 oz (185 g) unsweetened chocolate, chopped

$^3/_4$ cup (6 oz/185 g) unsalted butter, cut into $^3/_4$-inch (2-cm) pieces

3 large eggs

1$^3/_4$ cups (14 oz/440 g) sugar

$^1/_4$ teaspoon salt

2 teaspoons vanilla extract (essence)

1 cup (5 oz/155 g) plus 2 tablespoons all-purpose (plain) flour

Pies and Tarts

About Pies and Tarts

Mastering the making of a flaky, buttery pie or tart pastry will make you feel like a pro. A bit of practice, a dash of patience, and before you know it, you will have a first-rate crust. If you follow the techniques here, you will find what works for you and be able to make pies with ease.

Tarts and pies share two basic characteristics—they combine a filling with one or two layers of crust—but there are many differences, too.

Most tarts do not call for a top crust and are traditionally baked in fluted metal tart pans with removable bottoms that are shallower than pie pans. Tarts often call for a crust enriched with sugar and egg, which makes it more tender than its flakier cousin, the pie crust. Called *pâte sucrée,* this sweetened tart crust resembles a crumbly butter cookie.

Tarts can also be free-form: A filled round of sturdy pastry dough is pleated to envelop the edges of the filling, leaving the center exposed. Free-form tarts are more rustic and are often called *galettes*. Savory tarts and *galettes* are popular, too, especially when filled with the sunny flavors of the Mediterranean, such as olives, tomatoes, and herbs.

The pie is the American answer to the French tart. Unlike tarts, which are removed from the pan before serving, pies are served right out of the pan in which they are baked. They work best with an easy-handling dough that contains both butter and shortening, producing delicious layers of flaky pastry.

Pies can be single crust or double crust, with the latter solid or lattice. Many single-crust pies—and tart crusts, too—are partially or fully baked before the filling is added. If the filling must be baked, the crust is partially baked beforehand to ensure a crisp, brown bottom on the finished pie. This is true of baked custard pies, such as pumpkin, or single-crust fruit pies, such as blueberry crumble.

Pie crusts that contain a pre-cooked filling that does not require further baking, such as lemon meringue or banana cream, are fully baked before being filled.

Choosing between a metal pie pan and a glass or ceramic pie dish depends on the type of pie you are baking. Double-crust and lattice-top pies, such as apple and peach pies, should be baked in metal pans. Metal, an even, dependable conductor of heat, produces the crisp, golden crusts these pies need for success. Glass pie dishes also conduct and retain heat rapidly and efficiently and are good choices for crusts that will be partially or fully baked before the filling is added. Ceramic pie dishes should only be used for cobblers, crisps, and other crustless fruit desserts. If using glass or ceramic in a recipe calling for a metal pan, reduce the oven temperature by 25°F (15°C).

Cobblers and crisps (along with pandowdy, buckles, and other whimsically named treats) are rustic relatives of the tart and pie. They each call for a deep base of fresh fruit. The cobbler is topped with a thick biscuitlike crust. The dough is dolloped over the hot fruit and then baked. The crisp has a crunchy crumb topping. Butter, sugar, and flour are the usual ingredients, sometimes with nuts or rolled oats for added texture and flavor.

TROUBLESHOOTING PIES AND TARTS

What happened	Why it happened
Pie or tart dough is sticky and hard to roll out.	Too much water was added, use extra flour when rolling; dough is too warm, chill dough in refrigerator for 30 minutes before proceeding.
Pie or tart dough is stiff and hard to roll out.	Not enough water was added to dough, or dough is too cold, let it warm up before proceeding.
Blind-baked single-crust pie or tart dough did not hold its shape.	Too few pie weights were used for blind baking; dough did not rest long enough or was too soft.
Blind-baked single-crust pie or tart dough shrank in pan.	Dough was not chilled long enough, or was stretched too much when lining the pan.
Pie or tart is browning too quickly.	Oven is too hot; cover loosely with aluminum foil and continue baking.
Pie crust is not fully baked on bottom.	Crust was not partially baked before filling was added; especially true for custard pies.
Pie or tart crust is dense rather than flaky.	Butter and dough were overworked.

Six All-Purpose Fruit Pie Fillings

Here are six seasonal fruit pie fillings. They can be used to fill double-crust, crumb-topped, or most lattice-topped pies. Use them in place of the apple, peach, and blueberry fillings in the recipes on pages 176–79, then experiment with creating your own fruit fillings.

PEACH-RASPBERRY FILLING

6 cups (2¼ lb/1.1 kg) sliced, peeled peaches (page 23)

¼ cup (1½ oz/45 g) all-purpose (plain) flour

3 tablespoons sugar

1 tablespoon fresh lemon juice, strained

1 teaspoon vanilla extract (essence)

1 cup (4 oz/125 g) raspberries

In a large bowl, combine the peaches, flour, sugar, lemon juice, and vanilla and stir until blended. Fold in the raspberries until evenly distributed. Proceed as directed.

THREE-BERRY FILLING

3 cups (12 oz/375 g) blueberries

1 cup (4 oz/125 g) blackberries

1 cup (4 oz/125 g) raspberries

¼ cup (1½ oz/45 g) all-purpose (plain) flour

¼ cup (2 oz/60 g) sugar

1 tablespoon fresh lemon juice, strained

In a large bowl, combine the berries, flour, sugar, and lemon juice and stir gently until blended. Proceed as directed.

PLUM FILLING

20 French prune plums or 15 Santa Rosa plums, pitted and cut into 1-inch (2.5-cm) thick slices

⅓ cup (2½ oz/75 g) firmly packed golden brown sugar

3 tablespoons all-purpose (plain) flour

1 tablespoon fresh lemon juice, strained

1 tablespoon amaretto liqueur

In a large bowl, combine the plums, brown sugar, flour, lemon juice, and liqueur and stir until blended. Proceed as directed.

SOUR CHERRY FILLING

5 cups (2 lb/1 kg) pitted sour cherries

½ cup (4 oz/125 g) sugar, or to taste

1½ tablespoons cornstarch (cornflour)

1 tablespoon fresh lemon juice, strained

¼ teaspoon almond extract (essence)

In a large bowl, combine the cherries, sugar, cornstarch, lemon juice, and almond extract and stir until blended. Proceed as directed.

APRICOT FILLING

5 cups (2 lb/1 kg) apricots, cut into quarters

½ cup (4 oz/125 g) sugar

¼ cup (1½ oz/45 g) all-purpose (plain) flour

2 tablespoons unsalted butter, melted

1 tablespoon fresh lemon juice, strained

1 tablespoon apricot liqueur (optional)

In a large bowl, combine the apricots, sugar, flour, melted butter, lemon juice, and the liqueur, if using, and stir until blended. Proceed as directed.

PEAR-CRANBERRY FILLING

6 cups (1½ lb/750 g) peeled, cored pears cut into 1-inch (2.5-cm) pieces

1 cup (4 oz/125 g) cranberries

2 tablespoons unsalted butter, melted

⅓ cup (3 oz/90 g) sugar

½ teaspoon ground cinnamon

In a large bowl, combine the pears, cranberries, butter, sugar, and cinnamon and stir until blended. Proceed as directed.

MASTER RECIPE Flaky Pie Pastry

For single-crust pie

5 tablespoons (2^1/$_2$ oz/75 g) cold unsalted butter

3 tablespoons cold vegetable shortening

1^1/$_3$ cups (7 oz/220 g) all-purpose (plain) flour

1 tablespoon sugar (optional)

^{1}/$_4$ teaspoon salt

4 tablespoons (2 fl oz/60 ml) ice water

For lattice-crust pie

^{1}/$_2$ cup (4 oz/125 g) cold unsalted butter

4 tablespoons (2 oz/60 g) cold vegetable shortening

2 cups (10 oz/315 g) all-purpose (plain) flour

4 teaspoons sugar (optional)

^{1}/$_4$ teaspoon salt

6 tablespoons (3 fl oz/90 ml) ice water

For double-crust pie

^{2}/$_3$ cup (5 oz/155 g) cold unsalted butter

6 tablespoons (3 oz/90 g) cold vegetable shortening

2^2/$_3$ cups (13^1/$_2$ oz/425 g) all-purpose (plain) flour

2 tablespoons sugar (optional)

^{1}/$_2$ teaspoon salt

8 tablespoons (4 fl oz/125 ml) ice water

Cut the butter and vegetable shortening into ^{3}/$_4$-inch (2-cm) pieces.

BY HAND: In a large bowl, combine the flour, sugar, and salt and stir to mix. Scatter the butter and shortening pieces over the flour mixture. Using a fork, toss to coat with the flour. Using a pastry blender or 2 knives, cut in the butter and shortening until the mixture forms large, coarse crumbs the size of large peas. Drizzle the ice water over the mixture and toss with the fork until the dough is evenly moist and begins to come together in a mass but does not form a ball.

BY FOOD PROCESSOR: Combine the flour, sugar, and salt. Pulse 2 or 3 times to mix. Add the butter and shortening pieces and pulse 8–10 times until the mixture forms large, coarse crumbs the size of large peas. Add the ice water a little at a time and pulse 10–12 times just until the dough begins to come together in a mass but does not form a ball.

BY STAND MIXER: In the large bowl of a stand mixer fitted with the paddle attachment, combine the flour, sugar, and salt. Mix on low speed until blended, about 10 seconds. Turn off the mixer, add the butter and shortening, and then continue mixing on low speed just until the mixture forms large, coarse crumbs the size of large peas, about 20 seconds. Add the ice water 1 tablespoon at a time, and mix on low speed just until the mixture begins to hold together, about 20 seconds. The dough will form large clumps and pull away from the sides of the bowl, but will not form a ball. To test, stop the mixer and squeeze a small piece of dough; it should hold together.

Transfer the dough to a work surface. If making the single-crust pie pastry, shape the dough into a 6-inch (15-cm) disk. For the lattice pie, divide the dough into 2 portions, one twice as large as the other; shape the larger portion into a 6-inch (15-cm) disk and the smaller one into a 3-inch (7.5-cm) disk. For the double-crust pie, divide the dough in half and form each half into a 6-inch (15-cm) disk. Wrap each disk tightly in plastic wrap and refrigerate until well chilled, about 1 hour or for up to overnight. To learn how to work with pie pastry, see page 162.

The rich flavor of butter and the flake-making quality of vegetable shortening produce a pie pastry that is both versatile and delicious. The butter and shortening should be very cold so that they will form the layers in the crust that contribute to the overall flakiness. Use ice water for the liquid to ensure that the shortening and butter do not soften during mixing.

If you are making a savory pie, such as a quiche or savory *galette*, omit the sugar.

To use up your dough scraps, press them together and roll them out again into a long, narrow rectangle. Brush the surface with softened butter and sprinkle it with cinnamon sugar. Working from a long side, roll up the rectangle into a log, then cut crosswise into slices 1 inch (2.5 cm) thick. Place the slices in a pan and bake alongside the pie. They are ready when the pastry is golden brown and the sugar starts to caramelize in the pan.

Working with Pie Pastry

TO ROLL OUT PIE DOUGH

Remove the dough disk(s) from the refrigerator. If the dough is cold and hard to roll out, let it stand at room temperature for 10–20 minutes. Dust a work surface and rolling pin with flour. For the bottom crust, use a 6-inch (15-cm) disk.

1 Rolling from the center toward the edges and in all directions, roll out the dough into a round 12 inches (30 cm) in diameter and $1/8$ inch (3 mm) thick. Use firm pressure and work quickly to prevent the dough from becoming warm.

2 Lift and turn the dough several times as you roll to prevent sticking, and dust the surface and the rolling pin with flour as needed. If the pastry sticks, loosen it with a bench scraper.

TO LINE A PIE PAN WITH DOUGH

1 Carefully roll the dough around the pin and position the pin over the pie pan.

2 Unroll the dough and center it in the pie pan, gently but firmly pressing it against the bottom and sides while taking care not to pull or stretch it. Repair any tears by pressing small scraps of dough over them.

3 Gently lift the edge of the dough with one hand, while pressing it into the edge of the pie pan with the other. Take care not to stretch the dough. If making a single-crust pie, using a small knife or a pair of kitchen scissors, trim the edge, leaving a $3/4$-inch (2-cm) overhang. Roll the overhang under itself to create a high edge on the pan rim. Using your index finger and thumb, pinch the dough around the rim to form a fluted edge or make another decorative edge (page 166). Freeze the pie crust until it is firm, about 30 minutes.

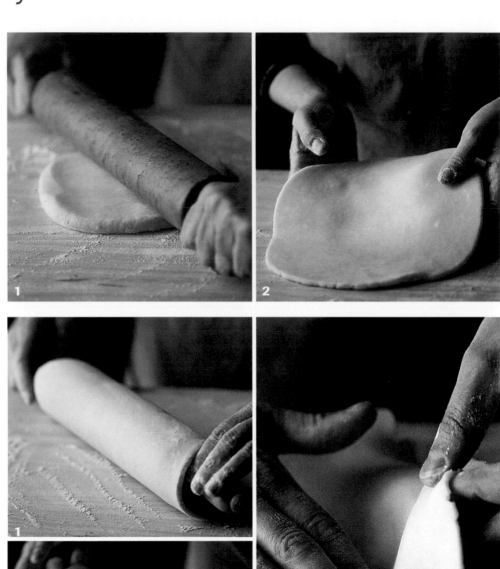

TO PREBAKE A SINGLE CRUST

1 Preheat the oven to 400°F (200°C). Line the frozen pie crust with a piece of heavy-duty aluminum foil. Fill the foil-lined crust with dried beans, uncooked rice, or ceramic or metal pie weights.

2 Bake the lined crust until it dries out, about 15 minutes. Check to see if the crust is ready by pulling up one corner of the foil. If the foil sticks, the crust is not fully dried out. Return it to the oven and check every 2 minutes. Carefully remove the weights and foil by gathering the foil edges toward the center and pulling up and out. Reduce the heat to 350°F (180°C).

3 For a partially baked crust, continue to bake until the crust is lightly browned on the edges and dry-looking on the bottom, about 5 minutes longer. Transfer the crust to a wire rack and use as directed in individual recipes.

4 For a fully baked crust, continue to bake until the entire crust is golden brown, about 10 minutes longer. Transfer the crust to a wire rack and use as directed in individual recipes.

TO MAKE A DOUBLE CRUST

Roll out 1 chilled dough disk and line the pie pan as directed on page 162, but do not trim the edges. Fill the lined pan with the pie filling as directed in the recipe. Then, roll out the second disk into a 12-inch (30-cm) round $^{1}/_{8}$ inch (3 mm) thick.

1 Carefully lift the dough round and place it over the filling, making sure to center the dough. You should have a slight overhang.

2 Using a sharp knife or a pair of kitchen scissors, trim the edge of the bottom and top crust together so they are even, leaving a $^{3}/_{4}$-inch (2-cm) overhang. Roll the overhang under itself to create an edge on the pan rim. Using your index finger and thumb, pinch the dough around the rim to form a fluted edge or make another decorative edge (see page 166).

3 To make steam vents, using a sharp knife, cut 3 or 4 slits in the center of the top crust. For a more decorative pattern, using the knife or a cookie cutter, cut out a shape such as a star or a heart. This will allow the steam to escape while the pie is baking.

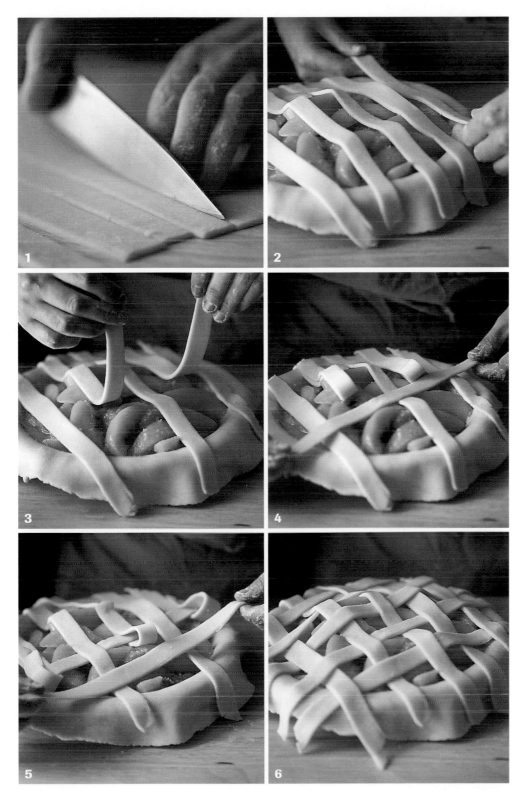

TO MAKE A LATTICE CRUST

Roll out the larger dough disk and line the pie pan as directed on page 162, but do not trim the edges.

1 Roll out the smaller dough disk into a rectangle about 8 by 11 inches (20 by 28 cm) and $^1/_8$ inch (3 mm) thick. Trim the edges evenly. Cut the rectangle into 10 strips, each 11 inches (28 cm) long and $^3/_4$ inch (2 cm) wide. Fill the lined pie pan with the pie filling.

2 Beginning 1 inch (2.5 cm) from the edge of the pie pan, lay 5 of the strips about 1 inch (2.5 cm) apart over the filling. Use a thin metal spatula to pick up the strips gently if they start to stick to the work surface.

3 Fold back every other strip halfway over itself. The first time you will fold back 2 strips, and the next time you will fold back the other 3 strips.

4 Place a strip at a slight angle across the unfolded strips. Return the 2 strips that have been folded back to their flat position.

5 Pull back the 3 alternate strips. Place the next strip across the unfolded (flat) strips about 1 inch (2.5 cm) from the last strip.

6 Continue folding back and weaving strips until the top of the pie is latticed. Using a sharp knife or scissors, trim the edge of the bottom crust and lattice strips so they are even, leaving a $^3/_4$-inch (2-cm) overhang. Roll the overhang under itself to create an edge on the pan rim. Using your index finger and thumb, pinch the dough around the rim to form a fluted edge or make another decorative edge (page 166).

Decorative Edges

Whether you have made a single crust, a lattice crust, or a double crust, you will need to create a finished edge on your pie. These four simple edges not only make your pie even more beautiful but help the crust stay in place during baking. For a more decorative look, try the dough cutouts.

CRIMPED EDGE

1 Use the tines of a fork to seal the dough around the edge of the pastry rim.

ROPE EDGE

2 Holding your left and right index fingers at a slight angle, press the pie dough together all along the pastry rim at $^1/_2$–1 inch (12 mm–2.5 cm) intervals.

SIMPLE FLUTED EDGE

3 Hold the thumb and index finger of one hand about 1 inch (2.5 cm) apart and press them against the outer edge of the pastry rim while pressing with your other index finger from the inside edge of the pastry rim through the opening. Repeat all along the pastry rim at 1-inch (2.5-cm) intervals.

DECORATIVE FLUTED EDGE

4 Follow the directions for making a simple fluted edge. Crimp each flute or every other flute with the tines of a fork all along the pastry rim.

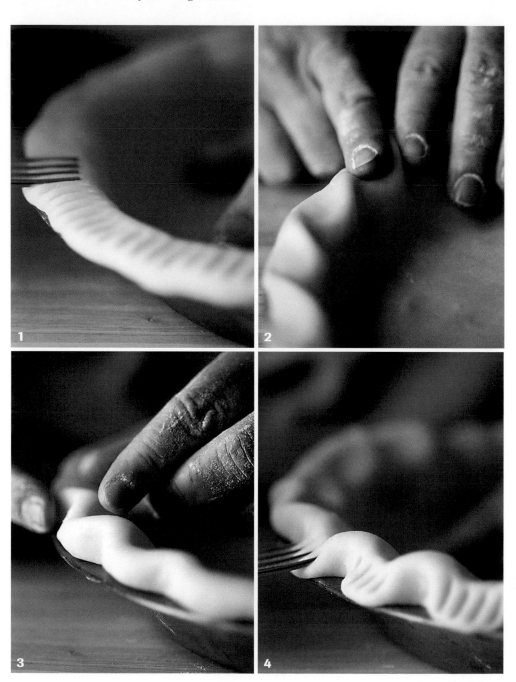

SIMPLE DOUGH CUTOUTS

1 Gather the remaining scraps of dough and press them together. Roll out ⅛ inch (3 mm) thick. Using a small cookie cutter or a sharp paring knife, cut out shapes from the dough.

2 Brush the back of each dough cutout with egg wash made by whisking together 1 egg with 1 tablespoon water.

3 Place the cutouts along the edge of a crimped crust or decoratively on the top of a double-crust pie. Press each cutout lightly to adhere it to the crust.

LEAF CUTOUTS

1 Gather the remaining scraps of dough and press them together. Roll out ⅛ inch (3 mm) thick. Using a small leaf-shaped cookie cutter, cut out shapes from the dough.

2 Using the back of a paring knife, gently press lines into the dough to resemble the veining on a leaf. Preheat the oven to 400°F (200°C). Place the cutouts on a half-sheet pan or rimless baking sheet lined with parchment (baking) paper.

3 Bake until golden brown, about 15 minutes. Let cool on the pan on a wire rack. Place the baked leaves decoratively on top of a baked custard pie, such as a pumpkin pie, just before serving.

MASTER RECIPE Rich Tart Pastry

1 1/4 cups (6 1/2 oz/200 g) all-purpose (plain) flour

1/2 cup (2 oz/60 g) confectioners' (icing) sugar

1/4 teaspoon salt

1/2 cup (4 oz/125 g) cold unsalted butter, cut into 3/4-inch (2-cm) pieces

2 large egg yolks

1 tablespoon heavy (double) cream

Butter-rich tart pastry, also known as *pâte sucrée*, results in a tender texture, rather than the flaky character of a successful pie crust. The dough is similar to a smooth cookie dough, and once baked, it is reminiscent of a good butter cookie. While the pastry is tender, it is also strong enough to support a baked tart outside of the pan. Gather up your dough scraps to make delicious cookies. Just roll out and use a cookie cutter or a paring knife to cut out shapes from the dough. Sprinkle the cutouts with sugar and bake at 350°F (180°C) until golden brown.

BY HAND: In a large bowl, sift together the flour, confectioners' sugar, and salt. Scatter the butter pieces over the flour mixture and toss with your fingers or a fork to coat with the flour. Using a pastry blender or 2 knives, cut in the butter until the mixture forms large, coarse crumbs the size of large peas. In a small bowl, lightly beat the egg yolks with the fork, then stir in the cream until blended. Drizzle the egg mixture over the flour mixture and stir with the fork until the dough is evenly moist and comes together in a smooth mass.

BY FOOD PROCESSOR: Combine the flour, confectioners' sugar, and salt. Pulse 1 or 2 times to mix. Add the butter pieces and pulse 7–8 times until the mixture forms large, coarse crumbs the size of large peas. In a small bowl, lightly beat the egg

yolks with a fork, then stir in the cream until blended. With the motor running, add the egg mixture and process just until the dough begins to come together, but does not form a ball.

BY STAND MIXER: In the large bowl of a stand mixer fitted with a paddle attachment, combine the flour, confectioners' sugar, and salt. Mix on low speed until blended, about 10 seconds. Turn off the mixer, add the butter pieces, and then continue mixing on low speed just until the mixture forms large, coarse crumbs the size of large peas, about 20 seconds. In a small bowl, lightly beat the egg yolks with a fork, then stir in the cream until blended. With the mixer on low speed, pour in the egg mixture and continue mixing until the dough is evenly moist and comes together in a smooth mass.

On a work surface, shape the dough into a 6-inch (15-cm) disk. Wrap in plastic wrap and refrigerate until firm, at least 45 minutes or for up to overnight. To learn how to work with tart pastry, see page 170.

VARIATIONS

Citrus Tart Pastry
Add 1 teaspoon grated lemon, lime, or orange zest with the liquid ingredients.

Vanilla Tart Pastry
Add 1 teaspoon vanilla extract (essence) with the liquid ingredients.

Almond Tart Pastry
Add 1 teaspoon almond extract (essence) with the liquid ingredients.

Working with Tart Pastry

TO ROLL OUT TART DOUGH

Remove the dough disk from the refrigerator. If the dough is too cold and hard to roll out easily, let it stand at room temperature for about 10–20 minutes. Lightly dust a work surface and rolling pin with flour.

1 Rolling from the center toward the edges and in all directions, roll out the chilled dough into a round about 13 inches (33 cm) in diameter and $^3/_{16}$ inch (5 mm) thick. Use firm and steady pressure and work quickly to prevent the dough from becoming warm.

2 Lift and turn the dough several times as you roll to prevent sticking, and dust the surface and the rolling pin with additional flour as needed. If the pastry round sticks, use a bench scraper or an icing spatula to loosen it.

TO LINE A TART PAN WITH DOUGH

1 Carefully roll the dough around the pin and position the pin over a tart pan with a removable bottom. Unroll the dough and center it in the tart pan.

2 Lift the edge of the dough and ease it into the outer edges of the pan, allowing the extra to flop over the sides. Repeat around the entire circumference of the pan, taking care not to stretch the dough. Repair any tears by pressing scraps of dough over them.

3 Using a small knife, trim the edges, leaving a $^1/_2$-inch (12-mm) overhang.

4 Roll the overhang back over itself and press it into the sides of the pan, creating a double thickness to reinforce the sides of the tart crust. Using your rolling pin, roll over the top of the dough along the rim of the tart pan to cut off any excess dough. Freeze the crust until it is firm, about 30 minutes.

TO PREBAKE A TART CRUST

Some recipes call for prebaking, also known as blind baking, a tart crust partially or fully before the filling is added.

1 Preheat the oven to 400°F (200°C). Line the frozen tart crust with a large piece of heavy-duty aluminum foil, making sure to press the foil into the fluted edges of the crust.

2 Fill the foil-lined crust with dried beans, uncooked rice, or ceramic or metal pie weights.

3 Bake the lined crust until it dries out, about 15 minutes. Check to see if the crust is ready by pulling up one corner of the foil. If the foil sticks, the crust is not fully dried out. Return it to the oven and check every 2 minutes. Carefully remove the weights and foil by gathering the foil edges toward the center and pulling up and out. Reduce the heat to 350°F (180°C).

4 For a partially baked crust, continue to bake until the crust is lightly browned on the edges, about 5 minutes longer. Transfer the crust to a wire rack and use as directed in individual recipes.

5 For a fully baked crust, continue to bake until the crust is golden brown, about 10 minutes longer. Transfer the crust to a wire rack and use as directed in individual recipes.

UNMOLDING

To unmold a fully baked tart crust or a filled tart, place the pan on a large can or inverted bowl and carefully slide the outer ring down. Using an offset spatula, carefully loosen the tart from the bottom of the tart pan and slide it onto a serving platter.

MASTER RECIPE Cream Cheese Tartlet Pastry

¹/₂ cup (4 oz/125 g) unsalted butter, at room temperature

3 oz (90 g) cream cheese, at room temperature

1 cup (5 oz/155 g) all-purpose (plain) flour, sifted

BY HAND: In a large bowl, using a large wooden spoon, stir together the butter and cream cheese until smooth and blended, about 2 minutes. Add the flour and continue stirring until a smooth dough forms.

BY STAND MIXER: In the large bowl of a stand mixer fitted with the paddle attachment, combine the butter and cream cheese. Mix on low speed until smooth and blended, about 45 seconds. Add the flour and continue mixing on low speed until a smooth dough forms.

Butter, cream cheese, and flour are the only ingredients needed for this foolproof pastry dough that is easily pressed into tartlet pans. The method is similar to how a cookie dough is made: You cream together the butter and cream cheese and then stir in the flour. You can double the ingredients to make dough for 12 tartlets.

Transfer the dough to a work surface and shape into a thick disk. Using a sharp knife, cut the dough into 6 equal portions. Roll each portion into a 2-inch (5-cm) ball. Place 1 ball in each of six 3¹/₂-inch (9-cm) tartlet pans.

Press the center of the dough to make an indentation, then, using your fingertips, press the dough evenly over the bottom and up the sides of each pan until it is even with the top edge of the pan. Use your fingers to "cut" away any overhang. Check to see that the bottom of each pan is completely covered with dough and the thickness of the sides looks even. Freeze the tartlet crusts until the dough is firm, about 30 minutes.

To prebake the crusts, follow the directions for prebaking a tart crust on page 171, putting the lined pans on a half-sheet pan for easy transport. Use as directed in individual recipes.

Fig and Raspberry Galette

Flaky Pie Pastry for single crust (page 160)

12 figs, stemmed and quartered lengthwise

1/4 cup (2 oz/60 g) firmly packed golden brown sugar

2 tablespoons all-purpose (plain) flour

1 tablespoon fresh lemon juice, strained

1/2 teaspoon almond extract (essence)

3 tablespoons granulated sugar

1 large egg beaten with 1 tablespoon heavy (double) cream

1 1/2 cups (6 oz/185 g) raspberries

Prepare the Flaky Pie Pastry and refrigerate to chill as directed.

Position a rack in the lower third of the oven, and preheat to 400°F (200°C). Line a half-sheet pan with parchment (baking) paper.

Lightly dust a work surface and a rolling pin with flour. Roll out the chilled dough into a round 13 inches (33 cm) in diameter and about 1/8 inch (3 mm) thick (page 162). Trim off any ragged edges to make an even 12-inch (30-cm) round. Carefully roll the dough around the pin and unroll it onto the prepared pan.

In a large bowl, gently toss together the figs, brown sugar, 1 tablespoon of the flour, the lemon juice, and the almond extract until evenly distributed. Leaving a 2-inch (5-cm) plain border, sprinkle the remaining 1 tablespoon flour and 1 tablespoon of the granulated sugar over the prepared pastry. Arrange the fig filling in the center of the pastry, keeping it off the border. Fold the border up and over the filling, forming loose pleats all around the edge and leaving the center open. Brush the pleated dough with the egg mixture, then sprinkle it with 1 tablespoon of the granulated sugar. You will not use all of the egg mixture.

Bake for 25 minutes. Scatter the raspberries over the figs, then sprinkle with the remaining 1 tablespoon granulated sugar. Continue baking until the crust is golden brown and the raspberries are just beginning to soften, 8–12 minutes more. Transfer to a wire rack and let cool. Serve warm or at room temperature.

With both a late spring and early fall harvest, fresh fig season is long enough to enjoy this *galette* throughout the year. Figs should be harvested when fully ripened, so look for plump, soft fruits that do not give off a milky substance when the stem is broken, and use them as soon as possible, storing them unwashed for no more than a day in the refrigerator. You can use virtually any variety of fig, such as Mission, Kadota, or Adriatic, in this recipe. The *galette* is best served the day it is baked.

Double-Crust Apple Pie

Whether it is for a family picnic, a holiday table, or a cozy family dinner, apple pie is always welcome. Granny Smith, Rome Beauty, and Baldwin apples are excellent cooking apples, as they hold their shape well during baking. Try to find apples that are ripe and crisp, and not mealy. A scoop of cinnamon or vanilla ice cream makes a good accompaniment.

Prepare the Flaky Pie Pastry and refrigerate to chill as directed.

To make the filling, peel, halve, and core the apples, then slice the apples ¼ inch (6 mm) thick. In a large bowl, combine the apples, lemon juice, melted butter, brown sugar, cinnamon, and nutmeg. Using a large spoon, stir until blended. Set the filling aside.

Position a rack in the lower third of the oven, and preheat to 400°F (200°C).

Roll out the 2 pastry disks and line a 9-inch (23-cm) pie pan with the bottom crust (page 162). Stir the apple mixture again, spoon it into the crust, and smooth the apples into an even layer. Position the top crust over the filling, and trim and flute the edges (page 164). Without brushing the fluted edges, brush the top of the pie with the egg mixture, then sprinkle with the cinnamon sugar. You will not use all of the egg mixture. Cut steam vents in the top crust.

Bake the pie for 15 minutes. Reduce the oven temperature to 350°F (180°C) and continue to bake until the top crust is lightly browned, the apple filling is bubbling, and the apples are tender when tested through the slit in the crust with a toothpick, 40–45 minutes. Transfer to a wire rack, let cool for about 20 minutes, and serve warm, or let cool completely and serve at room temperature. Store covered at room temperature for up to 2 days. The pie can be rewarmed, uncovered, in a preheated 275°F (135°C) oven for about 15 minutes.

Flaky Pie Pastry for double crust (page 160)

6 apples (2½ lbs/1.25 kg)

1 tablespoon fresh lemon juice, strained

2 tablespoons unsalted butter, melted

¼ cup (2 oz/60 g) firmly packed golden brown sugar

1½ teaspoons ground cinnamon

⅛ teaspoon freshly grated nutmeg

1 large egg beaten with 2 tablespoons heavy (double) cream

1 tablespoon granulated sugar mixed with ¼ teaspoon ground cinnamon

Blueberry Crumble Pie

Flaky Pie Pastry for single crust (page 160)

³/₄ cup (4 oz/125 g) plus 5 tablespoons (1¹/₂ oz/45 g) all-purpose (plain) flour

²/₃ cup (6 oz/180 g) firmly packed golden brown sugar

¹/₃ cup (3 oz/90 g) granulated sugar, plus 1 tablespoon for the filling

2 teaspoons ground cinnamon

¹/₈ teaspoon salt

¹/₂ cup (4 oz/125 g) cold unsalted butter, cut into ³/₄-inch (2-cm) pieces

5 cups (1¹/₄ lb/625 g) blueberries

Prepare the Flaky Pie Pastry and refrigerate to chill as directed. Roll out the dough, line a 9-inch (23-cm) pie dish or pan (page 162), and prebake partially (page 163).

In a large bowl, stir together the ³/₄ cup flour, ¹/₃ cup (2¹/₂ oz/75 g) of the brown sugar, the ¹/₃ cup (3 oz/90 g) granulated sugar, 1 teaspoon of the cinnamon, and the salt. Scatter the butter pieces on top and toss with a fork or your fingers to coat with the flour mixture. Using your fingertips or a pastry blender, work the ingredients together until the mixture forms large, coarse crumbs the size of large peas. Set the topping aside.

Position a rack in the lower third of the oven, and preheat to 375°F (190°C).

In a large bowl, combine the blueberries, the remaining brown sugar, the remaining cinnamon, and 4 tablespoons (1 oz/30 g) of the flour. Stir gently to coat the blueberries evenly. Sprinkle the remaining flour and granulated sugar over the bottom of the prebaked crust. Pour the filling into the crust, spreading it evenly.

Sprinkle the topping evenly over the blueberry filling. Bake the pie until the topping is golden brown and the blueberry filling just begins to bubble, 50–60 minutes. Transfer to a wire rack and let cool completely. Serve at room temperature. The pie is best served the day it is baked.

A crisp and crunchy crumb topping is the perfect match for a juicy berry pie filling. You can substitute fresh, wild blueberries for the more standard, domestic cultivated berries in this pie. These intensely-flavored wild berries are usually available during the heat of summer.

Lattice-Top Peach Pie

In some areas, peach season can run for nearly four months, making this recipe indispensable to your pie repertoire. Beauty in peaches is more than skin deep. If they have been bruised in shipping or handling, they rot easily where they have been damaged, so check them carefully before purchase. Make sure you choose ripe, juicy peaches that give slightly when gently squeezed. Other good filling choices for lattice-top pies include sour cherry or pear-cranberry (page 159).

Prepare the Flaky Pie Pastry and refrigerate to chill as directed.

To make the filling, bring a large saucepan three-fourths full of water to a boil. Working in batches, immerse the peaches in the boiling water for 30 seconds, then transfer them to a work surface. When cool enough to handle, slip off the skins, using your fingertips or a small knife (page 23). Halve and remove the pits, then cut the flesh lengthwise into slices about $^1/_2$ inch (12 mm) thick. In a large bowl, combine the peaches, 4 tablespoons (2 oz/60 g) of the sugar, the lemon juice, and the tapioca. Stir gently to coat the peaches evenly. Set aside.

Position a rack in the lower third of the oven, and preheat to 400°F (200°C). Roll out the larger dough disk for the bottom crust and line a 9-inch (23-cm) pie pan (page 162). Sprinkle the flour and the remaining sugar over the bottom crust. Spoon in the filling, spreading it evenly. Roll out the smaller dough disk, cut into lattice strips, and place over the filled crust (page 165). Gently brush the lattice with the egg mixture, then sprinkle with sugar.

Bake the pie until the edges of the crust begin to brown, about 15 minutes. Reduce the heat to 350°F (180°C) and continue to bake until the crust is lightly browned and the peach filling is bubbling, 40–45 minutes. Transfer to a wire rack and let cool completely.

Flaky Pie Pastry for lattice crust (page 160)

For the filling

6 peaches (3 lb/1.5 kg)

5 tablespoons (2$^1/_2$ oz/75 g) sugar

2 teaspoons fresh lemon juice, strained

3 tablespoons quick-cooking tapioca

1 tablespoon all-purpose (plain) flour

For the topping

1 large egg beaten with 1 tablespoon heavy (double) cream

2 teaspoons sugar

French Apple Tart

A chunky, homemade applesauce is baked under a layer of concentrically arranged apple slices in this classic French apple tart. The different textures of the apples add layers of taste and interest, making this the ultimate apple tart. Use firm, crisp apples, such as Granny Smith, Rome Beauty, or Northern Spy.

Prepare the Rich Tart Pastry and refrigerate to chill as directed. Roll out the dough, line a 9¹/₂-inch (24 cm) tart pan with removable bottom (page 170), and prebake the crust partially (page 171).

Position a rack in the middle of the oven, and preheat to 375°F (190°C).

To make the filling, line a half-sheet pan with 1-inch (2.5-cm) sides with parchment (baking) paper. In a large bowl, stir together the apple pieces, sugar, lemon juice, and melted butter until well mixed. Spread the apple mixture on the prepared pan.

Bake the apples until they are soft, about 20 minutes, stirring once halfway through the baking time. Remove from the oven and scrape the apples into a bowl. Using a spoon, mash the warm apples until only a few chunks remain and they look like chunky applesauce. Let cool to room temperature, about 30 minutes. Spread the cooled filling evenly in the prebaked crust.

To make the topping, arrange the apple slices in 2 circular rows, slightly overlapping them to cover the filling completely. Drizzle the apple slices with the melted butter and sprinkle with the sugar.

Bake the tart until the apple slices are soft when pierced with the tip of a knife or a toothpick and the edges of the crust are browned, 45–50 minutes. Transfer to a wire rack and let cool for 30 minutes.

In a small pan over medium heat, warm the apricot preserves, stirring constantly, until melted, about 3 minutes. Strain the preserves through a medium-mesh sieve into a small bowl. Using a pastry brush, brush the apple slices gently and generously with the strained preserves. Unmold the tart (page 171) and serve at room temperature. This tart is best served the day it is baked.

Rich Tart Pastry (page 168)

For the filling

5 apples(2 lbs/1 kg), peeled, cored, and cut into 1-inch (2.5 cm) pieces

2 tablespoons sugar

2 teaspoons fresh lemon juice, strained

1 tablespoon unsalted butter, melted

For the topping

2 cups (8 oz/250 g) peeled, thinly sliced apples (about 2 apples)

1 tablespoon unsalted butter, melted

1 tablespoon sugar

¹/₄ cup (2¹/₂ oz/75 g) apricot preserves

Strawberry and Mascarpone Cream Tart

Rich Tart Pastry (page 168)

For the filling

1 cup (8 oz/250 g) cold mascarpone cheese

3/4 cup (6 fl oz/180 ml) cold heavy (double) cream

1/4 cup (1 oz/30 g) confectioners' (icing) sugar

1 teaspoon vanilla extract (essence)

3 tablespoons seedless raspberry jam or strawberry jelly

About 20 strawberries, hulled

Although this impressive strawberry tart looks as if it takes hours to make, the opposite is true. Simply pick out the nicest-looking and ripest strawberries that you can find and arrange them in a prebaked tart crust filled with a light mascarpone cream. You can bake the crust a day ahead, cool it, cover with plastic wrap, and store at room temperature overnight. Use a long, thin serrated knife for slicing this tart.

Prepare the Rich Tart Pastry and refrigerate to chill as directed. Roll out the dough, line a 9 1/2-inch (24-cm) tart pan (page 170), and prebake fully (page 171).

To make the filling, in a large bowl, combine the mascarpone cheese, cream, confectioners' sugar, and vanilla. Using a stand mixer fitted with the whip attachment or a hand mixer, beat on medium speed until firm peaks form, about 2 minutes. Using an icing spatula, spread the filling evenly in the cooled crust.

To assemble the tart, in a small saucepan over low heat, warm the jam until melted. Remove from the heat. Carefully arrange the strawberries, pointed end up and placed closely together, on top of the cream filling. Using a pastry brush, gently brush the strawberries with the melted jam. Cover and refrigerate until cold or for up to 1 day. Unmold the tart (page 171) and serve cold.

VARIATION

Strawberry and Pastry Cream Tart
Substitute Pastry Cream (page 309) for the mascarpone filling.

Plum and Almond Frangipane Tart

VARIATIONS

Pear and Frangipane Tart
Substitute 2 pears, peeled, halved, cored, and sliced, for the plums.

Apple and Frangipane Tart
Substitute 2 apples, peeled, halved, cored, and sliced, for the plums.

Frangipane, a mixture of ground almonds, sugar, eggs, and butter, bakes into a soft, macaroon-like layer in this summertime tart. Although sophisticated in taste and appearance, it takes only minutes to make. You can substitute other full-flavored plums for the French prune plums.

Prepare the Rich Tart Pastry and refrigerate to chill as directed. Roll out the dough, line a 9½-inch (24-cm) tart pan (page 170), and prebake partially (page 171). Position a rack in the middle of the oven, and preheat to 350°F (180°C).

In a food processor, process the almonds and the ²/₃ cup sugar until the almonds are finely ground. Add the salt, vanilla and almond extracts, and egg and process until blended. Add the butter and process until it is smoothly blended into the mixture. Using a rubber spatula, scrape the almond mixture into the prebaked crust, spreading it evenly. Arrange the plum quarters, cut side up, in 2 circular rows on top of the frangipane. Sprinkle the remaining sugar over the plums.

Bake the tart until the frangipane is golden and set when you give the pan a gentle shake, 30–35 minutes. Transfer to a wire rack and let cool completely. Unmold the tart (page 171) and serve at room temperature or refrigerate and serve cold.

Rich Tart Pastry (page 168)

1 cup (5½ oz/170 g) blanched almonds

²/₃ cup (5 oz/155 g) plus 1 tablespoon sugar

¼ teaspoon salt

1 teaspoon vanilla extract (essence)

½ teaspoon almond extract (essence)

1 large egg

4 tablespoons (2 oz/60 g) unsalted butter, at room temperature

8 French prune plums, pitted and quartered

Tarte Tatin

Tarte Tatin, an upside-down caramel-apple tart, is a popular specialty from the Sologne region of France. Sometimes called *la tarte des demoiselles Tatin,* it is named after the two sisters who ran a small hotel in the village of Lamotte-Beuvron. Legend has it that one day when making an apple tart for the hotel restaurant, Stephanie Tatin forgot to put in the bottom crust. Not wanting to waste the sugared apples already in the pan, she covered them with pastry and baked them into this now famous upside-down tart. Choose a tart baking apple for this classic, such as Granny Smith, Rome Beauty, or Arkansas Black. Standing the apples on end allows you to pack in the maximum number of apples.

Flaky Pie Pastry for single crust (page 160)

6 tablespoons (3 oz/90 g) unsalted butter, at room temperature

1 cup (8 oz/250 g) sugar

10 apples (4¹/₂ lbs/2.25 kg), peeled, cored, and quartered lengthwise

Crème fraîche (page 20) or vanilla ice cream for serving (optional)

Prepare the Flaky Pie Pastry and refrigerate to chill as directed.

Spread the butter evenly over the bottom of a heavy, 10-inch (25-cm) nonstick ovenproof frying pan. Reserve 1 tablespoon of the sugar and sprinkle the remaining sugar evenly over the butter. Place over medium-low heat and heat until the butter melts and the sugar begins to melt, about 4 minutes.

Remove the pan from the heat and arrange the apple quarters so they are standing upright in the pan, placing them close together so that the bottom of the pan is fully covered. Sprinkle the reserved tablespoon of sugar evenly over the apples.

Return the pan to medium-high heat and cook until the butter and sugar mixture caramelizes, becoming syrupy and golden and bubbling up around the apples, 20–25 minutes. Remove the pan from the heat. Set aside to cool slightly.

Position a rack in the middle of the oven, and preheat to 400°F (200°C). Lightly dust a work surface and a rolling pin with flour.

Roll out the chilled dough into a round 11 inches (28 cm) in diameter and ¹/₈ inch (3 mm) thick (page 162). Carefully roll the dough around the pin and position the pin over the frying pan. Unroll the dough, placing it on top of the apples. Tuck the excess dough edge inside the pan. Be careful not to burn yourself on the hot pan.

Bake the tart until the crust is golden brown, 20–25 minutes. Remove from the oven and let cool for 1 minute. Using a small knife, loosen the edges of the crust from the pan sides. Invert a large, flat serving plate on top of the pan. Holding the pan and plate together, carefully invert them so that the tart comes to rest on the plate. Lift off the pan. Straighten any apples that may have dislodged and serve.

Blood Orange Tartlets

Cream Cheese Tartlet Pastry (page 172)

2 large whole eggs plus 3 large egg yolks

1/2 cup (4 fl oz/125 ml) fresh blood orange juice, strained

2 tablespoons fresh lemon juice, strained

1 cup (8 oz/250 g) sugar

1/2 cup (4 oz/125 g) unsalted butter, cut into 1/2-inch (12-mm) pieces

2 teaspoons grated orange zest

1 cup (8 fl oz/250 ml) Whipped Cream (page 306)

Prepare the Cream Cheese Tartlet Pastry, line six 3 1/2-inch (9-cm) tartlet pans with removable bottoms (page 172), and prebake fully (page 171). Leave the prebaked crusts on the sheet pan for filling and baking.

Position a rack in the lower third of the oven, and preheat to 325°F (165°C).

To make the filling, in the top of a double boiler over (not touching) barely simmering water, whisk together the whole eggs, egg yolks, orange juice, lemon juice, and sugar. Stir constantly with the whisk until the mixture is thick enough to coat the back of a spoon and registers 160°F (71°C) on an instant-read thermometer, about 12 minutes. Remove from over the water and pour through a medium-mesh sieve into a bowl. Stir in the butter and orange zest until the butter melts and is incorporated. Let stand for 10 minutes. Spoon the filling into the cooled tartlet crusts, dividing it evenly.

Bake the tartlets until the centers are set, 12–15 minutes. Transfer the half-sheet pan to a wire rack and let the tartlets cool for 20 minutes, then cover and refrigerate for at least 3 hours or for up to overnight. The filling will thicken further.

Spoon the whipped cream into a pastry (piping) bag fitted with a large star tip and pipe small swirls on top of each chilled tartlet (page 213). Unmold and serve.

Blood oranges have a dark red pulp that lends a stunning ruby-rose color to the orange curd that fills these tartlets. Their slightly tart flavor often includes a hint of berries. Although the season varies, blood oranges are usually in markets from December to mid-March. If you cannot find them, the juice of regular oranges can be substituted. Blood orange juice is typically more tart than the juice of other varieties, however, so you will need to reduce the amount of sugar in the filling to 3/4 cup (6 oz/185 g).

Classic Pumpkin Pie

This American custard pie dates back to colonial times. The first pumpkin pie baked by early settlers was probably made by removing the seeds from a whole pumpkin, filling it with milk, honey, and spices, and then baking it until the inside was soft. Pumpkin, milk, and spices remain the major ingredients in the dark golden filling of today's traditional pie. Check the pie often toward the end of baking so that it does not overbake, as the filling can quickly become grainy.

Prepare the Flaky Pie Pastry and refrigerate to chill as directed. Roll out the larger dough disk, line a 9-inch (23-cm) pie pan (page 162), and trim and finish the edges as for a single-crust pie (page 166). Prebake the crust partially (page 163).

Roll out the smaller disk and use to make dough cutouts (page 167), then bake them as directed. Let cool on the pan on a wire rack.

Position a rack in the middle of the oven, and preheat to 350°F (180°C).

In a large bowl, combine the pumpkin purée, eggs, brown sugar, and evaporated milk. Whisk until smooth. Slowly whisk in the melted butter, vanilla, cinnamon, ginger, nutmeg, and salt until the mixture is smooth and well blended. Pour the filling into the prebaked crust.

Bake the pie until the filling is set, 50–55 minutes. The center should jiggle slightly when the pan is given a gentle shake. Transfer to a wire rack and let cool completely. Place the dough cutouts decoratively along the edge of the pie. Serve at room temperature or slightly chilled, topped with whipped cream.

Flaky Pie Pastry for lattice crust (page 180)

1 can (15 oz/470 g) pumpkin purée (not pie filling)

3 large eggs

³/₄ cup (6 oz/185 g) firmly packed dark brown sugar

1 cup (8 fl oz/250 ml) evaporated milk

2 tablespoons unsalted butter, melted

1 teaspoon vanilla extract (essence)

1 teaspoon ground cinnamon

¹/₂ teaspoon ground ginger

¹/₄ teaspoon freshly grated nutmeg

¹/₄ teaspoon salt

Whipped Cream (page 306)

Banana Cream Pie

Flaky Pie Pastry for single crust (page 160)

Pastry Cream (page 309)

4 ripe bananas, peeled and cut into slices ¹/₄ inch (6 mm) thick

1 tablespoon fresh orange juice, strained

Whipped Cream (page 306)

Rich and creamy, with slices of fresh bananas pocketed between layers of pastry cream and whipped cream, this pie is the definition of comfort food. It is easy to use this recipe as a starting point for other cream pies, such as the variations to the right, or even for chocolate-banana cream pie or coconut-banana cream pie. Or leave out the bananas for a smooth, delicious vanilla cream pie.

Prepare the Flaky Pie Pastry and refrigerate to chill as directed. Roll out the dough, line a 9-inch (23-cm) pie dish or pan (page 162), and prebake fully (page 163).

Prepare the pastry cream as directed, cover with plastic wrap, and let cool slightly until it is still warm, 10–20 minutes.

To assemble the pie, in a bowl, combine the bananas and orange juice and toss to mix. Pour half of the pastry cream into the cooled crust. Arrange the bananas in a thick layer over the pastry cream. Spoon the rest of the pastry cream over the bananas and spread evenly with the back of the spoon. Cover the filled pie with plastic wrap placed directly on the pastry cream and chill completely in the refrigerator, about 5 hours.

Remove the plastic wrap from the pie and, using an icing spatula, spread the whipped cream over the pastry cream, mounding it slightly toward the center. Refrigerate for up to 1 day before serving. Serve cold.

VARIATIONS

Coconut Cream Pie

Omit the bananas. Prepare the Pastry Cream. When making the Pastry Cream, just after you add the butter and it melts, stir in 1 cup (4 oz/125 g) sweetened shredded dried coconut, toasted (page 21). Garnish the whipped cream with extra toasted coconut.

Chocolate Cream Pie

Omit the vanilla bean in the pastry cream. Add 6 oz (185 g) semisweet (plain) or bittersweet chocolate, melted and cooled (page 21), to the Pastry Cream with the butter. Garnish the whipped cream topping with chocolate shavings (page 21).

Lemon Meringue Pie

Classic and refreshing, this lemony pie is always a showstopper. The key to a crisp crust and a stable meringue that does not separate and "weep" is to add the hot lemon filling to the fully baked crust and then immediately top it with the meringue. Make sure that the meringue is spread all the way to the edge so that it touches the crust. This will help prevent it from shrinking during baking.

Prepare the Flaky Pie Pastry and refrigerate to chill as directed. Roll out the dough, line a 9-inch (23-cm) pie dish or pan (page 162), and prebake fully (page 163).

Position a rack in the middle of the oven, and preheat to 350°F (180°C).

To make the lemon filling, in a small bowl, combine the cornstarch and $^1/_2$ cup (4 fl oz/125 ml) of the water and stir until the cornstarch dissolves. In a saucepan, whisk together the egg yolks, granulated sugar, lemon juice, and the remaining 1 cup (8 fl oz/250 ml) water until well blended. Whisk in the cornstarch mixture and bring to a boil over medium heat while whisking constantly, about 8 minutes. Boil for 1 minute until the mixture thickens and looks clear. Remove from the heat and stir in the lemon zest. Using a rubber spatula, scrape the filling into a medium bowl and place plastic wrap directly on the surface of the filling to keep it hot and to prevent a skin from forming.

To make the meringue, in a large bowl, combine the egg whites and cream of tartar. Using a stand mixer fitted with a whip attachment or a hand mixer, beat on medium speed until the whites begin to thicken. Increase the speed to medium-high and beat just until soft peaks form. Slowly add the superfine sugar and continue to beat until stiff, shiny peaks form (page 27).

Remove the plastic wrap from the hot lemon filling and pour it into the prebaked crust. Using the rubber spatula, distribute the meringue evenly over the filling, mounding it toward the center and spreading it to the edge to seal the crust. Use the back of a spoon to form peaks and swirls on the meringue. Bake until the meringue is lightly browned, 12–17 minutes. Transfer to a wire rack and let cool for 1 hour. Place in an airtight container and refrigerate until cold, at least 5 hours or for up to overnight. Serve cold.

Flaky Pie Pastry for single crust (page 160)

For the filling

6 tablespoons (1$^1/_2$ oz/45 g) cornstarch (cornflour)

1$^1/_2$ cups (12 fl oz/375 ml) water

5 large egg yolks

1$^3/_4$ cups (14 oz/440 g) granulated sugar

$^1/_2$ cup (4 fl oz/125 ml) fresh lemon juice, strained

2 teaspoons grated lemon zest

For the meringue

6 large egg whites, at room temperature

$^1/_2$ teaspoon cream of tartar

6 tablespoons (3 oz/90 g) superfine (caster) sugar

Southern Pecan Pie

Pecans are harvested in late fall. When you first see new-crop pecans in the market, buy a big supply to have on hand for baking the rest of the year. Freshly shelled pecans can be sealed in a plastic freezer bag and stored for a month in the refrigerator, or for up to a year in the freezer. Here, pecans are mixed into the pie filling, but during baking they float to the surface, covering the pie with a wonderfully crunchy topping.

Prepare the Flaky Pie Pastry and refrigerate to chill as directed. Roll out the crust, line a 9-inch (23-cm) pie pan (page 162), and prebake partially (page 163).

Position a rack in the middle of the oven, and preheat to 350°F (180°C).

To make the filling, in a large bowl, combine the eggs, sugar, corn syrup, and vanilla. Whisk until blended, then whisk in the melted butter. Using a spoon, stir in the pecans. Pour the filling into the prebaked crust.

Bake the pie until the filling is set, 45–50 minutes. The center of the pie should jiggle slightly if the pan is given a gentle shake. Transfer to a wire rack and let cool. Serve warm or at room temperature, topped with whipped cream, if desired. The pie can be covered with plastic wrap and stored at room temperature for up to 2 days.

Flaky Pie Pastry for single crust (page 160)

For the filling

3 large eggs

$^1/_2$ cup (4 oz/125 g) sugar

1 cup (10 oz/315 g) dark corn syrup

1 teaspoon vanilla extract (essence)

$^1/_4$ cup (2 oz/60 g) unsalted butter, melted

1$^1/_2$ cups (6 oz/185 g) large pecan pieces, cut into halves and quarters

Whipped Cream (page 306), optional

Caramel-Macadamia Tartlets

Cream Cheese Tartlet Pastry (page 172)

For the filling

$1/2$ cup (4 fl oz/125 ml) heavy (double) cream

$2/3$ cup (5 oz/155 g) sugar

$1/2$ teaspoon fresh lemon juice, strained

3 tablespoons water

$1/8$ teaspoon salt

$3/4$ cup (4 oz/125 g) unsalted roasted macadamia nuts, cut into quarters

A traditional caramel sauce fills these individual tartlets. It is made by melting sugar with water and letting it boil until it reaches the desired color, and then adding warm cream. You must, however, watch the bubbling caramel carefully so that it does not burn. The addition of macadamia nuts makes these tartlets even richer. The deep gold caramel sauce is also delicious poured over ice cream or drizzled over cakes. ♀

Prepare the Cream Cheese Tartlet Pastry, line six $3^1/2$-inch (9-cm) tartlet pans with removable bottoms (page 172), and prebake partially (page 171). Leave the pre-baked crusts on the half-sheet pan for filling and baking.

To make the caramel filling, in a small saucepan, heat the cream over low heat until it registers 150°F (65°C) on an instant-read thermometer. Keep the cream over very low heat to maintain this temperature.

In a large, heavy saucepan over medium heat, combine the sugar, lemon juice, and water and stir with a wooden spoon until the sugar dissolves. As soon as the sugar dissolves, stop stirring and wash down the sides of the pan with a pastry brush dipped in water. Raise the heat to medium-high and bring the mixture to a boil. Boil until the sugar melts and turns a dark golden color, about 4 minutes. Watch carefully, swirling the pan occasionally to ensure that the sugar cooks evenly. Remove the pan from the heat.

Slowly pour the warm cream into the hot caramelized sugar. The mixture will bubble up, so be careful to avoid spatters. Return the pan to low heat, add the salt, and stir with the wooden spoon until the caramel completely dissolves and is smooth, about 1 minute. Remove from the heat and set aside to cool and thicken slightly, about 30 minutes.

Position a rack in the middle of the oven, and preheat to 350°F (180°C).

Stir the nuts into the slightly cooled filling. Pour the filling into the cooled tartlet crusts, dividing it evenly and filling the crusts to just below the rim.

Bake the tartlets until the filling begins to bubble, 10–15 minutes. Transfer the half-sheet pan to a wire rack and let the tartlets cool completely before unmolding. The tartlets can be covered with plastic wrap and stored at room temperature for up to 2 days before serving.

VARIATION

Chocolate-Caramel Macadamia Tartlets
When the tartlets are cooled, pour 2 tablespoons Ganache Filling (page 309) over the top of each tartlet. Swirl the tartlet to make sure the chocolate coats the top evenly. Allow the ganache to set at room temperature for about 30 minutes before serving.

Bing Cherry Cobbler

VARIATION

Fruit Cobbler

Nearly any fruit can be used for a cobbler, and the juicier it is, the better. If you are lucky enough to catch the very short season for sour, or tart, cherries, by all means use them, adding more sugar to taste. Blueberries, peaches, berries with peaches, apples, pears, cranberries, rhubarb, or rhubarb with strawberries can bake you through a year of cobblers. Use the same dough for the topping with about 5 cups (2 lb/1 kg) of any of these fruits. Sweeten the fresh fruit to taste, then add lemon juice, if desired, and any appropriate spices or grated citrus zest.

Cobblers call for a biscuit topping baked over fresh fruit. The dough beneath the crisply baked surface stays tender over the warm, cooked fruit. This recipe uses a soft biscuit dough that spreads as it bakes to cover the fruit completely. Cold heavy (double) cream, Whipped Cream (page 306), or ice cream makes a good accompaniment to the warm cobbler.

Position a rack in the middle of the oven, and preheat to 375°F (190°C). For individual servings, place six 1-cup (8–fl oz/250-ml) ramekins or custard cups on a half-sheet pan. For a large cobbler, have ready a 9-inch (23-cm) glass or ceramic pie dish or baking dish with sides at least 2³/₄ inches (7 cm) high.

To make the filling, in a large bowl, stir together the cherries, lemon juice, and sugar until well mixed. Divide the fruit among the ramekins or pour into the pie dish or baking dish. Bake the fruit for 10 minutes while you prepare the topping.

BY HAND: To make the topping, in a small bowl, stir together the buttermilk and vanilla and set aside. In a large bowl, sift together the flour, sugar, baking powder, baking soda, salt, and cinnamon. Using a pastry blender or 2 knives, cut in the butter until the mixture forms large, coarse crumbs the size of small peas. Pour the buttermilk mixture over the flour mixture and, using a large wooden spoon, stir just until combined and a soft, sticky, evenly moistened dough forms.

BY STAND MIXER: To make the topping, in a small bowl, stir together the buttermilk and vanilla and set aside. In the large bowl of a stand mixer, sift together the flour, sugar, baking powder, baking soda, salt, and cinnamon. Add the butter pieces. Using the paddle attachment, mix on low speed until the mixture forms large, coarse crumbs the size of small peas, about 30 seconds. Slowly pour in the buttermilk mixture and continue to mix just until combined and a soft, sticky, evenly moistened dough forms.

Drop the dough by heaping spoonfuls onto the hot fruit, spacing it evenly over the surface. The topping will not cover the fruit but will spread during baking to cover it. Sprinkle the cinnamon-sugar mixture evenly over the dough.

Bake the cobbler until the fruit filling is bubbling, the topping is browned, and a toothpick or cake tester inserted into the topping comes out clean, 30–35 minutes. Transfer to a wire rack and let cool 15 minutes. Serve warm.

For the filling

5 cups (2 lb/1 kg) pitted fresh Bing cherries or other sweet cherries (about 3 lb/1.5 kg unpitted)

1 tablespoon fresh lemon juice, strained

3 tablespoons sugar

For the topping

²/₃ cup (5 fl oz/160 ml) buttermilk

1 teaspoon vanilla extract (essence)

1¹/₂ cups (7¹/₂ oz/235 g) all-purpose (plain) flour

¹/₃ cup (3 oz/90 g) sugar

1 teaspoon baking powder

¹/₂ teaspoon baking soda (bicarbonate of soda)

¹/₂ teaspoon salt

¹/₂ teaspoon ground cinnamon

6 tablespoons (3 oz/90 g) cold unsalted butter, cut into ¹/₂-inch (12-mm) pieces

1 tablespoon sugar mixed with ¹/₄ teaspoon ground cinnamon

Strawberry-Rhubarb Crisp

For the filling

6 medium stalks rhubarb, cut into ¹/₂-inch (12-mm) pieces

2 cups (8 oz/250 g) strawberries, hulled and halved lengthwise

¹/₂ cup (4 oz/125 g) granulated sugar

For the topping

1 cup (5 oz/155 g) all-purpose (plain) flour

¹/₂ cup (1¹/₂ oz/45 g) old-fashioned rolled oats

¹/₃ cup (3 oz/90 g) granulated sugar

¹/₃ cup (2¹/₂ oz/75 g) firmly packed golden brown sugar

¹/₂ teaspoon ground cinnamon

¹/₄ teaspoon salt

¹/₂ cup (4 oz/125 g) unsalted butter, melted

Botanically speaking, rhubarb is classified as a vegetable, but it is used so often as a fruit, especially in pies, that its nickname is "pieplant." Be sure to remove and discard any leaves remaining on the rhubarb stems, as they are toxic. When using different fruits for making this crisp (see variations, right), the amount of sugar and the baking time often change. Also, some fruits benefit from the addition of lemon juice or cinnamon. Since fruits vary in sweetness, mix in a small amount of sugar, then taste and add more sugar as needed. Serve this sweet yet slightly tart crisp with a scoop of vanilla ice cream.

Position a rack in the middle of the oven, and preheat to 350°F (180°C). Have ready a 2¹/₂-qt (2.5 l) ceramic or glass pie dish or baking dish.

To make the filling, in a large bowl, stir together the rhubarb, strawberries, and granulated sugar until well mixed. Pour into the baking dish and set aside.

To make the topping, in a large bowl, stir together the flour, rolled oats, granulated sugar, brown sugar, cinnamon, and salt until blended. Stir in the melted butter until evenly moistened crumbs form. Spoon the crumb mixture evenly over the filling.

Bake the crisp until the rhubarb is tender when tested with a toothpick, the juices are bubbling, and the topping is golden brown, 35–40 minutes. Transfer to a wire rack and let cool for 10 minutes. Serve warm. The crisp can be cooled, covered with plastic wrap, and stored at room temperature for up to 2 days, then rewarmed in a 250°F (120°C) oven for 15 minutes before serving.

VARIATIONS

Apple or Pear Crisp
Omit the strawberry-rhubarb filling. Stir together 6 cups (1¹/₂ lb/ 750 g) chopped, peeled apples or pears; 2 tablespoons granulated sugar; 1 tablespoon fresh lemon juice, strained; and ¹/₂ teaspoon ground cinnamon.

Berry Crisp
Omit the strawberry-rhubarb filling. Stir together 5 cups (1¹/₄ lb/625 g) blueberries or mixed berries, ¹/₂ teaspoon ground cinnamon and 3–5 tablespoons granulated sugar. Top as directed and bake for 30–35 minutes.

Peach Crisp
Omit the strawberry-rhubarb filling. Stir together 6 cups (2¹/₈ lb/1 kg) sliced, peeled peaches and 3–4 tablespoons granulated sugar. Top as directed and bake for 25–30 minutes.

Provençal Tomato, Olive, and Goat Cheese Galette

Stop by any Provençal village on a summer market day and you will find a colorful profusion of ingredients for making the local specialties: baskets of ripe tomatoes, barrels of olives and jugs of olive oil, long braids of garlic, and tables topped with neatly arranged rows of cheeses. This *galette* makes a nice first course, or a light dinner when served with a salad.

Prepare the Flaky Pie Pastry and refrigerate to chill as directed.

Position a rack in the lower third of the oven, and preheat to 400°F (200°C). Oil a half-sheet pan or a 14-inch (35-cm) pizza pan with olive oil.

Lightly dust a work surface and a rolling pin with flour. Roll out the chilled dough into a round 13 inches (33 cm) in diameter and about $^1/_8$ inch (3 mm) thick. Trim off any ragged edges to make an even 12-inch (30-cm) round. Carefully roll the dough around the pin and unroll it onto the prepared pan. Fold about $^1/_2$ inch (12 mm) of the edge inward to form a small rolled rim around the entire edge of the round. Prick the pastry lightly all over with a fork. Bake until firm, 7–10 minutes. Transfer the pan to a wire rack.

Bring a saucepan three-fourths full of water to a boil. Cut a small, shallow X in the blossom end of each tomato. Immerse half of the tomatoes in the boiling water and leave for 30 seconds. Using a slotted spoon, transfer them to a work surface. Repeat with the remaining tomatoes. When cool enough to handle, using your fingertips or a small knife and starting at the X, slip off the skins. Cut the tomatoes lengthwise into slices about $^1/_2$ inch (12 mm) thick and place in a bowl.

In a frying pan over medium heat, warm 1 tablespoon of the oil. Add the onion and sauté until soft, about 6 minutes. Stir in the garlic, 2 tablespoons of the basil, the thyme, and the parsley. Sauté until the garlic softens, about 3 minutes. Transfer to a small bowl and let cool slightly, about 15 minutes.

Leaving the rolled rim of the pastry uncovered, spread the cooled onion mixture evenly over the prebaked crust. Using a teaspoon, dot the onion mixture with about two-thirds of the goat cheese. Discard any accumulated juice from the tomatoes. Arrange the tomato slices, tightly touching, to cover the crust completely, except for the rolled rim. Dot the tomatoes with the remaining cheese and the remaining 3 tablespoons chopped basil. Drizzle the surface evenly with 1 tablespoon of the oil. Sprinkle lightly with salt and pepper. Place the olives evenly over the top. Sprinkle evenly with the bread crumbs, and then drizzle with the remaining 1 tablespoon oil.

Bake the *galette* until the edges of the crust are brown and the bread crumbs are crisp and golden, 30–35 minutes. Transfer to a wire rack and let cool on the pan for 30 minutes before serving.

Flaky Pie Pastry for single crust, made without sugar (page 160)

10 plum (Roma) tomatoes

3 tablespoons olive oil

1 yellow onion, thinly sliced

2 cloves garlic, finely chopped

5 tablespoons ($^1/_2$ oz/15 g) chopped fresh basil

1 teaspoon chopped fresh thyme

2 tablespoons chopped fresh flat-leaf (Italian) parsley

6 oz (185 g) fresh goat cheese

Sea salt and freshly ground pepper

24 oil-cured black olives, pitted

$^1/_2$ cup (2 oz/60 g) coarse dried bread crumbs

Quiche Lorraine

Flaky Pie Pastry for single crust, made without sugar (page 160)

4 slices thick-cut lean bacon, about ¹/₄ lb (125 g) total weight

3 large eggs

¹/₂ teaspoon salt

¹/₈ teaspoon freshly ground pepper

Pinch of freshly grated nutmeg

³/₄ cup (6 fl oz/180 ml) heavy (double) cream

³/₄ cup (6 fl oz/180 ml) whole milk

1 tablespoon unsalted butter, cut into ¹/₄-inch (6-mm) pieces

Prepare the Flaky Pie Pastry and refrigerate to chill as directed. Roll out the dough, line a 9-inch (23-cm) quiche dish or glass or ceramic pie dish (page 162), and prebake partially (page 163).

Position a rack in the middle of the oven, and preheat to 350°F (180°C).

In a frying pan over medium heat, fry the bacon until the edges are crisp, about 8 minutes. Transfer to paper towels to drain, then pat dry with more paper towels. Cut crosswise into 1-inch (2.5-cm) pieces. Arrange the bacon pieces evenly in the prebaked crust. Set aside.

In a large bowl, whisk together the eggs, salt, pepper, and nutmeg until blended. Whisk in the cream and milk until well mixed. Pour through a medium-mesh sieve into a pitcher. Slowly and carefully pour the egg mixture over the bacon in the crust, trying not to disturb the bacon layer. Dot the top with the butter pieces.

Bake the quiche until the top is lightly browned and the filling is set when you give the dish a gentle shake, 40–45 minutes. Transfer a the wire rack and let cool for 5 minutes. Serve hot.

Both France and Germany play roles in the history of the classic quiche Lorraine. Since sovereignty over Lorraine, now a province of northern France, has bounced back and forth between the two countries, the word *quiche* (sometimes spelled *kiche*) may have originated with the German *Kuchen*, meaning "cake" or "pastry." Although grated Gruyère cheese can be included, the true quiche Lorraine is a simple egg-and-cream custard dotted with bits of bacon. Traditionally offered as a first course, nowadays it is more commonly served as the main course at lunchtime or for a light supper.

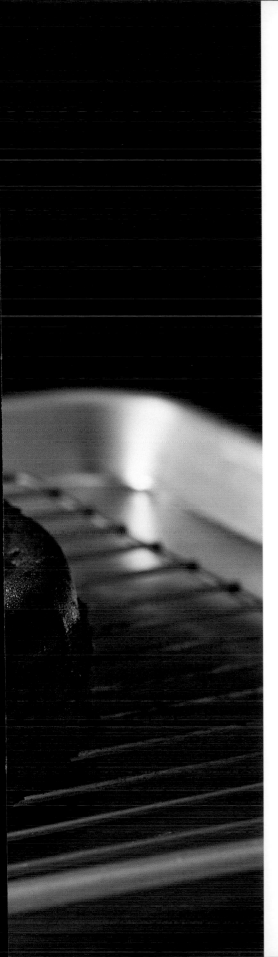

Cakes

About Cakes

Cakes vary dramatically in flavor, texture, complexity, and dramatic effect. From a whisper-light angel food cake to a dense flourless chocolate cake to a sky-high layer cake, a slice of cake can be the perfect afternoon snack or the grand finale to a celebration.

No matter what kind of cake you are making, before you even start, a few simple tips will come in handy. First, measure every ingredient carefully; too much flour or too little butter invites disappointment. Make sure that the ingredients are at room temperature, unless otherwise specified in the recipe. Always mix together dry ingredients thoroughly before continuing on to the next step. Finally, the moment you combine the wet and dry ingredients, heed the directions on folding or stirring only until mixed. In general, the best cakes have a tender texture, so the less movement, the better.

If you are new to cake baking, butter cakes, such as pound cake, are an excellent place to start. The three most important steps in making them are the beating together, or creaming, of the butter and sugar until light in color and fluffy, and the beating in of each egg thoroughly before adding the next. When these steps are done correctly, tiny air pockets develop that help the cakes rise as they bake. The third step, the gentle folding of the dry ingredients into the aerated butter and egg mixture, will keep your butter cake tender.

Chiffon cakes call for oil instead of butter, while angel food cakes call for no fat at all. Both of them are also good cakes for beginning bakers to make. Their appealing loft depends on properly beaten egg whites, a technique that, like creaming, is mastered with a little practice. Tortes, also known as flourless cakes, are made with ground nuts or cookie crumbs and little or no flour. A generous addition of eggs contributes a rich texture and delicious flavor that make tortes at once simple and showstopping.

While layered cakes may look complicated, they are no more than an assembly of simple elements. The key to their success is attention to detail. Dacquoise, a heavenly cake made of nut-meringue layers spread with buttercream, calls for no flour at all. Its texture is a product of beaten egg whites baked very slowly until crisp and dry. Cakes like génoise and sponge cake are the base for countless layer cakes and charlottes, roulades, and trifles. They are essential tools in a cake baker's repertoire.

Cheesecakes, among the most popular of all the cakes, are built on a base of ricotta or cream cheese, rather than flour. Unlike most other cakes, these dense, creamy creations have a crust, usually made from finely crushed cookies or graham crackers, often with the addition of nuts.

Once your cake is ready to come out of the oven, a few more tips will ease the trip to the table. Some recipes call for cooling cakes in their pans; others call for unmolding them while still hot and cooling them on a rack. In either case, run a thin knife blade around the edge of the cake to loosen it from the pan sides. Plain cakes need no more adornment than a light dusting of confectioners' (icing) sugar or perhaps a thin citrus glaze.

If you are frosting a cake, precede the top coat with a thin crumb coating to prevent stray crumbs from marring the icing. If you like, add some simple decorations, such as crystallized flowers, shaved chocolate, toasted coconut, or chopped nuts. The result of all your efforts— a beautiful cake—is now ready to serve.

TROUBLESHOOTING CAKES

What happened	Why it happened
Cake is dry.	Cake was overbaked, or ingredients were overmixed or overwhipped.
Cake did not rise.	Ingredients were overmixed, knocking too much air out of batter.
Cake is cracked in the middle.	Oven temperature was too low.
Cake is high on the edges but is sunken in the middle.	Oven temperature was too high.
Cake stuck to pan.	Cake was too hot when removed from pan, or pan was not properly prepared.
Cake is soggy on the bottom.	Cake was left to cool too long in pan.

Layer Cake Variations

Layer cakes offer countless variations: a vanilla génoise can be layered with berries and cream or become a robust mocha mousse cake. The possibilities are limited only by your imagination. This section will get you started with combinations for one 8- or 9-inch (20- or 23-cm) cake.

LAYER CAKE BASE

First, determine what kind of base you want to use. Start with a Génoise (page 232), Sponge Cake (page 234), or Dacquoise (page 226). You can make a classic vanilla-flavored cake or choose from a variety of flavor variations: chocolate, nut, citrus, liqueur, ginger, or espresso.

CAKE SYRUP

Next, decide on the flavor of the syrup (page 308). The syrup should enhance the flavor of the cake base, so choose a compatible flavor: vanilla, espresso, lemon, orange, almond, ginger, an infused spice, a liqueur such as Grand Marnier, or a spirit such as rum.

FILLING

With the base and syrup determined, select a filling that complements these flavors.

Among your choices are:

^{1}/$_3$ cup (3^1/$_2$ oz/105 g) strained raspberry, strawberry, or apricot preserves

^{1}/$_3$ cup (3^1/$_2$ oz/105 g) orange marmalade

Ganache Mousse (page 309)

Ganache Filling (page 309)

Lemon Curd (page 309)

Pastry Cream (page 309)

Sour Cream Chantilly (page 307) or Whipped Cream (page 306)

Sour Cream Chantilly (page 307) or Whipped Cream (page 306) mixed with 1 cup (4 oz/125 g) berries

FROSTING OR GLAZE

Finally, choose a frosting or a glaze, again selecting it with the other already chosen flavors in mind. The standard base frostings are Vanilla Meringue Buttercream (page 306), Rich Vanilla Buttercream (page 307), and Sour Cream Chantilly (page 307). All three of these frostings can be flavored with almond, chocolate-orange, chocolate, citrus, espresso, or liqueur or other spirits, among other flavorings. Other frostings include Chocolate Frosting (page 242), Cream Cheese Frosting (page 237), and Maple Frosting (page 229). You can also glaze the cake with Chocolate Glaze (page 308).

SUGGESTED FLAVOR COMBINATIONS

Here are six ideas to get you started on putting together a successful flavor combination.

Strawberries and Cream Cake

Start with a vanilla génoise (or sponge cake). Split and brush the cake base with kirsch syrup, and fill the layers with vanilla pastry cream and sliced strawberries. Frost the cake with kirsch-flavored Sour Cream Chantilly or Whipped Cream.

Chocolate-Espresso Cake

Start with a chocolate sponge cake (or génoise). Split the cake base and brush with espresso syrup. Fill the layers with espresso-flavored rich buttercream. You could also include a round of hazelnut (filbert) dacquoise in the middle. Frost with Chocolate Frosting or glaze with Chocolate Glaze.

Orange-Flower Cake

Start with a génoise (or sponge cake) flavored with orange-flower water. Split the cake base into thirds and brush with orange-flower syrup. Sandwich the cake layers with thin layers of apricot preserves and frost with Vanilla Meringue Buttercream.

Nutty Chocolate Cake

Start with a hazelnut or almond sponge cake (or génoise). Split the cake base and brush with brandy syrup. Fill the cake layers with Ganache Mousse and frost with espresso-flavored rich buttercream. Glaze with Chocolate Glaze.

Raspberry-Lemon Cake

Start with a vanilla sponge cake (or génoise). Split and brush the cake base with framboise syrup. Fill the layers with lemon curd and frost with framboise buttercream.

Almond Crunch Cake

Start with an espresso génoise. Split the cake base and brush with espresso syrup. Layer the cake with a layer of dacquoise and Rich Almond Buttercream. Frost with the buttercream and decorate with toasted almonds.

Mixing Techniques for Cakes

There are two types of cake, defined according to two mixing techniques. The creaming method is used with butter cakes and calls for beating air into butter and sugar. The foaming method is used for foam cakes and calls for beating air into egg whites, which are then folded into the batter.

THE CREAMING METHOD

1 Using a hand mixer or stand mixer fitted with the paddle attachment on medium-high speed, or a sturdy wire whisk or wooden spoon, beat together room-temperature butter and sugar until light in color and fluffy.

2 Add the eggs one at a time, mixing well after each addition until thoroughly incorporated. It is important to beat each egg in separately and completely so that the batter remains an emulsion. Scrape down the sides of the bowl with a rubber spatula before adding the next egg.

3 Using the spatula, fold the dry ingredients into the butter-egg mixture, taking care not to force out the incorporated air, just until fully combined. Some batters will look slightly lumpy.

THE FOAMING METHOD

If directed in the recipe, beat whole eggs or egg yolks with sugar to the ribbon stage (see page 26 for more information on ribbon stage).

1 Using a handheld mixer, a stand mixer fitted with the whip attachment, or a balloon whisk, beat the egg whites until they form medium peaks (page 27), or as directed in the recipe. Some recipes call for adding cream of tartar and sugar to the whites to help stabilize them.

2 Using a rubber spatula, fold the egg whites in three equal batches into the egg-sugar mixture alternately with the dry ingredients, beginning and ending with the egg whites (see page 26 for more information on folding).

3 The egg whites and dry ingredients should be evenly incorporated. Be careful not to overmix; a tiny bit of streaking is fine. The batter should look fluffy and aerated.

Assembling Layer Cakes

This step-by-step section shows you what happens once you have mixed and baked your layer cake. The following techniques will walk you through removing a cake from the pan, cooling a cake, slicing a cake base into layers, filling a layer cake, and frosting and glazing a cake.

TO REMOVE A CAKE FROM A CAKE PAN

1 If you are making a foam cake, such as a sponge or génoise, run a thin knife along the inside edge of the pan. Keep the knife against the pan side so you do not cut into the cake.

2 Place a cooling rack upside down on top of the cake. Holding the cake and cooling rack together, invert them and set the rack on the work surface. Lift off the pan, then let the cake cool completely before slicing or decorating.

TO SLICE A CAKE INTO LAYERS

1 Place the cooled cake base on a flat surface. Hold a ruler up to the side of the cake base and, using toothpicks, mark the midpoint at regular intervals around the cake.

2 Using a long, thin serrated cake knife and a sawing motion, split the cake horizontally into even layers. If you are slicing on a turntable, turn the cake while you cut. Put one layer, cut side up, on a cardboard circle. Place the other layer, cut side down, on a sheet of plastic wrap.

TO FILL A LAYER CAKE

When filling a layer cake, the thickness of the filling is determined by the type of filling. Jams should be spread thinly, while rich fillings, such as curd, pastry cream, or buttercream, should be thicker. Lighter fillings, such as mousse, should be thick, but never thicker than the cake layer.

1 Place the cake layer on its cardboard circle on a turntable or work surface. Using a pastry brush, coat the cake layer with cake syrup. Mound the filling in the center of the layer and, using an icing spatula, spread it to the edge.

2 Flip the other layer over onto the filling, cut side up. Remove the plastic wrap and gently push the layer evenly into place. Brush the top layer with cake syrup.

TO MAKE A CRUMB COATING

1 Before you frost or glaze a cake, make a crumb coating (a thin layer of frosting that adheres crumbs to the cake so they do not mar the finish). Place the filled layer cake on a turntable or work surface. Put a small amount of frosting (no more than one-third of the frosting) on top of the cake. Using an icing spatula, smooth a thin layer of frosting over the cake.

2 The crumb coating should be a thin, even layer that covers the entire surface of the cake. Refrigerate the cake until firm, 15 to 30 minutes.

TO FROST A LAYER CAKE

1 Place the layered cake, still on its cardboard, on a serving plate. Cut 4 strips of waxed or parchment (baking) paper or aluminum foil, and tuck a strip under each side of the cake to protect the plate from drips. Set the plate on the cake turntable or a work surface. If you plan to glaze the cake after frosting, do not put it on a serving plate; frost it directly on the cake turntable or work surface. If some of the frosting will be used to decorate the finished cake, set that portion aside before you begin. Mound the remaining frosting in the center of the cake and, using an icing spatula, smooth it gently and evenly over the top.

2 Using the cardboard as a guide to how thick the frosting should be, smooth the frosting down the sides of the cake with the icing spatula, employing broad strokes and holding the spatula nearly perpendicular to the top. Do not touch the spatula to the cake without frosting on the spatula, or you might pick up crumbs from the cake.

3 Dip the spatula in warm water and wipe with a damp, clean kitchen towel. Holding the spatula perpendicular to the top, smooth the frosting on the sides, wiping the spatula with the towel before each stroke. If you are using a turntable, rotate it as you work.

4 Holding the spatula parallel to the top, sweep it across the top to smooth the frosting. Continue to rotate the turntable, if using, wiping the spatula after each stroke. The top should be flat and the sides straight on the finished cake.

If you are glazing the cake over the frosting, refrigerate the cake for 30 minutes to firm up the frosting before glazing it. Otherwise, remove the strips of paper or foil from beneath the cake and then decorate the cake (see page 212).

TO GLAZE A CAKE WITH CHOCOLATE GLAZE

1 Place the cake on a cooling rack set on a half-sheet pan. Make sure that the glaze is the right temperature (92°F/33°C) and consistency before you begin to pour it. If it is too cold, warm it up slightly over hot water. If it is too thick, and warming does not thin it, gently stir in a few tablespoons of melted butter until the glaze flows from a spoon. Pour the glaze onto the center of the cake.

2 Immediately tilt the rack back and forth until the glaze covers the top and falls evenly over the sides.

3 Use an icing spatula to smooth the top and sides and to remove excess puddles. Don't worry if the sides of the cake are bumpy. Refrigerate the cake for about 30 minutes to set up the first coat of glaze completely. It is ready for the second coat when you can touch the glaze and it does not smear. Scrape up the drippings from the pan, return them to the bowl that held the glaze, and rewarm the glaze. Pour the glaze on the cake and immediately tilt the rack back and forth once or twice to cover evenly. This time do not use the spatula. Let the cake sit until the glaze sets up, then transfer to a serving plate using a wide metal spatula.

STORING CAKES

Most cakes, with the exception of cakes frosted with whipped cream, can be stored in a covered cake plate or in a box covered with plastic wrap at room temperature for up to 4 hours or in the refrigerator for up to 2 days before serving. Cakes frosted with whipped cream should be refrigerated immediately and served chilled.

SERVING CAKES

Most cakes taste best when served at room temperature. The exceptions are cakes filled and frosted with whipped cream and mousse cakes, both of which should be served chilled. To cut most cakes, use a thin-bladed serrated knife and a smooth, continuous stroke. For angel food cakes and sponge cakes, use the same knife but apply a sawing motion. If the cake is frosted and/or filled or if it is a cheesecake, dip the blade in hot water and wipe clean with a clean kitchen towel before each cut. Serve the cake as is or with Chocolate Sauce (page 284), Berry Coulis (page 306), or a pool of Crème Anglaise (page 306).

Decorating Techniques for Cakes

A variety of simple decorations can dress up any cake, from layer cakes to simple butter cakes. If you are decorating the cake with a flavored item, such as nuts, choose a flavor that complements the cake. Plain cakes can be served as is or dressed up with modest adornments.

SIMPLE DECORATIONS FOR LAYER CAKES

1 To decorate a frosted cake with chocolate shavings, make chocolate shavings as described on page 21, using dark, milk, or white chocolate, and place in a shallow pan. Place shavings directly on the frosted cake. Alternatively, apply as you would the nuts in step 3.

2 To decorate the top of a cake with raspberries, blackberries, or hulled strawberries, place the berries, stem ends down, in the frosting or glaze, arranging them in concentric circles or in a decorative arrangement.

3 To decorate the sides of a frosted cake with chopped toasted nuts, fill a shallow pan with about 2 cups (8–10 oz/250–315 g) of nuts. Hold the cake over the pan with one hand. Press the nuts into the sides of the cake with the other hand, rotating the cake as you work.

EASY ADORNMENTS FOR PLAIN CAKES

1 A light sifting of confectioners' (icing) sugar is an easy way to add a finishing touch to a cake. Just before serving, place the cake on a cooling rack set on your work surface. Using a fine-mesh sieve, sift ½ cup (2 oz/60 g) confectioners' sugar over the top of the cake, gently tapping the sieve while moving it to apply a light dusting. For a more festive decoration, place a stencil on top of the cake before sifting.

2 Make your cake even more delicious with a drizzle of Vanilla Glaze (page 68) or Citrus Glaze (page 214). Place the cake on a cooling rack set on a half-sheet pan. Dip a whisk, fork, or spoon into the glaze and drizzle over the top.

TO PIPE WITH A PASTRY BAG

Piping may seem intimidating, but the more you practice, the easier it becomes. If using melted chocolate, use a parchment cone (page 10).

1 Fit a canvas pastry (piping) bag with a plain or fluted tip. Use smaller tips for buttercream and larger tips for whipped cream. Hold the bag in one hand and fold down the top, forming a cuff. Use a rubber spatula to fill it half full.

2 Unfold the pastry bag and press the frosting down toward the tip. Twist the top half of the bag so the frosting is snug in the lower half. Hold the bag with one hand near the tip and the other holding the bulk of the bag. The tip should be just above the place you want to pipe. Before you decorate the cake, practice on a piece of parchment (baking) or waxed paper.

3 To pipe shells along the top or bottom edge of the cake, fit the pastry bag with a fluted tip. Hold the bag at a slight angle. Using your upper hand, apply gentle pressure so that the frosting adheres to the surface, then pull the bag up and toward you, lessening the pressure as you lift away. Release the pressure and bring the tip down and up to cut off the flow of frosting. Repeat the movement at the tip of each shell to create a border.

4 To pipe rosettes along the top or bottom edge of the cake, fit the pastry bag with a fluted tip. Hold the bag perpendicular to the surface. Using your upper hand, apply gentle pressure so that the frosting adheres to the surface, then slowly pull up. Release the pressure to cut off the flow of frosting. Repeat the movement next to each rosette to create a border.

5 To pipe pearls along the top or bottom edge of the cake, fit the pastry bag with a plain tip. Hold the bag perpendicular to the surface. Using your upper hand, apply gentle pressure so that the frosting adheres to the surface, then slowly turn the bag in a circular motion to form the pearl. Release the pressure and bring the tip around and up to cut off the flow of frosting. Repeat next to each pearl to create a border.

Lemon Chiffon Cake

3 or 4 lemons

2¹/₄ cups (9 oz/280 g) cake (soft-wheat) flour

1¹/₂ cups (12 oz/375 g) granulated sugar

1 tablespoon baking powder

1 teaspoon salt

¹/₂ cup (4 fl oz/125 ml) canola oil or vegetable oil

¹/₄ cup (2 fl oz/60 ml) water

6 large eggs, separated, at room temperature

¹/₂ teaspoon cream of tartar

For the citrus glaze

2 cups confectioners' (icing) sugar, sifted, plus extra if needed

2 tablespoons lemon juice, strained, plus extra if needed

1 tablespoon heavy (double) cream

Position a rack in the middle of the oven, and preheat to 325°F (165°C). Grate the zest from the lemons and set aside. Juice the lemons and strain the juice into a liquid measuring pitcher. You should have ¹/₂ cup (4 fl oz/125 ml) juice. Have ready an ungreased 10-inch (25-cm) tube pan with a removable bottom.

Sift together the flour, granulated sugar, baking powder, and salt onto a sheet of parchment (baking) paper or onto a plate. In a bowl, combine the oil, water, egg yolks, lemon juice, and lemon zest. Using a whisk, beat until well mixed. Using a large rubber spatula, gently fold the dry ingredients into the wet ingredients until the batter is smooth.

BY HAND: In a large, clean bowl, stir together the egg whites and cream of tartar. Using a balloon whisk, beat the egg whites until soft peaks form (page 27). Be careful not to overbeat.

BY MIXER: In a clean bowl, combine the egg whites and cream of tartar. Using a stand mixer fitted with the whip attachment or a hand mixer, beat on medium-high speed until soft peaks form (page 27).

Using a rubber spatula, gently fold one-half of the whites into the batter until almost fully incorporated. Add the remaining whites and gently fold in just until combined. The batter should be smooth but foamy. Pour the batter evenly into the tube pan.

Bake the cake until a toothpick inserted into the center comes out clean, 45–50 minutes. Remove from the oven and invert the pan onto a wire rack. Make sure that air can circulate freely all around the cake. Let cool completely upside down in the pan, about 45 minutes.

To loosen the cake from the pan sides, rotate and tap the pan against the countertop until the cake disengages. Using the center tube, pull the cake out of the pan. Invert the cake onto the rack and, using your fingers, disengage it gently from the pan bottom. Pull the pan bottom and tube out from the cake.

To make the citrus glaze, in a small bowl, whisk together the confectioners' sugar, lemon juice, and cream until the sugar dissolves and the glaze is smooth. Add a few more drops of lemon juice if it is too thick, or a little more sugar if it is too thin. Place the cake on the rack, and slip a half-sheet pan under the rack to catch the glaze. Pour the glaze over the top of the cake, letting it drizzle down the sides. When the glaze dries, slide 2 icing spatulas under the cake and transfer it to a serving platter. The cake is best served the day it is baked.

This moist, lemony version of a chiffon cake is simple, delicate, and delicious. The texture falls somewhere between a dense butter cake and a light and airy sponge cake. Be careful not to overwhip the egg whites, or the cake will be dry. Serve with fresh blueberry ice cream for a great summertime dessert.

Pound Cake

VARIATIONS

Chocolate Pound Cake

Reduce the cake flour to 1¹/₄ cups (5 oz/155 g). In a small, heatproof bowl, stir together ¹/₄ cup (³/₄ oz/20 g) Dutch-process cocoa powder and 1 teaspoon instant espresso powder. Pour in ¹/₄ cup (2 fl oz/60 ml) boiling water and stir until smooth. Let cool, then add to the creamed butter mixture after the eggs.

Orange-Espresso Pound Cake

Omit the vanilla. In a small bowl, dissolve 2 teaspoons instant espresso powder in 1 tablespoon fresh orange juice. Add it along with the grated zest of 1 orange to the creamed butter mixture before incorporating the eggs.

Lemon–Poppy Seed Pound Cake

Omit the vanilla. Add the grated zest of 1 lemon to the creamed butter mixture. Add 1 tablespoon poppy seeds to the sifted dry ingredients before folding them into the creamed mixture.

Position a rack in the middle of the oven, and preheat to 350°F (180°C). Butter the bottom and sides of 9-by-5-inch (23-by-13-cm) loaf pan or an 8-inch (20-cm) round cake pan. Line the bottom with parchment (baking) paper cut to fit (page 10). Butter the paper, then dust the bottom and sides of the pan with flour.

Sift together the flour, salt, and baking powder onto a sheet of parchment paper or onto a plate. Set aside.

BY HAND: In a large, deep bowl, combine the butter and granulated sugar. Using a sturdy wire whisk, beat vigorously until the mixture is light in color and fluffy, about 5 minutes. Whisk in the eggs one at a time, beating well after each addition. The mixture may look slightly curdled, but this normal. Whisk in the vanilla.

BY MIXER: In a large bowl, combine the butter and granulated sugar. Using a stand mixer fitted with the paddle attachment or a hand mixer, beat on medium-high speed until the mixture is light in color and fluffy, about 5 minutes. Beat in the eggs one at a time, beating well after each addition. Mix in the vanilla. Remove the bowl from the mixer.

Using a rubber spatula, gently fold in one-half of the dry ingredients until almost fully incorporated. Add the remaining dry ingredients and, using a light lifting motion and turning the bowl continuously, fold in until the batter is smooth and the dry ingredients are incorporated. Do not fold the batter too vigorously, or the cake will be tough.

Pour the batter into the prepared pan and smooth with the rubber spatula. Bake the cake until a toothpick inserted into the center comes out clean, 60–70 minutes. Watch the time closely at the end so that the cake does not overbake.

Let the cake cool in the pan on a wire rack for 5 minutes. Place a rack on top of the cake and invert them together. Lift off the pan and peel off the parchment. Turn the cake domed side up and let cool completely on the rack. Cover the cake with a clean, slightly damp kitchen towel so that the outside does not dry out as it cools.

Using a fine-mesh sieve, liberally dust the top of the cooled cake with confectioners' sugar, then transfer it to a serving plate. Serve with the coulis and whipped cream, if desired.

2¹/₄ cups (9 oz/280 g) cake (soft-wheat) flour

¹/₄ teaspoon salt

2 teaspoons baking powder

1 cup (8 oz/250 g) unsalted butter, at room temperature

1¹/₂ cups (12 oz/375 g) granulated sugar

5 large eggs, slightly cool

2 teaspoons vanilla extract (essence)

Confectioners' (icing) sugar for dusting

Berry Coulis (page 306) (optional)

Whipped Cream (page 306) (optional)

Angel Food Cake

1¹/₄ cups (10 oz/315 g) granulated sugar

1 cup (4 oz/125 g) cake (soft-wheat) flour

¹/₂ teaspoon salt

10 large egg whites, cold

Juice of 1 lemon, strained

2 tablespoons lukewarm water

1 teaspoon cream of tartar

1 teaspoon vanilla extract (essence)

¹/₂ teaspoon almond extract (essence)

Confectioners' (icing) sugar for dusting (optional)

Position a rack in the middle of the oven, and preheat to 350°F (180°C). Have ready an ungreased 9-inch (23-cm) tube pan with a removable bottom.

Sift together ¹/₂ cup (4 oz/125 g) plus 2 tablespoons of the granulated sugar, the flour, and the salt onto a sheet of parchment (baking) paper. Sift a second time. In a large, clean stainless steel or copper bowl, combine the egg whites, lemon juice, and lukewarm water. Place the bowl in a sink of warm water. Stir the whites until they no longer feel chilly, but still feel cool. Stir in the cream of tartar.

BY HAND: Using a balloon whisk, whisk the whites as fast as you can. When they have taken in enough air to form soft peaks, they will have tripled in volume. Continue to whisk vigorously while pouring in the remaining granulated sugar and the vanilla and almond extracts. Whisk until the mixture firms up slightly. When the whisk is lifted, the whites should fall over gently.

BY MIXER: Using a stand mixer fitted with the whip attachment or a hand mixer, beat the whites on medium-high speed until soft peaks form and they have tripled in volume. Slowly pour in the remaining granulated sugar and the vanilla and almond extracts and beat until the mixture firms up slightly. When the whip or beaters are lifted, the whites should fall over gently.

Sift one-third of the dry ingredients over the whipped whites. Using a rubber spatula, fold in the dry ingredients gently but quickly with as few strokes as possible. When almost fully incorporated, sift another one-third of the dry

This heavenly batter bakes into a light, sweet, fat-free cake. The triple sifting called for in the recipe aerates the dry ingredients, helping to ensure a light-textured cake. The air trapped in the egg whites expands from the heat of the oven, giving the cake its characteristic height. If you are lucky enough to own an unlined copper bowl, omit the cream of tartar and whip your egg whites in the bowl. Copper produces a reaction in the egg whites that causes them to whip up higher and lighter, and gives them good stability. Serve this cake plain or with fruit sorbet and fresh berries.

ingredients onto the batter and fold it in until almost fully incorporated. Sift in the remaining dry ingredients and fold in gently. Be careful not to overfold, or you will deflate the whites, and the cake will not rise well in the oven.

Using the spatula, scrape the batter into the tube pan and smooth the surface. Bake the cake until the top is golden and a toothpick inserted into the center comes out clean, 40–45 minutes. Remove from the oven and immediately invert the pan. If the pan does not have legs on which it can stand, position the tube of the pan over the neck of a bottle. Make sure that air can circulate freely all around the cake. Let cool completely upside down, about 45 minutes. To loosen the cake from the pan sides, rotate and tap the pan against the countertop until the cake disengages. Using the center tube, pull the cake out of the pan. Invert the cake onto a wire rack and, using your fingers, disengage it gently from the pan bottom. Pull the pan bottom and tube out from the cake.

If desired, using a fine-mesh sieve, dust the top of the cake with confectioners' sugar before placing it on a serving plate. Using a thin-toothed serrated cake knife and a gentle sawing motion, cut the cake into slices. Store in an airtight container at room temperature for up to 2 days.

Ginger Butter Cake

3/4 cup (4¹/₂ oz/140 g) crystallized ginger, minced

1/3 cup (3 fl oz/80 ml) Grand Marnier or other orange liqueur

2 cups (8 oz/250 g) cake (soft-wheat) flour

2 teaspoons baking powder

2 teaspoons ground ginger

3/4 cup (6 oz/185 g) unsalted butter, at room temperature

1¹/₄ cups (5 oz/155 g) confectioners' (icing) sugar, plus extra for dusting

1 tablespoon light corn syrup

4 large eggs, at room temperature

Grated zest of 1 orange

3-inch (7.5-cm) piece fresh ginger, peeled and grated

1/2 teaspoon almond extract (essence)

1/2 cup (4 fl oz/125 ml) whole milk, at room temperature

In a small bowl, soak the crystallized ginger in the Grand Marnier for 10 minutes.

Position a rack in the middle of the oven, and preheat to 350°F (180°C). Butter the bottom and sides of a 9-by-5-inch (23-by-13 cm) loaf pan. Line the bottom with parchment (baking) paper cut to fit. Butter the paper and dust the bottom and sides of the pan with flour.

Sift together the cake flour, baking powder, and ground ginger onto a sheet of parchment paper or onto a plate. Set aside.

BY HAND: In a large, deep bowl, combine the butter, confectioners' sugar, and corn syrup. Using a sturdy wire whisk, beat vigorously until the mixture is light in color and fluffy, about 5 minutes. Whisk in the eggs one at a time, beating well after each addition. Whisk in the orange zest, grated ginger, and almond extract.

BY MIXER: In a large bowl, combine the butter, confectioners' sugar, and corn syrup. Using a stand mixer fitted with the paddle attachment or a hand mixer, beat on medium-high speed until the mixture is light in color and fluffy, about 5 minutes. Beat in the eggs one at a time, beating well after each addition. Beat in the orange zest, grated ginger, and almond extract. Remove the bowl from the mixer.

Using a rubber spatula, gently fold in one-third of the dry ingredients until almost fully incorporated. Fold in half of the milk, then fold in another third of the dry ingredients, followed by the remaining milk. Add the remaining dry ingredients and the liqueur-soaked crystallized ginger and, using a light lifting motion and turning the bowl continuously, fold in until the batter is smooth and the dry ingredients are incorporated. Do not fold too vigorously, or the cake will be tough.

Spread the batter in the prepared pan. Bake the cake until a toothpick inserted into the center comes out clean, 50–60 minutes. Watch the time closely at the end so that the cake does not overbake. Let cool in the pan on a wire rack for 5 minutes. Place a wire rack on top of the cake and invert them together. Lift off the pan and peel off the parchment. Turn the cake domed side up and let cool completely on the rack. Cover the cake with a clean, slightly damp kitchen towel so that the outside does not dry out as it cools.

Using a fine-mesh sieve, liberally dust the top of the cooled cake with confectioners' sugar, then transfer it to a serving plate.

As its name suggests, this cake combines lots of ginger with butter to make a hearty, flavorful dessert. If you want a less bold flavor, omit the freshly grated ginger from the batter. Juxtapose the richness of this cake with fresh tropical fruits, such as chilled slices of mango, papaya, and kiwifruit, or with warm poached pears. Unlike most cakes, the flavor of this cake improves after several days.

Hazelnut-Cornmeal Cake

1 cup (5 oz/155 g) hazelnuts (filberts), toasted and skinned (page 21)

$^1/_2$ cup ($2^1/_2$ oz/75 g) corn flour or finely ground cornmeal

$^1/_2$ cup (2 oz/60 g) cake (soft-wheat) flour

1 teaspoon baking powder

$^1/_4$ teaspoon salt

1 cup (8 oz/250 g) unsalted butter, at room temperature

$^3/_4$ cup (6 oz/185 g) granulated sugar

4 large eggs, separated

1 teaspoon vanilla extract (essence)

Juice of $^1/_2$ lemon, strained

Confectioners' (icing) sugar for dusting

Position a rack in the middle of the oven, and preheat to 350°F (180°C). Butter the bottom and sides of an 8-inch (20-cm) round cake pan. Line the bottom with a circle of parchment (baking) paper cut to fit (page 10). Butter the paper and dust the bottom and sides of the pan with flour.

In a food processor or blender, combine the hazelnuts and corn flour. Process until the nuts are finely ground. Sift together the cake flour, baking powder, and salt onto a sheet of parchment paper or onto a plate. Stir in the ground nut mixture. Set aside.

BY HAND: In a large, deep bowl, combine the butter and sugar. Using a sturdy wire whisk, beat vigorously until the mixture is light in color and fluffy, about 3 minutes. Whisk in the egg yolks and vanilla. In another clean bowl, stir together the egg whites and lemon juice. Using a balloon whisk, beat until soft peaks form (page 27). Do not overwhip the whites, or the cake will be dry.

BY MIXER: In a large bowl, combine the butter and granulated sugar. Using a stand mixer fitted with the paddle attachment or a hand mixer, beat on medium-high speed until the mixture is light in color and fluffy, about 5 minutes. Beat in the egg yolks and vanilla. In another clean bowl, stir together the egg whites and lemon juice. Using the whip attachment or a hand mixer, beat on medium-high speed until soft peaks form (page 27). Remove the bowl from the mixer.

Italian in origin, this butter cake gets both crunch and flavor from toasted hazelnuts and cornmeal. Eat it any time of day. Have a wedge with an espresso for breakfast, or with a glass of grappa for dessert. If some remains after a day or two, slice and toast it and spread with raspberry jam.

Using a rubber spatula, gently fold one-third of the dry ingredients into the butter mixture until almost fully incorporated. Fold in one-half of the egg whites. Fold in another third of the dry ingredients, followed by the remaining whites. Add the remaining dry ingredients and, using a light lifting motion with the spatula and continuously turning the bowl, fold in until the batter is smooth and the dry ingredients are incorporated. The batter should be quite light, almost foamy. Do not overmix, or the whites will deflate and the cake will be dense.

Spread the batter in the prepared pan. Bake the cake until a toothpick inserted into the center comes out clean, 35–40 minutes. Watch the time closely at the end so that the cake does not overbake.

Let the cake cool in the pan on a wire rack for 5 minutes. Place a wire rack on top of the cake and invert them together. Lift off the pan and peel off the parchment. Let the cake cool completely on the rack. Cover the cake with a clean, slightly damp kitchen towel so that the outside does not dry out as it cools.

Using a fine-mesh sieve, lightly dust the top of the cooled cake with confectioners' sugar, then transfer it to a serving plate. Store wrapped with plastic wrap and aluminum foil at room temperature for up to 2 days, or freeze for up to 1 month.

Almond Cake

Simple to make, this cake is deceptively rich. The almond paste gives it a bold, straightforward flavor that highlights the butter and almonds. Make sure that the paste is fresh, soft, and at room temperature before using it. Garnish thin slices of the cake with chilled orange segments and sliced strawberries.

Position a rack in the middle of the oven, and preheat to 350°F (180°C). Butter and flour a 9-inch (23-cm) decorative tube pan or Bundt pan.

Sift together the flour, baking powder, and salt onto a sheet of parchment (baking) paper or onto a plate. Set aside.

BY MIXER: In a large bowl, break up the almond paste with a spoon, then add the granulated sugar and butter. Using a stand mixer fitted with the paddle attachment or a hand mixer, beat on medium-high speed until the mixture is light and creamy, about 5 minutes. Add the eggs one at a time, beating well after each addition. The mixture may look curdled, but this is normal. Beat in the vanilla.

BY FOOD PROCESSOR: Combine the almond paste, sugar, and butter. Pulse to break up the ingredients, then process until the mixture is light and creamy, about 2 minutes. Add the eggs and the vanilla and process until thoroughly mixed. The mixture may look slightly curdled, but this is normal. Transfer the creamed mixture to a large bowl.

Add one-half of the dry ingredients and, using a rubber spatula, fold in gently until almost fully incorporated. Add the remaining dry ingredients and, using a light lifting motion with the spatula and continuously turning the bowl, fold in until the batter is smooth and the dry ingredients are thoroughly incorporated. Do not fold too vigorously, or the cake will be tough.

Spread the batter in the prepared pan. Bake the cake until a toothpick inserted into the center comes out clean, 40–45 minutes. Watch the time closely at the end so that the cake does not overbake.

Let the cake cool on a wire rack for 10 minutes. Place a wire rack on top of the cake and invert them together. Lift off the pan. Let the cake cool completely on the rack. Cover the cake with a clean, slightly damp kitchen towel so that the outside does not dry out as it cools.

Using a fine-mesh sieve, liberally dust the top of the cooled cake with confectioners' sugar, then transfer it to a serving plate. Store the cake wrapped with plastic wrap and aluminum foil at room temperature for up to 3 days or freeze for up to 1 month.

1 cup (4 oz/125 g) cake (soft-wheat) flour

1 teaspoon baking powder

$1/4$ teaspoon salt

7 oz (220 g) almond paste, at room temperature

1 cup (8 oz/250 g) granulated sugar

1 cup (8 oz/250 g) unsalted butter, at room temperature

6 large eggs, at room temperature

1 teaspoon vanilla extract (essence)

Confectioners' (icing) sugar for dusting

Almond Dacquoise

1¹⁄₃ cups (7 oz/220 g) plus ¹⁄₄ cup (1¹⁄₂ oz/45 g) whole almonds, toasted (page 21)

1 cup (8 oz/250 g) granulated sugar

2 tablespoons cornstarch (cornflour)

6 large egg whites, at room temperature

1 teaspoon vanilla extract (essence)

Rich Almond Buttercream (page 307)

Confectioners' (icing) sugar for dusting

Position a rack in the middle of the oven, and preheat to 300°F (150°C). Lightly butter the bottom and sides of 2 half-sheet pans. Using an 8-inch (20-cm) round cake pan as a guide, trace 2 circles on a sheet of parchment (baking) paper cut to fit the bottom of a half-sheet pan. Repeat on a second sheet, drawing 2 more circles. Place each sheet, circle side down, on a prepared pan. Butter the paper, then dust the bottom and sides of the pan with flour. You should be able to see the circle markings through the paper.

In a food processor or blender, combine the 1¹⁄₃ cups almonds, ¹⁄₂ cup (4 oz/125 g) of the granulated sugar, and the cornstarch. Process to grind the almonds to a powder.

BY HAND: In a large bowl, using a balloon whisk, whisk the egg whites as fast as you can. When they have taken in enough air to form soft peaks, they will have tripled in volume. Continue to whisk vigorously while pouring in the remaining ¹⁄₂ cup (4 oz/125 g) granulated sugar and the vanilla until the whites are stiff and glossy. Be careful not to overwhip the whites, or they will be dry and powdery.

BY MIXER: In a large bowl, using a stand mixer fitted with the whip attachment or a hand mixer, beat the egg whites on medium-high speed until they form soft peaks and have tripled in volume. Slowly pour in the remaining ¹⁄₂ cup (4 oz/125 g) granulated sugar and the vanilla and beat until the whites are stiff and glossy. Be careful not to over-whip the whites, or they will be dry and powdery. Remove the bowl from the mixer.

Pour the almond-sugar mixture over the egg whites. Using a rubber spatula, fold it in gently and quickly, with as few strokes as possible. Spoon some of the batter into a pastry (piping) bag fitted with a ¹⁄₂-inch (12-mm) plain tip (page 213). Holding the bag upright just above the half-sheet pan, and starting in the middle of a circle, pipe spirals of the batter until you reach the edge of the circle. Refill the bag as necessary and pipe 3 solid circles. Pipe the fourth circle as full as possible with the batter you have left.

Bake the layers until they are crisp, dry, and beginning to brown, 50–60 minutes. They will feel crisp on top when done, but they might give a little while they are still warm. Transfer the pans to wire racks and let cool. The dacquoise layers will become crisp as they cool.

The queen of nut meringue cakes, dacquoise boasts a multitude of variations and uses. You can sandwich the layers with buttercream, as in this classic version, or you can slip a round of dacquoise into the middle of a layer cake for crunch and flavor. This is also a great cake to make when you need a delicious wheat-free option in your repertoire. Serve with a compote of chilled citrus.

VARIATIONS

Chocolate-Hazelnut Dacquoise

Use toasted, skinned hazelnuts (filberts) (page 21) in place of the almonds. Add 3 tablespoons Dutch-process cocoa powder to the nuts when grinding them. Fill and frost with a double recipe of Ganache Filling (page 309) in place of the Rich Almond Buttercream.

Chocolate-Orange Dacquoise

Use Chocolate-Orange Buttercream (page 308) in place of the Rich Almond Buttercream.

To assemble the cake, gently peel the cooled layers away from the parchment paper. Using a serrated knife and a sawing motion, trim the 3 solid rounds so that they are exactly the same size. Using a rolling pin, crush any trimmings along with the fourth round. Place in a bowl. Finely chop the remaining $1/4$ cup almonds and add to the crushed trimmings. Set aside.

Place 1 layer on a cardboard circle or a cake platter. Using an icing spatula, spread about $1/3$ cup (3 fl oz/80 ml) buttercream in a thin, even layer on the layer. Place a second layer on top of the buttercream, and spread with the same amount of buttercream. Place the third layer on top. Using as much of the remaining buttercream as needed, spread the top and sides of the cake with a thin coating, smoothing it as evenly as possible.

Coat the entire cake with the crumb-nut mixture, pressing it against the sides and top of the cake with your hands. Using a fine-mesh sieve, sift a light dusting of confectioners' sugar over the top. If desired, fit a clean pastry bag with a small star tip, fill with any remaining buttercream, and pipe a border of rosettes on the top of the cake (page 213). Slip a wide metal spatula underneath the cake and transfer it to a serving plate.

The cake can be cut right away, but it is easier to cut if it is first allowed to soften for several hours in the refrigerator. It will keep, well covered in the refrigerator, for up to 2 days. Slice into wedges with a sharp chef's knife or a serrated knife and serve at room temperature.

Apple Cake

This extremely versatile cake can be dressed up or down depending on the occasion. Bake in a rectangular pan and cut into squares for a school lunch box, or frost it with a rich maple frosting and take it to a picnic. Bake it in a 10-inch (25-cm) round cake pan, and serve it in wedges with warm Crème Anglaise (page 306) at Thanksgiving. If you like, add 1/2 cup (3 oz/90 g) golden raisins (sultanas), plumped in hot water (page 23) and drained, with the apples. Use a soft, tart apple in this cake, such as Gravenstein or McIntosh. Pippin or Granny Smith apples work well, too.

Position a rack in the middle of the oven, and preheat to 350°F (180°C). Butter the bottom and sides of a 9-by-13-by-2-inch (23-by-33-by-5-cm) baking pan. Sift together the flour, baking powder, baking soda, cinnamon, nutmeg, cloves, and salt onto a sheet of parchment (baking) paper or onto a plate.

BY HAND: In a large bowl, combine the butter and granulated sugar. Using a sturdy wire whisk, beat vigorously until the mixture is light in color and fluffy, 3–5 minutes. Whisk in the eggs one at a time, beating well after each addition.

BY MIXER: In a large bowl, combine the butter and granulated sugar. Using a stand mixer fitted with the paddle attachment or a hand mixer, beat on medium-high speed until the mixture is light and fluffy, 3–5 minutes. Beat in the eggs one at a time, beating well after each addition. Remove the bowl from the mixer.

Using a rubber spatula, gently fold in one-third of the flour mixture until almost fully incorporated. Fold in one-half of the buttermilk, then fold in another third of the flour mixture, followed by the remaining buttermilk. Add the remaining flour mixture, the apples, and the walnuts, if using. Using a light lifting motion and turning the bowl continuously, fold in until the batter is smooth and the flour is thoroughly incorporated. Do not fold too vigorously, or the cake will be tough.

Spread the batter in the prepared pan. Bake the cake until the top is brown and a toothpick inserted into the center comes out clean, 35–40 minutes. Watch the time closely at the end so that the cake does not overbake.

Transfer to a wire rack and let cool for at least 15 minutes. Cut into squares and serve warm, or let cool completely and frost with maple frosting. Store wrapped with plastic wrap and aluminum foil at room temperature for up to 3 days, or freeze for up to 1 month.

To make the maple frosting, if using, in a saucepan over medium-high heat, simmer the maple syrup until it reduces by half, about 15 minutes. Stir in the butter. Remove from the heat and stir in the cream and vanilla. Sift the confectioners' sugar into a bowl. Pour in the warm maple mixture and beat with a whisk until smooth and creamy. Let cool completely before using it to frost the cake.

2 cups (10 oz/315 g) all-purpose (plain) flour

1 teaspoon baking powder

1 teaspoon baking soda (bicarbonate of soda)

1 teaspoon ground cinnamon

1/2 teaspoon freshly grated nutmeg

1/2 teaspoon ground cloves

1/2 teaspoon salt

3/4 cup (6 oz/185 g) unsalted butter, at room temperature

1 1/2 cups (12 oz/375 g) granulated sugar

3 large eggs, at room temperature

1/2 cup (4 fl oz/125 ml) buttermilk, at room temperature

2 cups (8 oz/250 g) diced, peeled apples

1/2 cup (2 oz/60 g) walnuts, toasted (page 21) and chopped (optional)

For the maple frosting (optional)

1 cup (11 oz/345 g) pure maple syrup

1/4 cup (2 oz/60 g) unsalted butter

1/2 cup (4 fl oz/125 ml) heavy (double) cream

1/2 teaspoon vanilla extract (essence)

2 cups (8 oz/250 g) confectioners' (icing) sugar

Pineapple Upside-Down Cake

For the topping

3 cups (24 fl oz/750 ml) water

1¹/₂ cups (12 oz/375 g) granulated sugar

3 cinnamon sticks

12 whole allspice

3 tablespoons (1 oz/30 g) crystallized ginger

1 ripe pineapple, peeled, cored, and sliced ¹/₂ inch (12 mm) thick (page 22)

¹/₂ lb (250 g) fresh cherries, pitted (optional)

¹/₄ cup (2 oz/60 g) unsalted butter, melted

1 cup (7 oz/220 g) firmly packed brown sugar

For the batter

1¹/₄ cups (5 oz/155 g) cake (soft-wheat) flour

¹/₂ teaspoon baking soda (bicarbonate of soda)

¹/₂ teaspoon salt

¹/₂ cup (4 oz/125 g) unsalted butter, at room temperature

³/₄ cup (6 oz/185 g) firmly packed brown sugar

3 large eggs, separated, at room temperature

1 teaspoon vanilla extract (essence)

¹/₂ cup (4 fl oz/125 ml) buttermilk, at room temperature

¹/₄ cup (2 oz/60 g) granulated sugar

In a large frying pan or wide saucepan, bring the water and granulated sugar to a boil, stirring to dissolve the sugar. Add the cinnamon sticks, allspice, crystallized ginger, and pineapple slices, making sure that the fruit is covered with the syrup. Cover and simmer until the pineapple is tender when pierced with a fork, 15–20 minutes. If using, add the cherries during the last 5 minutes. Remove from the heat, drain the pineapple and cherries, and set the fruits aside.

Butter the bottom and sides of a 10-inch (25-cm) round cake pan or heavy frying pan. Line the bottom with a circle of parchment (baking) paper cut to fit (page 10). Pour the melted butter into the pan and use a fork to spread the brown sugar evenly over it. Top with 7 or 8 of the poached pineapple slices, slightly overlapping them for a snug fit. Reserve any remaining pineapple for another use. Put a whole poached cherry, if using, in the center of each pineapple slice. Reserve the remaining cherries for serving.

Position a rack in the middle of the oven, and preheat to 325°F (165°C). To make the batter, sift together the flour, baking soda, and salt onto a sheet of parchment paper or onto a plate. In a large, deep bowl, combine the butter and brown sugar. Using a sturdy wire whisk, beat vigorously until the mixture is light in color and fluffy, about 5 minutes. Whisk in the egg yolks and vanilla.

Using a rubber spatula, gently fold in one-third of the dry ingredients until almost fully incorporated. Fold in one-half of the buttermilk, then fold in another third of the dry ingredients, followed by the remaining buttermilk. Add the remaining dry ingredients and, using a light lifting motion and turning the bowl continuously, fold in until the batter is smooth and the dry ingredients are thoroughly incorporated. Do not fold too vigorously, or the cake will be tough.

In a clean bowl, using a stand mixer fitted with the whip attachment, or a hand mixer, beat the egg whites until soft peaks form (page 27). Slowly pour in the granulated sugar while continuing to beat until the mixture firms up slightly. The whites should fall over gently when the beaters are lifted. Using a rubber spatula, fold the egg whites into the batter. Spread the batter in the prepared pan.

Bake the cake until it is golden brown and a toothpick inserted into the center comes out clean, 35–40 minutes. The top should feel slightly firm to the touch. Transfer to a wire rack and let cool in the pan for 10 minutes. Invert a serving plate on top of the pan and, holding the plate and pan together, invert them. Gently pull off the pan, being careful not to burn yourself. If the parchment has adhered to the cake, carefully peel it off. Serve warm.

When the pan is lifted off this cake, a beautiful display of glistening fruit is revealed. Poach fresh, ripe pineapple slices, rather than canned, for the best flavor. In the summer, garnish the cake with fresh cherries that you poach along with the pineapple. Other seasons, use good-quality jarred Morello cherries and omit the poaching.

Classic Génoise

³/₄ cup (3 oz/90 g) cake (soft-wheat) flour

4 large eggs

²/₃ cup (5 oz/155 g) granulated sugar

4 tablespoons (2 oz/60 g) unsalted butter, melted and cooled

¹/₂ teaspoon vanilla extract (essence)

VARIATIONS

Citrus, Orange Flower, Rose Water, or Almond Génoise
Omit the vanilla. Add the grated zest of 1 lemon or 1 orange, 1 teaspoon orange-flower water or rose water, or ¹/₂ teaspoon almond extract (essence) with the butter.

Chocolate Génoise
Reduce the cake flour to ¹/₂ cup (2 oz/60 g). Sift the flour twice with 3 tablespoons cocoa powder. Reduce the sugar to ³/₄ cup (6 oz/185 g). Add 2 large egg yolks with the whole eggs.

Nut Génoise
Increase the cake flour to 1 cup (4 oz/125 g). In a food processor or blender, combine the flour with ¹/₄ cup (1¹/₂ oz/45 g) toasted almonds, (1 oz/30 g) walnuts, or (1¹/₄ oz/35 g) skinned hazelnuts (filberts), page 21. Grind to a powder in a food processor or blender. Reduce the sugar to ³/₄ cup (6 oz/185 g). Add 1 large egg yolk with the whole eggs.

Position a rack in the middle of the oven, and preheat to 350°F (180°C). Butter a 9-inch (23-cm) round cake pan. Line the bottom with a circle of parchment (baking) paper cut to fit (page 10). Butter the paper and dust the bottom and sides of the pan with flour.

Sift the flour onto a sheet of parchment paper or onto a plate. Set aside. Put the eggs and sugar in a deep stainless-steel or copper bowl or in the bowl of a stand mixer. Choose a pan in which the bowl will fit snugly in the rim, fill it halfway with water, and bring to a simmer. Set the bowl of eggs and sugar over (not touching) the simmering water. Stir gently with a whisk for a few minutes until the mixture is warm (160°F/71°C on an instant-read thermometer) and the sugar dissolves.

BY HAND: With the bowl over the simmering water, whisk the eggs vigorously with a balloon whisk until the batter is light, has tripled in volume, and is thick enough to fall back on itself like a ribbon when the whisk is lifted, 8–10 minutes (page 26). Remove from over the water.

BY MIXER: Remove the bowl from over the water. Using a stand mixer fitted with the paddle attachment or a hand mixer, beat on high speed until the batter is light, has tripled in volume, and is thick enough to fall back on itself like a ribbon when the whisk is lifted, about 5–7 minutes (page 26).

Sift the flour a second time over the batter. Using a long-handled rubber spatula, fold in gently but quickly with as few strokes as possible while turning the bowl continuously. When the flour is almost incorporated, gently but quickly fold in the butter and vanilla. Be careful not to overfold, or the eggs will deflate and the batter will lose its volume. Pour the batter into the prepared pan.

Bake the cake until it springs back when lightly touched with a fingertip or a toothpick inserted into the center comes out clean, 20–30 minutes. Remove the cake from the oven. Immediately run a small, thin knife around the inside of the pan to loosen the cake, pressing the knife against the pan to avoid gouging the cake. Place a wire rack on top of the cake and invert them together. Carefully lift off the pan and peel off the parchment. Turn the cake back over onto another rack and let cool completely. Use the cake immediately, or wrap well and store at room temperature for up to 2 days, or in the freezer for up to 2 weeks. For ideas on syrups, fillings, and frostings, see page 207. To assemble the cake, see pages 209–10.

This is arguably the most important cake in a baker's repertoire. Mastering génoise allows you the possibility of making a vast array of different layer cakes, always using this cake as the base. It gets most of its personality from the cake syrup, which is used to flavor and moisten it, as it tends to be drier than most other cakes. A génoise comes to life when it is assembled: Brushed with syrup, filled with one of a variety of delicious options, and frosted with a complementary flavor, it is both versatile and impressive. You can also bake this recipe in an 8-inch (20-cm) round cake pan if you want a taller cake, or if you want to split it into three layers.

Classic Sponge Cake

³/₄ cup (3 oz/90 g) cake (soft-wheat) flour

4 large eggs, separated, at room temperature

³/₄ cup (6 oz/185 g) sugar

¹/₂ teaspoon vanilla extract (essence)

Position a rack in the middle of the oven, and preheat to 350°F (180°C). Butter the bottom and sides of a 9-inch (23-cm) round cake pan. Line the bottom with a circle of parchment (baking) paper cut to fit (page 10). Butter the paper and dust the bottom and sides of the pan with flour.

Sift the flour onto a sheet of parchment paper or onto a plate. Set aside.

In a large, deep bowl, combine the egg yolks and ¹/₂ cup (4 oz/125 g) of the sugar. Using a sturdy wire whisk, beat vigorously until the mixture is light in color and thick, about 5 minutes. Whisk in the vanilla. Set aside.

BY HAND: In a large bowl, using a balloon whisk, beat the egg whites as fast as you can. When they have taken in enough air to form soft peaks, they will have tripled in volume (page 27). Continue to whisk vigorously while pouring in the remaining ¹/₄ cup (2 oz/60 g) sugar until the whites are stiff and glossy. You should be able to hold the bowl upside down without the whites falling out. Be careful not to over-whip the whites, or they will be dry.

BY MIXER: In a large bowl, using a stand mixer fitted with the whip attachment or a hand mixer, beat the egg whites on medium-high speed until they form soft peaks and have tripled in volume (page 27). Slowly pour in the remaining ¹/₄ cup (2 oz/60 g) sugar and beat until the whites are stiff and glossy. You should be able to hold the bowl upside down without the whites falling out. Be careful not to over-whip the whites, or they will be dry.

This cold-method sponge cake, traditionally known as biscuit (pronounced bis-kwee), can be used interchangeably with génoise for most recipes. Classic sponge cake is lighter in color and texture, a little moister (although like génoise, it must be soaked with a cake syrup), and a little more forgiving to make. If you pipe the same batter out of a pastry bag into short strips, they are called lady-fingers. You can bake this recipe in an 8-inch (20-cm) round cake pan if you want a taller cake, or if you want to split it into three layers.

Chocolate Sponge Cake

Reduce the cake flour to $^1/_2$ cup (2 oz/60 g) plus 2 tablespoons. Sift it twice with 2 tablespoons Dutch-process cocoa powder.

Nut Sponge Cake

Reduce the cake flour to $^1/_2$ cup (2 oz/60 g). In a food processor or blender, combine the flour and 1$^1/_4$ cups (5 oz/155 g) walnuts, (7 oz/220 g) almonds, or (6$^1/_2$ oz/200 g) skinned hazelnuts (filberts), page 21. Grind to a powder. Increase the sugar to $^2/_3$ cup (5 oz/155 g).

Using a rubber spatula, gently but quickly fold one-third of the beaten egg whites into the yolk-sugar mixture. Fold in one-half of the flour. Fold in the another third of the whites, followed by the remaining flour. Finally, fold in the remaining whites until the batter is smooth. Be careful not to overfold, or the eggs will deflate and the batter will lose its volume. Pour the batter into the cake pan.

Bake the cake until it springs back when lightly touched with a fingertip or a toothpick inserted into the center comes out clean, 20–30 minutes. Remove the cake from the oven. Immediately run a small, thin knife around the inside of the pan to loosen the cake, pressing the knife against the pan to avoid gouging the cake. Place a wire rack on top of the cake and invert them together. Carefully lift off the pan and peel off the parchment paper. Turn the cake back over onto another rack and let cool completely.

Use the cake immediately, or wrap well and store at room temperature for up to 2 days, or in the freezer for up to 2 weeks. For ideas on syrups, fillings, and frostings, see page 207. To assemble the cake, see pages 209–10.

Carrot Cake

One of the most requested cakes for birthdays, carrot cake, frosted with a thick layer of cream cheese frosting, is a hearty celebratory dessert that became popular in the 1970s. Whether baked in a rectangular baking pan for an afternoon snack or as a layer cake for a birthday celebration, it is surprisingly simple to make. You can also leave the cake in the pan and frost just the top for easy transport to a family picnic. To make it truly decadent, serve with vanilla or maple nut ice cream.

Position a rack in the middle of the oven, and preheat to 350°F (180°C). Butter and flour a 9-by-13-by-2-inch (23-by-33-cm) baking pan or two 10-inch (25-cm) round cake pans to make a layer cake.

Peel and grate the carrots. You should have about 3 cups (1 lb/500 g). Set aside. Sift together the flour, baking powder, baking soda, salt, cinnamon, and mace onto a sheet of parchment (baking) paper or onto a plate. Set aside.

In a large bowl, combine the sugar, eggs, oil, and orange zest. Whisk thoroughly to combine. Stir in the carrots. With a rubber spatula, fold the dry ingredients into the wet ingredients until almost fully incorporated. Add the raisins and nuts and fold to mix thoroughly. Pour the batter into the prepared pan(s).

Bake the cake until a toothpick inserted into the center comes out clean, 35–40 minutes. Watch the time closely at the end so that the cake does not overbake. Remove the cake from the oven and let cool in the pan on a wire rack for 15 minutes. Place a cake rack on top of the pan and invert them together. Lift off the pan. Let the cake cool completely. Cover the cake with a clean, slightly damp kitchen towel so that the outside does not dry out as it cools.

To make the cream cheese frosting, in a bowl, using a stand mixer fitted with the paddle attachment or a hand mixer, cream the butter and cream cheese on medium speed until thoroughly mixed. Pour in the melted white chocolate and mix on low speed until fully combined. Beat in the orange juice and vanilla.

Transfer the cooled cake to a serving platter. Using an icing spatula, frost the cake with a thick layer of cream cheese frosting. If you want to make a layer cake and have baked cake layers, assemble as directed on pages 209–10. Serve immediately, or store in an airtight container at room temperature for up to 3 days.

4 large carrots

2 cups (8 oz/250 g) cake (soft-wheat) flour

2 teaspoons baking powder

2 teaspoons baking soda (bicarbonate of soda)

1 teaspoon salt

1 teaspoon ground cinnamon

1/4 teaspoon ground mace

1 1/2 cups (12 oz/375 g) sugar

4 large eggs

1 1/4 cups (10 fl oz/310 ml) canola oil

Grated zest of 1 orange

1/2 cup (3 oz/90 g) raisins, plumped in hot water (page 23) and drained

1 cup (4 oz/125 g) walnuts or pecans, toasted (page 21) and chopped

For the cream cheese frosting

1/2 cup (4 oz/125 g) unsalted butter, at room temperature

1 lb (500 g) cream cheese, at room temperature

10 oz (315 g) white chocolate, melted (page 21)

Juice of 1 orange, strained

2 teaspoons vanilla extract (essence)

Coconut Layer Cake

For the cake

2¹/₄ cups (9 oz/280 g) cake (soft-wheat) flour

2 teaspoons baking powder

¹/₂ teaspoon salt

³/₄ cup (6 oz/185 g) unsalted butter, at room temperature

1¹/₂ cups (12 oz/375 g) sugar

3 large eggs, separated, at room temperature

1 teaspoon vanilla extract (essence)

1 cup (8 fl oz/250 ml) canned coconut milk

1 cup (4 oz/125 g) loosely packed sweetened coconut

For the frosting and filling

2 large egg whites, at room temperature

³/₄ cup (6 oz/185 g) sugar

1 tablespoon corn syrup

¹/₈ teaspoon cream of tartar

2 tablespoons water

Juice of ¹/₂ lemon, strained

¹/₂ teaspoon vanilla extract (essence)

2 cups (8 oz/250 g) loosely packed sweetened coconut

Lemon Curd (page 309)

Position a rack in the middle of the oven, and preheat to 350°F (180°C). Butter two 9-inch (23-cm) round cake pans. Line the bottoms with circles of parchment (baking) paper cut to fit (page 10). Butter the paper and dust the bottoms and sides of the pans with flour.

Sift together the flour, baking powder, and salt onto a sheet of parchment paper or onto a plate. Set aside.

BY HAND: In a large, deep bowl, combine the butter and sugar. Using a sturdy wire whisk, beat vigorously until the mixture is light in color and fluffy, about 5 minutes. Whisk in the egg yolks and vanilla.

BY MIXER: In a large bowl, combine the butter and sugar. Using a mixer, beat on medium-high speed until the mixture is light in color and fluffy, about 5 minutes. Beat in the egg yolks and vanilla. Remove the bowl from the mixer.

Using a rubber spatula, gently fold in one-third of the dry ingredients until almost fully incorporated. Fold in one-half of the coconut milk, then fold in another third of the dry ingredients, followed by the remaining coconut milk. Add the remaining dry ingredients and, using a light lifting motion and turning the bowl continuously, fold in until the batter is smooth and the dry ingredients are thoroughly incorporated. Do not fold too vigorously, or the cake will be tough.

In a clean bowl, using a balloon whisk, a stand mixer fitted with the whip attachment, or a hand mixer, beat the egg whites until medium peaks form (page 27). The whites should fall over gently when the whisk or beaters are lifted. Using a rubber spatula, fold the egg whites into the batter, then fold in the coconut.

Pour the batter into the prepared pans, dividing it evenly. Bake the cake layers until a toothpick inserted into the center of a layer comes out clean, 20–25 minutes. Transfer to wire racks and let cool in the pans for 3 minutes. Place a wire rack on top of a cake layer and invert them together. Lift off the pan and peel off the parchment. Repeat with the remaining layer. Let cool completely on the racks. Cover the cake layers with a clean, slightly damp kitchen towel so that the outsides do not dry out as they cool.

To make the frosting (see the photographs to the right), combine the egg whites, sugar, corn syrup, cream of tartar, water, and lemon juice in a deep stainless-steel bowl or in the bowl of a stand mixer. Stir gently with a whisk to mix.

This is one of the American South's most spectacular traditional cakes. Clouds of coconut meringue frosting conceal a rich coconut butter cake and a tangy, velvety lemon curd. Make the lemon curd ahead to save time on baking day. The soft frosting is a nice contrast to the chewy coconut cake. Serve this memorable dessert to a crowd who will eat it right up, as the frosting lasts only a few hours.

Choose a saucepan in which the bowl will fit snugly in the rim, fill it halfway with water, and bring to a simmer. Set the bowl holding the egg whites over (not touching) the simmering water. Stir gently with the whisk for a few minutes until the mixture is quite warm (160°F/75°C on an instant-read thermometer) and the sugar has dissolved. Remove from the heat and, using a hand mixer or a stand mixer fitted with the whip attachment, beat the mixture at high speed until stiff and glossy (page 27), about 7 minutes. Using the rubber spatula, fold in the vanilla and one-half of the coconut.

To assemble the cake (pages 209–10), put a cooled cake layer, cut side up, on a 9-inch (23-cm) cardboard circle. Using an icing spatula, evenly spread the lemon curd on top of the cake. Place the second layer on top of the curd. Transfer the cake to a serving platter. Using an icing spatula or a small spoon, frost the sides and top of the cake with the frosting. Make dramatic indentations with the spoon so that the frosting is fluffy and textured. When the cake is covered, sprinkle the remaining coconut all over the cake. Serve at once, or refrigerate the cake for up to 2 hours before serving.

Mocha Roulade

Espresso cake syrup (page 308)

For the mocha
ganache mousse

8 oz (250 g) semisweet (plain) chocolate, finely chopped

¹/₂ cup (4 fl oz/125 ml) whole milk

1 tablespoon instant espresso powder

1 cup (8 fl oz/250 ml) heavy (double) cream

For the cake

¹/₃ cup (1¹/₂ oz/45 g) cornstarch (cornflour)

¹/₃ cup (1¹/₂ oz/45 g) cake (soft-wheat) flour

2 tablespoons Dutch-process cocoa powder

5 large eggs, separated

¹/₃ cup (3 oz/90 g) sugar

1 teaspoon vanilla extract (essence)

Rich Espresso Buttercream (page 307)

Milk chocolate shavings (pages 21 and 212) for decorating (optional)

Have ready the espresso cake syrup.

To make the mocha ganache mousse, put the chocolate in a heatproof bowl. In a small saucepan, bring the milk just to a boil over medium-high heat. Pour the milk over the chocolate. Add the espresso powder and stir with a whisk until the chocolate is melted and the mixture is smooth. Set aside to cool slightly. In another bowl, using a balloon whisk, whip the cream just until it holds soft peaks (page 27). With a rubber spatula, lightly fold the cream into the chocolate just until incorporated. Do not overfold, or the mousse will be gritty. Cover with plastic wrap and refrigerate. The mousse will firm up and become spreadable.

To make the cake, position a rack in the middle of the oven, and preheat to 375°F (190°C). Butter the bottom and sides of a half-sheet pan. Line the bottom with parchment (baking) paper and butter the paper. Dust the bottom and sides of the pan with flour.

Sift together the cornstarch, flour, and cocoa powder onto a sheet of parchment paper or onto a plate. Set aside. In a large, deep bowl, combine the egg yolks and 3 tablespoons of the sugar. Using a sturdy wire whisk, whisk vigorously until the mixture is light in color and thick, about 5 minutes. Whisk in the vanilla. Set aside.

In a large bowl, using a stand mixer fitted with the whip attachment or a hand mixer, beat the egg whites on medium-high speed until they form soft peaks and have tripled in volume (page 27). Slowly pour in the remaining sugar and beat until the mixture is stiff and glossy. You should be able to hold the bowl upside down without the whites falling out. Be careful not to overwhip the whites, or they will be dry and powdery. Remove the bowl from the mixer. Using a rubber spatula, gently but quickly fold one-third of the whites into the yolk-sugar mixture. Fold in one-half of the dry ingredients. Fold in another third of the whites, followed by the remaining dry ingredients. Finally, fold in the remaining whites just until combined.

Pour the batter into the prepared pan. Using an offset spatula, quickly and lightly spread the batter evenly, being careful not to press too hard or you will deflate the egg whites. Bake the cake until it puffs up and feels slightly firm to the touch, 6–8 minutes. Transfer to a wire rack and let cool completely in the pan.

Run a thin knife around the inside edge of the pan to loosen the cooled cake. Lay a piece of plastic wrap about 6 inches (15 cm) longer than the sheet pan lengthwise to cover half of the cake. Place a second piece over the other half,

Here, chocolate and coffee, a natural pair, flavor a classic roulade, or rolled cake. Although the cake and the whipped mocha filling are both light, the combination delivers a bold taste. Use this traditional sponge cake as a base for other fillings and frostings (see page 206). You may not need all of the buttercream; cover the remainder tightly and freeze for up to 1 month, then bring to room temperature and beat again before using.

overlapping it slightly with the first piece. The whole cake should be covered. Flip the pan over and tap it so that the cake falls out onto the plastic wrap. Lift off the pan and peel off the parchment.

Using a pastry brush, generously moisten the entire surface of the cake with the cake syrup. Using the rubber spatula, scrape all of the mousse into the center of the cake. Spread it evenly over the surface with an icing spatula. Starting at the long end closest to you, roll up the cake into a cylinder, using the plastic wrap to help. Wrap the plastic wrap around the rolled cake, twist the ends to seal, and slide the roll onto a rimless baking sheet. Refrigerate for at least 2 hours to firm up the filling. Meanwhile, make the espresso buttercream.

Unwrap the cake and place on a serving plate. Using a small icing spatula, frost the top and the sides with a thin layer of the buttercream. With a sharp, serrated cake knife, neatly trim off the ends of the cake. Arrange the chocolate shavings on the top and/or down the sides, if using. Serve the cake at once, or refrigerate in an airtight container for up to 3 days. Let stand at room temperature for 5 minutes before serving.

Classic Chocolate Cake

4 oz (125 g) semisweet (plain) chocolate, finely chopped

$^1/_2$ cup (4 fl oz/125 ml) boiling water

$2^1/_2$ cups (10 oz/315 g) cake (soft-wheat) flour

1 teaspoon baking soda (bicarbonate of soda)

$^1/_2$ teaspoon salt

1 cup (8 oz/250 g) unsalted butter, at room temperature

2 cups (1 lb/500 g) granulated sugar

4 large eggs, separated, at room temperature

1 teaspoon vanilla extract (essence)

1 cup (8 fl oz/250 ml) buttermilk, at room temperature

For the chocolate frosting

$1^1/_2$ lb (750 g) bittersweet chocolate, finely chopped

2 cups (1 lb/500 g) unsalted butter, at room temperature

3 cups (12 oz/375 g) confectioners' (icing) sugar

2 teaspoons vanilla extract (essence)

Position a rack in the middle of the oven, and preheat to 350°F (180°C). Butter two 9-inch (23-cm) round cake pans. Line the bottoms with circles of parchment (baking) paper cut to fit (page 10). Butter the paper and dust the bottoms and sides of the pans with flour.

Place the chopped chocolate in a small, heatproof bowl. Pour the boiling water over the chocolate and stir to melt. Set aside to cool.

Sift together the flour, baking soda, and salt onto a sheet of parchment paper or onto a plate. Set aside.

BY HAND: In a large, deep bowl, combine the butter and granulated sugar. Using a sturdy wire whisk, whisk vigorously until the mixture is light in color and fluffy, about 5 minutes. Whisk in the egg yolks and vanilla, then whisk in the cooled chocolate mixture.

BY MIXER: In a large bowl, combine the butter and granulated sugar. Using a stand mixer fitted with the paddle attachment or a hand mixer, beat on medium-high speed until the mixture is light in color and fluffy, about 5 minutes. Beat in the egg yolks and vanilla, then beat in the cooled chocolate mixture. Remove the bowl from the mixer.

Using a rubber spatula, gently fold in one-third of the dry ingredients until almost fully incorporated. Fold in one-half of the buttermilk, then fold in another third of the dry ingredients, followed by the remaining buttermilk. Add the remaining dry ingredients and, using a light lifting motion and turning the bowl continuously, fold in until the batter is smooth and the dry ingredients are thoroughly incorporated. Do not fold too vigorously, or the cake will be tough.

In a clean bowl, using a balloon whisk, a stand mixer fitted with the whip attachment, or a hand mixer, beat the egg whites until medium peaks form (page 27). The whites should fall over gently when the whisk or beaters are lifted. Using a rubber spatula, gently fold the egg whites into the batter.

Pour the batter into the prepared pans, dividing it evenly. Bake the cake layers until a toothpick inserted into the center of a layer comes out clean, 30–35 minutes.

This dramatically tall cake pays tribute to the recipient. Dress up this moist and chocolatey special-occasion dessert with some chocolate shavings (pages 21 and 212), party candles, and, of course, a scoop of vanilla bean ice cream. For an even more elaborate—and more chocolatey—presentation, try the Decadent Mocha Cake variation. It is a bit more time-consuming to make, but it is guaranteed to please even the most discriminating chocolate connoisseur.

VARIATION

Decadent Mocha Cake

Prepare the cake and frosting as directed. Prepare the Mocha Ganache Mousse (page 240). To assemble the cake (pages 209–10), cut each layer in half horizontally, for a total of 4 layers. Using an icing spatula, evenly spread equal amounts of the mousse between the layers. Transfer the cake to a serving plate. Frost the sides and top of the cake with a thin, smooth layer of the frosting. Refrigerate the cake for 30 minutes. Make the Chocolate Glaze (page 308) and cool slightly. Place the layered and frosted cake on a rack and glaze the cake (page 211). Serve slices of the cake with Raspberry Coulis (page 306).

Transfer to wire racks and let cool in the pans for 5 minutes. Place a wire rack on top of a cake and invert them together. Lift off the pan and peel off the parchment. Repeat with the remaining cake layer. Let cool completely on the racks. Cover the cake layers with a clean, slightly damp kitchen towel so that the outsides do not dry out as they cool.

To make the chocolate frosting, place the chocolate and butter in the top of a double boiler placed over (not touching) barely simmering water. Heat, stirring often, until the butter and chocolate melt (page 21). Remove from over the water and set aside to cool and thicken for about 10 minutes. Sift the confectioners' sugar onto a plate, then whisk it into the chocolate along with the vanilla.

To assemble the cake (pages 209–10), cut each layer in half horizontally, for a total of 4 layers. Using an icing spatula, spread equal amounts of the chocolate frosting between the layers. Transfer the cake to a serving plate, then frost the sides and top. Serve at once, or store in an airtight container at room temperature for up to 1 day.

Flourless Chocolate Cake

Keep it simple when serving this sinfully rich chocolate cake. A light shower of confectioners' sugar and a dollop of whipped cream are all that it needs. Depending on your taste, you can use all semisweet or all bittersweet chocolate in the recipe. In either case, make sure to purchase the highest-quality chocolate you can find.

Position a rack in the middle of the oven, and preheat to 300°F (150°C). Butter the bottom and sides of a 9-inch (23-cm) springform pan. Line the bottom with a circle of parchment (baking) paper cut to fit (page 10). In a food processor or blender, process together the nuts and granulated sugar until powdery.

Place the chocolates and butter in the top of a double boiler placed over (not touching) barely simmering water. Heat, stirring often, until the butter and chocolate melt (page 21). Remove from over the water.

BY HAND: In a bowl, using a balloon whisk, beat the egg whites until soft peaks form (page 27). Do not overwhip the whites, or the cake will be dry.

BY MIXER: In a bowl, using a stand mixer fitted with the whip attachment or a hand mixer, beat the egg whites on medium-high speed until soft peaks form (page 27).

Whisk the egg yolks into the chocolate. Using a rubber spatula, stir one-fourth of the whites into the chocolate mixture. Gently fold in the ground nut mixture. Add the remaining egg whites, folding gently and thoroughly. Pour the batter into the prepared pan, using the spatula to scrape all of it into the pan.

Bake the cake until it puffs up a little and jiggles only very slightly when the pan is gently shaken, 30–35 minutes. If the center looks soupy, bake for another 5 minutes. Transfer to a wire rack and let cool in the pan for 3 minutes, then release and lift off the pan sides. Using an icing spatula, gently slide the cake from the bottom of the pan onto a cardboard cake circle or serving plate. Be careful, as the cake is very fragile when warm. Place on a rack and let cool completely. Cover the cake with a clean, slightly damp kitchen towel so that the outside does not dry out as it cools.

Using a fine-mesh sieve, dust the top of the cooled cake with confectioners' sugar. Serve each slice with a dollop of whipped cream, if desired. Store in an airtight container at room temperature for up to 1 day.

1/2 cup (2 oz/60 g) walnuts or whole, unblanched almonds

1/2 cup (4 oz/125 g) granulated sugar

5 oz (155 g) semisweet (plain) chocolate, finely chopped

5 oz (155 g) bittersweet chocolate, finely chopped

1/2 cup (4 oz/125 g) unsalted butter

8 large eggs, separated, at room temperature

Confectioners' (icing) sugar for dusting

Whipped Cream (page 306), optional

Chocolate-Raspberry Torte

1 cup (5 oz/155 g) all-purpose (plain) flour

8 oz (250 g) bittersweet chocolate

³/₄ cup (6 oz/185 g) unsalted butter

1 cup (8 oz/250 g) sugar

6 large eggs, separated, at room temperature

1 cup (10 oz/310 g) seedless raspberry preserves

Chocolate Glaze (page 308)

Raspberry Whipped Cream (page 306), optional

Position a rack in the middle of the oven, and preheat to 350°F (180°C). Butter the bottom and sides of a 9-inch (23-cm) springform pan. Line the bottom with a circle of parchment (baking) paper cut to fit (page 10). Sift the flour onto a piece of parchment paper or onto a plate. Set aside.

Place the chocolate and butter in the top of a double boiler placed over (not touching) barely simmering water. Heat, stirring often, until the butter and chocolate melt (page 21). Remove from over the water. Whisk ¹/₂ cup (4 oz/125 g) of the sugar into the egg yolks, then stir the egg mixture into the melted chocolate.

BY HAND: In a bowl, using a balloon whisk, beat the egg whites until soft peaks form, while slowly adding the remaining ¹/₂ cup sugar (page 27).

BY MIXER: Using a stand mixer fitted with the whip attachment or a hand mixer, beat the egg whites on medium-high speed until soft peaks form, while slowly adding the remaining ¹/₂ cup sugar (page 27).

Using a rubber spatula, stir one-fourth of the whites into the chocolate mixture. Gently fold in the flour. Add the remaining egg whites, folding gently and thoroughly. Scrape the batter into the prepared pan using the spatula.

Bake the cake until it puffs up and feels firm to the touch in the center, 25–30 minutes. If the center looks soupy, bake for another for 5 minutes. Transfer to a wire rack and let cool in the pan for 3 minutes, then release and lift off the pan sides. Place a wire rack on top of the cake and carefully invert them together. Lift off the pan bottom and peel off the parchment. Gently turn the cake back over onto another rack and let cool completely. Cover the cake with a clean, slightly damp kitchen towel so that the outside does not dry out as it cools.

To assemble the cake (pages 209–10), put it on a 9-inch (23-cm) cardboard circle and cut in half horizontally. Remove the top half. Using an icing spatula, spread ¹/₃ cup (4 oz/125 g) of the preserves on the bottom layer. Replace the top round. Spread the remaining preserves over the top and sides of the cake. Refrigerate the cake for 30 minutes to firm up the preserves. Meanwhile, make the chocolate glaze.

Glaze the cake with the warm chocolate glaze (page 211). Refrigerate the cake for 30 minutes to set the glaze. Scrape up any drippings from the sheet pan, rewarm the glaze, and add a second coat. When the glaze sets up slightly, transfer the cake to a serving plate. Serve immediately with the whipped cream.

The inspiration for this cake comes from the Sachertorte, a famous chocolate cake that was created in the kitchen of Vienna's renowned Hotel Sacher. The dense cake is coated with apricot preserves and then topped with a chocolate glaze. This version features raspberry preserves, which provide a good counterpoint to the intense chocolate. Traditionally, Sachertorte is eaten with lots of whipped cream. Here, raspberry-flavored whipped cream adds extra interest to the plate.

Lemon Ricotta Cheesecake

Light and subtle and not too sweet, this cheesecake is very Italian. You can substitute the same amount of orange zest and candied peel for the lemon zest and peel. Serve slices of the cheesecake with fresh raspberries and blueberries, or dress it up with Berry Coulis (page 306).

BY HAND: To make the crust, in a bowl, combine the flour, sugar, baking powder, salt, and lemon zest. Using a pastry blender or your fingers, cut in the butter until the mixture resembles coarse crumbs the size of small peas. Pour in the cream and continue to work in with the pastry blender or with a fork until the mixture is light yellow but crumbly.

BY FOOD PROCESSOR: To make the crust, combine the flour, sugar, baking powder, salt, and lemon zest. Pulse briefly to mix. Add the butter and pulse just until the mixture looks crumbly. Pour in the cream and continue to pulse just until the mixture is light yellow but still crumbly. Do not pulse too long, or the mixture will come together into a dough.

Measure out 1 cup (3 oz/90 g) of the crust mixture (to be used as topping), and set aside in a bowl in the freezer until needed. Pour the remaining crust mixture into a 9-inch (23-cm) springform pan. Using your hand, press the mixture evenly onto the bottom and halfway up the sides of the pan. Place the crust in the refrigerator while you make the filling.

Position a rack in the lower third of the oven, and preheat to 350°F (180°C).

BY HAND: To make the filling, press the ricotta through a fine-mesh sieve placed over a bowl. Using a sturdy wire whisk, stir in the sugar until the mixture is creamy. Whisk in the eggs, then stir in the crème fraîche, vanilla, flour, cinnamon, and lemon zest, mixing well.

BY FOOD PROCESSOR: To make the filling, combine the ricotta and the sugar. Process until the mixture is creamy. Add the eggs, crème fraîche, vanilla, flour, cinnamon, and lemon zest and pulse to mix well.

Remove the crust from the refrigerator and immediately pour the filling into it, using a rubber spatula to scrape all of it into the pan. Sprinkle the frozen crust crumbs evenly over the surface. Bake the cheesecake until the crust is golden, the filling puffs up slightly, and the center jiggles very slightly when the pan is gently shaken, 45–50 minutes. If the center looks soupy, continue to bake for a few more minutes. Transfer to a wire rack and let cool completely.

To unmold, set the cheesecake on an inverted tall, narrow can or bowl. Release the pan sides, opening them widely and carefully so that they fall away from the cake. Set the cheesecake on a serving plate. Serve at room temperature. Store in an airtight container in the refrigerator for up to 2 days. Bring to room temperature before serving.

For the crust

2 cups (10 oz/315 g) all-purpose (plain) flour

1/4 cup (2 oz/60 g) sugar

1/2 teaspoon baking powder

1/4 teaspoon salt

Grated zest of 1 lemon

3/4 cup (6 oz/185 g) cold unsalted butter, cut into 3/4-inch (2-cm) pieces

1/4 cup (2 fl oz/60 ml) heavy (double) cream

For the filling

2 cups (15 oz/470 g) whole-milk or part-skim ricotta cheese

1/2 cup (4 oz/125 g) sugar

2 large eggs

1/3 cup (3 fl oz/80 ml) crème fraîche (page 20) or heavy (double) cream

1 teaspoon vanilla extract (essence)

1 tablespoon all-purpose (plain) flour

1/4 teaspoon ground cinnamon

Grated zest of 3 lemons

1/4 cup (1 1/2 oz/45 g) candied lemon peel, minced

Vanilla Bean Cheesecake

For the crust

1 cup (3 oz/90 g) honey graham cracker crumbs (about 5 crackers)

4 tablespoons (2 oz/60 g) unsalted butter, melted

2 tablespoons sugar

$1/4$ teaspoon freshly grated nutmeg

$1/2$ cup (2 oz/60 g) walnuts, pecans, or almonds

For the filling

2 lb (1 kg) cream cheese, at room temperature

1 cup (8 oz/250 g) sugar

3 large eggs, at room temperature

2 vanilla beans, split lengthwise

Juice of 1 lemon, strained

2 teaspoons vanilla extract (essence)

For the topping

2 cups (16 fl oz/500 ml) sour cream

$1/4$ cup (2 oz/60 g) sugar

1 vanilla bean, split lengthwise

To make the crust, position a rack in the middle of the oven, and preheat to 350°F (180°C). Line a half-sheet pan with parchment (baking) paper. In a food processor or blender, combine the cracker crumbs, butter, sugar, nutmeg, and nuts. Process until mixed thoroughly.

Butter the bottom and sides of a 9-inch (23-cm) springform pan. Pour the crumb mixture into the pan and, using your hand, press it evenly into the pan bottom. Bake the crust until it is a little bit darker brown and smooths out, 10–12 minutes. Transfer to a wire rack and let cool completely.

Reduce the heat to 325°F (165°C).

BY HAND: To make the filling, in a large bowl, combine the cream cheese and sugar. Using a sturdy wire whisk, beat together until smooth and creamy, about 5 minutes. Add the eggs one at a time, beating gently but thoroughly after each addition. Try to incorporate as little air as possible. Using the tip of a small knife, scrape out the tiny seeds from the inside of each vanilla bean (page 19). Add to the cream cheese mixture along with the lemon juice and vanilla. Continue to whisk the mixture until it is smooth, creamy, and free of lumps.

BY MIXER: To make the filling, in a large bowl, using a stand mixer fitted with the paddle attachment or a hand mixer, mix the cream cheese on low speed until creamy. Add the sugar and mix slowly until smooth. Turn off the mixer and scrape down the bowl and beater with a rubber spatula. On low speed, add the eggs one at a time, beating gently after each addition. Scrape down the bowl again. Using the tip of a small knife, scrape out the tiny seeds from the inside of each vanilla bean (page 19). Add to the cream cheese mixture along with the lemon juice and vanilla. Mix again on the lowest speed until smooth and creamy.

It is important to whip as little air into the mixture as possible to prevent the cheesecake from sinking in the middle once it is baked.

Place the cooled crust on the prepared half-sheet pan and pour the batter into the crust. Cover the cake pan with a pot lid or another sheet pan to insulate the cake while it bakes. Bake the cheesecake until the center jiggles very slightly when the pan is gently shaken, 45–50 minutes. If the center looks soupy, re-cover the cheesecake and continue to bake for a few more minutes.

Even people who say they seldom eat dessert always seem to have room for cheesecake. This version of an American classic is a beauty. Its satiny texture and color come from proper mixing and a generous dose of vanilla. Let the cream cheese sit out for several hours or overnight so that it reaches true room temperature, to ensure even mixing. Serve plain or with fresh berries scattered on the plate.

Meanwhile, make the topping. In a small bowl, combine the sour cream and sugar. Scrape the seeds from the vanilla bean and add to the bowl. Stir well. Cover with plastic wrap and set aside at room temperature until needed.

Remove the cheesecake from the oven and uncover it. Carefully pour the topping around the edge of the cheesecake. Using a small offset spatula, gently spread the topping out evenly over the entire surface of the hot cheesecake. Do not press down too hard, or the topping will sink into the cake.

Re-cover the cheesecake, return it to the oven, and bake for another 5 minutes just to set the topping. Transfer the cheesecake to a rack and let cool, covered, for 1–2 hours. Remove the lid or sheet pan. Cover the cooled cheesecake with a 10-inch (25-cm) cardboard circle covered with plastic wrap or with a large, flat plate. Refrigerate overnight.

To unmold, set the cheesecake on a tall, narrow can or on a bowl. Release the pan sides, opening them widely so that they fall away from the cake. Set the cheesecake on a serving plate and serve chilled. Store in an airtight container in the refrigerator for up to 5 days.

Pastries

About Pastries

Puff pastry, Danish pastry, and croissant doughs are versatile, offering myriad possibilities for sweet and savory treats. All three doughs bake up into hundreds of delicate layers of buttery pastry. Choux and filo are building blocks for other treats that round out the pastry repertoire.

There are subtle differences among puff pastry, Danish pastry, and croissant doughs, primarily that croissant and Danish are yeasted doughs and puff pastry is not. More similarities unite them, however, the most important of which is that they are made by repeatedly rolling and folding a flexible, cool block of butter into a tender dough, the *détrempe*, until the butter is divided into scores of layers within the mass. This technique is known as laminating, and when the dough is baked, the water in the butter turns into steam, causing the layers to rise and create a light and flaky pastry.

Working a block of butter into a mound of flour is one of the most masterful turns of hand in all of pastry making. And the result of that hard, skilled work, puff pastry, is one of the best loved of all desserts. Buttery, flaky, multilayered puff pastry is arguably the queen of pastries. it can serve as a base for a tart, a wrapper for a turnover, the layers of a napoleon, or big or small cases for savory or sweet fillings. Classic puff pastry will give the baker the most layers, but it is time-consuming to make. Quick puff pastry, which requires fewer turns, also results in fewer layers, but still delivers respectable results. The recipes in this chapter are just a starting point for your exploration into the world of puff pastry.

Danish and croissant doughs are yeast-raised doughs that require a series of techniques similar to those used for making puff pastry. Also, like puff pastry, these doughs can be shaped in many ways—pinwheels, braids, crescents, oblongs—and paired with many different fillings—chocolate, cheese, fruit, pastry cream, frangipane, jam. Yet regardless of shape or filling, the best examples always result in finished pastries that shatter into flaky, delicious shards when you break into them.

Choux pastry is less buttery than other pastry doughs, but just as delectable, rising into rich puffs in the oven. The dough is soft enough to be piped, yet bakes into crisp, irregular-shaped, hollow shells. It is the base for éclairs, profiteroles, cream puffs, and the savory French cheese-flavored cream puffs known as *gougères*.

Filo pastry, big, paper-thin sheets of dough, is the pastry maker's key to baklava and strudel and one of the few instances in which opting for a commercial product is perfectly acceptable—and more practical. The delicate sheets need careful handling, however: You must bring them to room temperature, keep them covered to prevent them from drying out, and work quickly.

Nearly everyone thinks of homemade pastries, whether a chocolate éclair, an apple turnover, a cheese Danish, or a wedge of strudel, as something special, and thinks of the pastry maker as an artist.

TROUBLESHOOTING PASTRIES

What happened	Why it happened
Pastry dough is sticky and hard to roll out.	Butter in pastry dough is too warm; chill pastry in refrigerator for 30 minutes before proceeding.
Pastries are browning too quickly.	Oven is too hot; cover loosely with aluminum foil and continue baking.
Pastries did not rise or did not develop distinctive layers in oven.	Butter was too warm when rolling and folding pastry dough and layers stuck together, or butter was too cold and did not form layers.
Dough for choux is too stiff to pipe.	Dough has cooled off too much, or there is not enough egg in it; remake the dough.
Choux are not puffing up in oven.	Oven is not hot enough.
Choux puffs are tough, not tender.	Dough was overworked, or too much egg was added.
Filo sheets are dry and cracking.	Filo sheets were left uncovered; always keep sheets covered with a kitchen towel until needed to prevent drying.

Rolling and Folding Techniques for Pastries

Puff pastry, Danish pastry, and croissant doughs are laminated; that is, a tender dough is repeatedly rolled and folded with a butter block until the butter is divided into scores of layers within the mass. These techniques will show you how to insert the butter and roll and fold the dough.

The following technique is one of a variety of ways you can insert the butter block into the dough. You will find that each of the master recipes for laminated doughs in this chapter contains a slightly different technique. These variations illustrate the range of methods possible, but the general rules remain the same. The dimensions given here for the square and rectangle are for a dough that calls for 1 pound (500 g) butter. You will need to adjust them for smaller or larger amounts. Regardless of the amounts, the butter square shaped in step 2 should always be $^3/_4$ inch (2 cm) thick.

TO INSERT THE BUTTER BLOCK

1 Using a rolling pin or the heel of your hand, beat or knead the butter on a clean work surface to flatten it and warm it until it is pliable, about 60°F (16°C). Sprinkle the butter with 2 tablespoons flour and gently beat the butter with the rolling pin to press the flour into the butter.

2 Shape the butter into a 6-inch (15-cm) square about $^3/_4$ inch (2 cm) thick. If the butter has become too warm, wrap and refrigerate just until firm but still pliable (60°F/16°C), 5 minutes.

3 Remove the dough disk from the refrigerator. On a lightly floured work surface, roll out the dough into a 12-inch (30-cm) square.

4 Place the butter at a diagonal in the center of the dough.

5 Fold over the corners of the dough to meet in the center, covering the butter completely. Pat the dough with your hands to form an 8-inch (20-cm) square.

TO LAMINATE THE DOUGH

Once you have inserted the butter block, you are only a series of rolls and folds away from your end result. Each recipe differs in the number of times you are required to roll and fold the dough, so check the recipe before you begin.

1 Place the 8-inch (20 cm) square dough package seam side down and roll out into a rectangle 24 inches (60 cm) long by 8 inches (20 cm) wide.

2 The dough is then folded into thirds. Fold the bottom third (narrow end) of the rectangle up past the center of the rectangle.

3 Then fold the top third down, as if folding a letter. Rotate the dough a quarter turn clockwise so that a fold is on your left. This is the first turn. Wrap the dough in plastic wrap and refrigerate for 20–30 minutes. Remove the dough from the refrigerator and repeat the 3 steps—rolling it into the rectangle, folding it into thirds, and wrapping and chilling—to complete 3 to 5 additional turns. Each time you start, make sure you have a fold on your left. After the final turn, wrap the dough in plastic wrap, place in a plastic bag, and refrigerate for at least 4 hours or for up to overnight before shaping.

■ Be sure the dough stays cool. If the butter starts to ooze, return the dough to the refrigerator immediately. This will help keep the butter layers intact.

■ When rolling out the dough, keep the overall thickness even, avoid rolling over the ends of the dough, and work neatly, making sure the edges of your rectangle are straight and parallel.

■ Always give the dough the number of turns called for in the recipe.

MASTER RECIPE Classic Puff Pastry

For the puff dough

3 cups (15 oz/470 g) unbleached all-purpose (plain) flour

1 cup (4 oz/125 g) cake (soft-wheat) flour

1 teaspoon salt

2 tablespoons cold unsalted butter, cut into 1/2-inch (12-mm) pieces

1 cup (8 fl oz/250 ml) ice water, or as needed

For the butter package

1 lb (500 g) unsalted butter

2 tablespoons unbleached all-purpose (plain) flour

BY HAND: In a large bowl, stir together the flours and the salt. Scatter the butter pieces over the flour and work in with your fingers until the mixture is crumbly. Make a well in the center and pour the ice water into the well. Using a wooden spoon, gradually stir in the flour from the sides of the bowl until fully incorporated and a rough mass that holds together forms. If the dough does not hold together easily, slowly add additional ice water, 1 tablespoon at a time.

BY STAND MIXER: In the large bowl of a stand mixer fitted with the dough hook, combine 2 cups (10 oz/315 g) of the all-purpose flour and the salt. Pour in the ice water and mix on low speed until a smooth batter forms. Scatter the butter pieces over the surface. With the mixer on medium-low speed, add the remaining all-purpose flour and cake flour, 1/2 cup (2 1/2 oz/75 g) at a time, until the dough comes away from the sides of the bowl, about 5 minutes.

Turn the dough out onto a lightly floured work surface and knead for 15–20 seconds to make sure it is smooth and not sticky. Flatten the dough, shape into a rectangle, wrap in plastic wrap, place in a plastic bag, and refrigerate for at least 1 hour or for up to overnight.

To make the butter package (page 256), using a rolling pin or the heel of your hand, beat or knead the butter on a work surface to flatten and warm it until it is cool and pliable, about 60°F (16°C). Sprinkle the butter with the flour and gently beat the butter with the rolling pin to press the flour into the butter. Shape the butter into a 6-inch (15-cm) square about 3/4 inch (2 cm) thick. If the butter has become too warm, wrap and refrigerate just until firm but still pliable (60°F/16°C).

To laminate the dough (page 257), on a lightly floured work surface, roll out the dough into a 12-inch (30-cm) square. Place the butter at a diagonal in the center of the dough. Fold over the corners of the dough to meet in the center, covering the butter completely. Pat with your hands to form an 8-inch (20-cm) square, then turn the square over so the seams are underneath. Roll out into a rectangle 24 inches (60 cm) long by about 8 inches (20 cm) wide, with a short side facing you. Fold the bottom third up, then fold the top third down, as if folding a letter. This is the first turn. Rotate the dough a quarter turn clockwise so that a fold is on your left. Wrap the dough in plastic wrap and refrigerate for 20–30 minutes. Repeat to make 5 more turns, rolling, folding, and chilling the dough each time, for a total of 6 turns. Each time you start, make sure you have a fold on your left. After the final turn, wrap the dough in plastic wrap, place in a plastic bag, and refrigerate for at least 4 hours or for up to overnight before shaping.

When making this versatile pastry dough, the temperature of the butter and the dough is critical for success. If either warms too much, the pastry will not have the desired flaky character when it is baked. If the butter softens or the dough gets sticky as you work with it, refrigerate it immediately. Try to purchase a block of butter, rather than sticks, to make it easier to form the butter package. It takes a little time and patience to make this dough, but the end result is a light, flaky pastry that is unmatched by faster methods. All of the puff pastry recipes in this book call for 1 lb (500 g) of dough, or half of this recipe. Puff pastry is easily stored for later use. Simply cut the finished dough into quarters, wrap tightly with plastic wrap, place in a zippered plastic bag, and freeze for up to 1 month.

MASTER RECIPE Quick Puff Pastry

1¹/₂ cups (7¹/₂ oz/235 g) unbleached all-purpose (plain) flour

¹/₂ cup (2 oz/60 g) cake (soft-wheat) flour

¹/₂ teaspoon salt

¹/₂ lb (250 g) cold unsalted butter, cut into ¹/₂-inch (12-mm) pieces

¹/₂ cup (4 fl oz/125 ml) ice water

BY HAND: In a bowl, stir together the flours and the salt. Using a pastry blender or 2 knives, cut in the butter until the mixture forms large, coarse crumbs the size of large peas. Sprinkle the ice water over the surface and toss and stir with a wooden spoon or a rubber spatula until it is absorbed. With your hands, pat the mixture into a loose ball.

BY FOOD PROCESSOR: Combine the flours and the salt and process briefly to mix. Scatter the butter over the flour and pulse about 10 times until the mixture forms large, coarse crumbs the size of large peas. Pour in the water and pulse 2 or 3 times until the dough starts to gather together, but before it forms a ball.

BY STAND MIXER: In the bowl of a stand mixer fitted with the paddle attachment, stir together the flours and salt. Scatter the butter over the flour and mix on low speed until the butter is coated with flour. Pour in the water and mix just until the water is absorbed and the butter is still in large pieces.

If you don't have time to make classic puff pastry dough, this is a great alternative. This fast, easy pastry goes together in minutes in a food processor and only a little longer if mixing by hand or in a stand mixer. Use a long metal spatula or a ruler to smooth and straighten the sides of the dough as you roll it into a large rectangle.

Transfer the dough to a lightly floured work surface, dust the top lightly with flour, and pat into a rectangle ³/₄-inch (2-cm) thick. Roll out the dough into a rectangle 12 inches (30 cm) long, about 7 inches (18 cm) wide, and ¹/₂ inch (12 mm) thick.

With a short side facing you, fold the bottom third up, then fold the top third down, as if folding a letter. Rotate the dough a quarter turn clockwise (so a seam is on your left) and repeat the process, rolling the dough into a 12-by-7-inch (30-by-18-cm) rectangle and folding into thirds. Repeat the process a third time.

If at any time the dough begins to warm up and the butter begins to soften, place the dough in the refrigerator to chill for 20–30 minutes. After the third and final turn, wrap the dough in plastic wrap, place in a plastic bag, and refrigerate for at least 4 hours or for up to overnight before shaping.

For longer storage, cut the puff into quarters, wrap tightly with plastic wrap, place in an airtight plastic bag, and freeze for up to 1 month.

Apple Turnovers

In the fall, when apple orchards are ready for harvest, these flaky triangular pastries—the perfect size to eat out of hand—are a good way to use some of the bounty. In the summertime, fresh apricots, berries, peaches, or nectarines can replace the apples.

You will need about 4 cups (1–1 1/2 lb/500–750 g) total.

Prepare the Puff Pastry and refrigerate to chill as directed.

Line a half-sheet pan or rimless baking sheet with parchment (baking) paper.

On a floured work surface, roll out the chilled pastry dough into a 9-by-18-inch (23-by-45-cm) rectangle. Cut in half lengthwise, and then cut each half crosswise into 4 squares, for a total of 8 squares. Place the squares on the prepared pan, cover with waxed paper, and refrigerate while preparing the filling.

To make the filling, in a large frying pan over medium-high heat, melt the butter. Add the apples and sauté until tender, 5–7 minutes. Sprinkle with the granulated sugar and brandy and sauté, stirring, for 1–2 minutes longer. Remove from the heat and let cool.

Remove the chilled puff pastry squares from the refrigerator and spread out on a clean work surface. Using a pastry brush, brush the surface of each square with some of the egg mixture, leaving a 1/4-inch (6-mm) border around the edge. Place 2 tablespoons of the filling almost in the middle of each square, fold over to make a triangle, and press the edges together with the tines of a fork to seal. Place on the prepared baking sheet. Repeat with the remaining squares and filling. Cover with waxed paper and refrigerate for 30 minutes.

Position a rack in the middle of the oven, and preheat to 425°F (220°C).

Brush the tops of the pastries with the remaining egg mixture and sprinkle with the sugar. Pierce the top of each pastry twice with the tines of a fork. Bake the turnovers for 20 minutes. Reduce the heat to 350°F (180°C) and continue baking until golden brown and puffed, 15–20 minutes longer. Transfer to a wire rack and let cool on the pan for 15 minutes. Serve warm. Store in an airtight container at room temperature for up to 2 days.

1 lb (500 g) Classic Puff Pastry (page 258) or Quick Puff Pastry (page 260)

For the filling

2 tablespoons unsalted butter

4 large tart apples such as Granny Smith or pippin, about 1 3/4 lbs (28 oz/875 g) total weight, peeled, cored, and thinly sliced

1/4 cup (2 oz/60 g) granulated sugar

2 teaspoons apple brandy or fresh lemon juice

1 large egg, beaten with 1 tablespoon whole milk

1/3 cup (3 oz/90 g) granulated or coarse sugar for topping

Cheese Straws

1 lb (500 g) Classic Puff Pastry (page 258) or Quick Puff Pastry (page 260)

$2/3$ cup ($2^1/2$ oz/75 g) coarsely grated Parmesan cheese

1 large egg, beaten

Coarse sea salt and freshly ground pepper

Prepare the Puff Pastry and refrigerate to chill as directed.

Line a half-sheet pan with parchment (baking) paper. On a lightly floured work surface, roll out the chilled pastry dough $1/2$ inch (12 mm) thick. Carefully lift the pastry and set aside. Remove any dusting flour from the work surface. Sprinkle the work surface with a light dusting of some of the cheese.

Return the pastry to the work surface and roll it out into a 14-inch (35-cm) square about $1/8$ inch (3 mm) thick. Brush the half of the pastry farthest from you with some of the beaten egg, and sprinkle half of the remaining cheese over the egg-brushed surface. Season with salt and pepper. Fold the bottom half of the pastry up over the cheese and press the edges to seal. Roll the rolling pin lightly over the pastry. Brush the pastry with the rest of the egg and sprinkle with the remaining cheese.

Cut the pastry vertically into strips $1/2$ inch (12 mm) wide. Pick up each strip and twist the ends in opposite directions 4 or 5 times to make a spiral. Place the strips on the prepared half-sheet pan, spacing them 1 inch (2.5 cm) apart, and press the ends down to seal. Cover the pan with parchment and refrigerate for 45 minutes.

Position a rack in the middle of the oven, and preheat to 400°F (200°C). Bake the twists until golden brown, 13–17 minutes. Transfer to a wire rack and let cool completely in the pan. Store in an airtight container at room temperature for up to 5 days.

Use a top-quality Parmesan such as Parmigiano-Reggiano for these ethereal savory twists. Freshly ground sea salt and black pepper will also enhance the flavor-packed bites. Be sure to refrigerate the twists until chilled before baking them. The delicate pastry spirals need time to rest, or they will unwind when they hit the hot oven.

Palmiers

Folds of sugar-coated puff pastry unfurl during baking to form these caramelized cookies, one of the best-loved French puff pastry treats. Sometimes known as pig's ears or, when large, elephant's ears, they come in all sizes, but diminutive ones are lovely for teatime or snacking.

Prepare the Puff Pastry and refrigerate to chill as directed.

On a lightly sugared work surface, roll out the pastry dough into a rectangle $^1/_2$ inch (12 mm) thick. Move the pastry to the side and sprinkle the work surface with more sugar.

Return the pastry to the work surface and roll it out into a rectangle 10 inches (45 cm) long, 9 inches (23 cm) wide, and $^1/_4$ inch (6 mm) thick, turning it once or twice as you roll and dusting with more of the sugar.

Position the pastry so that the long side is in front of you. Fold one long end over onto itself halfway across the pastry. Fold the opposite end onto itself halfway across the pastry so that the two ends meet in the center of the rectangle. Sprinkle the pastry with more sugar. Roll the pin across the pastry lightly and sprinkle again with sugar. Fold each long side lengthwise again onto itself so they meet in the center of the rectangle, and roll the pin across the pastry lightly.

Using a pastry brush, brush the egg mixture lightly over half of the folded pastry rectangle. You will not use all of the egg mixture. Fold the egg-brushed half over onto the other half of the pastry to form a long, thick rectangle. Roll the pin across the pastry lightly to seal. Place the rectangle on a half-sheet pan, cover with parchment (baking) paper, and refrigerate until well chilled, at least 45 minutes.

Position 2 racks evenly in the oven, and preheat to 400°F (200°C). Line 2 half-sheet pans with parchment (baking) paper.

Place the pastry on a cutting board and cut crosswise into slices $^1/_4$ inch (6 mm) thick. Dust the work surface with sugar. Lay a cut side of a slice on the sugared surface and then flip it over to coat the other cut side. Place the slices cut side down on the prepared pan, spacing them 2 inches (5 cm) apart.

Bake the cookies until they are caramelized and brown, 13–17 minutes, turning once halfway through baking to ensure even caramelization. Transfer to wire racks and let cool completely in the pans. Store in an airtight container at room temperature for up to 5 days.

1 lb (500 g) Classic Puff Pastry (page 258) or Quick Puff Pastry (page 260)

1 cup (8 oz/250 g) sugar for dusting

1 large egg beaten with 1 tablespoon water

Strawberry Napoleons

For this impressive dessert, sheets of puff pastry are sandwiched with whipped cream and sugared berries—a lighter version of the classic napoleon. The filling contains just a hint of framboise, a raspberry liqueur. In France, this multilayered treat is known as *mille feuille*; it is typically filled with Pastry Cream (page 309) and drizzled with Vanilla Glaze (page 68) and zigzags of melted chocolate (page 21). Once you have the method down, experiment with the same amount of other fruits, such as poached pears or apricots, mixed berries, or caramelized banana slices.

Prepare the Puff Pastry and refrigerate to chill as directed.

Line a 9-inch (23-cm) square baking pan with parchment (baking) paper.

On a lightly floured work surface, roll out the chilled pastry 1/8 inch (3 mm) thick. Let it rest for a few minutes to relax. Using a ruler and a sharp knife, trim the pastry to fit the prepared pan. Carefully drape the pastry over the rolling pin and transfer it to the pan. Press the pastry into the bottom of the prepared pan. Pierce the surface of the pastry at 1/2- to 1-inch (12-mm to 2.5-cm) intervals with the tines of a fork. Cover the pastry with waxed paper and refrigerate for 1 hour.

Position a rack in the middle of the oven, and preheat to 400°F (200°C). Bake the pastry until golden brown, 20–25 minutes. Transfer to a wire rack and let cool completely in the pan.

To make the filling, in a bowl, whisk the cream until soft peaks form. Beat in the confectioners' sugar and framboise until stiff peaks form (page 27). In another bowl, stir the granulated sugar into the berries. Fold the berries into the cream.

Remove the cooled pastry from the pan by inverting it onto the cooling rack, then place it on a work surface. Using a long, sharp serrated knife, carefully cut the cooled pastry in half. Cut each half into 4 pieces. Spread the filling on half of the pastry pieces. Top with the remaining pieces.

Using a fine-mesh sieve, dust the tops with confectioners' sugar. Refrigerate for at least 20 minutes or for up to 2 hours before serving.

1 lb (500 g) Classic Puff Pastry (page 258) or Quick Puff Pastry (page 260)

For the filling

1 cup (8 fl oz/250 ml) heavy (double) cream

2 tablespoons confectioners' (icing) sugar

1 tablespoon framboise or brandy or 1/2 teaspoon vanilla extract (essence)

3 tablespoons granulated sugar

1 1/2 cups (6 oz/185 g) strawberries, hulled and sliced

Confectioners' (icing) sugar for dusting

MASTER RECIPE Danish Pastry

For the Danish dough

2 packages (5 teaspoons) active dry yeast

$1/3$ cup (3 oz/90 g) sugar

$1/2$ cup (4 fl oz/125 ml) warm water (105–115°F/ 40–46°C)

1 teaspoon salt

$1/2$ teaspoon ground cardamom (optional)

$1/4$ cup (2 oz/60 g) unsalted butter, melted

1 large whole egg, plus 2 large egg yolks

1 cup (8 fl oz/250 ml) whole milk

$1/2$ teaspoon vanilla extract (essence)

$3^1/2$ cups ($17^1/2$ oz/545 g) all-purpose (plain) flour, plus extra as needed

For the butter package

1 cup (8 oz/250 g) unsalted butter

$1/4$ cup ($1^1/2$ oz/45 g) all-purpose (plain) flour

In a small bowl, dissolve the yeast and a pinch of the sugar in the warm water. Let stand until foamy, about 5 minutes.

BY HAND: In a large bowl, using a wire whisk, whisk together the remaining sugar, the salt, cardamom (if using), melted butter, and eggs. Whisk in the milk, vanilla, and the yeast mixture. Using a wooden spoon, gradually stir in the flour, $1/2$ cup ($2^1/2$ oz/75 g) at a time, and mix just until the dough clings together in a rough mass. If the dough is still very soft, add up to $1/4$ cup ($1^1/2$ oz/45 g) additional flour.

BY STAND MIXER: In the bowl of a stand mixer fitted with the paddle attachment, combine the remaining sugar, salt, cardamom (if using), melted butter, eggs, milk, and vanilla and mix on medium speed until combined. Add the yeast mixture and then add the flour, $1/2$ cup ($2^1/2$ oz/75 g) at a time, and mix just until the dough clings together in rough mass. If it is still very soft, add up to $1/4$ cup ($1^1/2$ oz/45 g) flour.

Turn the dough out onto a lightly floured work surface and pat into a rectangle about 1 inch (2.5 cm) thick. Place on a half-sheet pan, cover with plastic wrap, and refrigerate until chilled, about 45 minutes.

To make the butter package (page 256), using a rolling pin or the heel of your hand, beat or knead the butter on a work surface to flatten it and warm it to about 60°F (16°C). Sprinkle the butter with the flour and gently beat the butter with the rolling pin to press the flour into the butter. Shape the butter into an 8-by-7-inch (20-by-18-cm) rectangle. If the butter has become too warm, wrap and refrigerate just until firm but still pliable (60°F/16°C).

To laminate the dough (page 257), on a lightly floured work surface, roll out the dough into a 10-by-16-inch (25-by-40-cm) rectangle. With a short side facing you, place the butter on the lower half, leaving a 1-inch (2.5-cm) border on all sides. Fold over the upper half to cover the butter and press the edges together to seal. Then, with a folded side to your left, roll out the dough into a 12-by-20-inch (30-by-50-cm) rectangle. With a short side facing you, fold the bottom third up, then fold the top third down, as if folding a letter. This completes the first turn. Return to the pan, cover with plastic wrap, and refrigerate for 15 minutes.

Return the chilled dough to the lightly floured work surface with a folded side to your left and repeat the process to make 3 more turns, rolling, folding, and chilling the dough each time, for a total of 4 turns. After the final turn, refrigerate the dough for at least $1^1/2$ hours or for up to overnight before shaping.

Danish pastry is a yeasted dough similar to croissant dough, but enriched with eggs and sugar. Like croissant and puff pastry, the technique of rolling and folding the dough so that it is interlaced with butter creates wonderfully flaky layers. The preparation is easy and fun once mastered, and the dough can be fashioned into a variety of pastries of different shapes. All of the Danish pastry recipes in this book call for 1 lb (500 g) of dough, or half of this recipe. You can use the extra to make pinwheels (page 273) or other shapes and freeze the formed and unbaked pastries. Simply line them up on a half-sheet pan, wrap the pan tightly with plastic wrap, and store in the freezer for up to 1 week. Bring the pastries to room temperature and let them rise to double in size as directed in the recipe before baking.

Apricot Pinwheels

With Danish pastry dough on hand, it is easy to form these delectable pastries. A simple apricot filling makes a bright and tasty center, but you can easily vary the filling by adding a dollop of Pastry Cream (page 309), a spoonful of jam, or both!

Prepare the Danish Pastry Dough and refrigerate to chill as directed.

Line 2 half-sheet pans with parchment (baking) paper, or butter lightly.

To make the apricot filling, in a small saucepan over medium heat, combine the apricots with water to cover. Bring to a simmer and cook until tender, about 15 minutes. Drain, reserving the water. In a food processor, combine the apricots, about 3 tablespoons of the reserved water, the granulated sugar, and the brandy and process to a smooth purée. You should have about 1 cup (8 fl oz/250 ml).

On a lightly floured work surface, roll out the pastry into an 8-by-16-inch (20-by-40-cm) rectangle. Cut in half lengthwise, and then cut each half crosswise into 4 squares, for a total of 8 squares.

Spread about 2 tablespoons of the filling in the center of each square. Using a sharp knife, make a diagonal cut from the corner of each square to within $3/4$ inch (2 cm) of the center. Fold over every other point to the center, overlapping them slightly and sealing the points together with a little of the egg mixture. Place the pastries on the prepared pans, spacing them about 2 inches (5 cm) apart. Place the pans in a warm, draft-free spot, cover them loosely with a kitchen towel, and let the pastries rise until doubled in size, about 45 minutes.

Position a rack in the middle of the oven, and preheat to 425°F (220°C).

Lightly brush the tops of the pastry with the egg mixture. Sprinkle with the coarse sugar, if desired. Bake the pastries, 1 sheet at a time, until golden brown, 15–18 minutes. Transfer to wire racks and let cool completely on the pans. Store in an airtight container at room temperature for up to 1 day.

1 lb (500 g) Danish Pastry Dough (page 270)

For the apricot filling

$2/3$ cup (4 oz/125 g) dried apricots

$1/4$ cup (2 oz/60 g) granulated sugar

1 tablespoon brandy or Cognac

1 egg beaten with 1 tablespoon water

$1/4$ cup (2 oz/60 g) coarse sugar (optional)

Chocolate Danish Braid

1 lb (500 g) Danish Pastry Dough (page 270)

For the filling

¹/₂ cup (4 oz/125 g) granulated sugar

¹/₄ cup (1¹/₂ oz/45 g) all-purpose (plain) flour

2 tablespoons unsalted butter

2 tablespoons Dutch-process cocoa powder

1 teaspoon ground cinnamon

1 large egg white

1 large egg beaten with 1 tablespoon water

Sliced (flaked) almonds and/or coarse sugar or Vanilla Glaze (page 68)

Here, Danish pastry dough encases a chocolate streusel filling in an elaborate lattice-topped braid. This pastry looks complex, but once the dough is made and chilled, the braid is easily shaped by crisscrossing strips of dough over the filling. Use a rimmed half-sheet pan in case the butter oozes out during baking.

Prepare the Danish Pastry Dough and refrigerate to chill as directed.

Line a half-sheet pan with parchment (baking) paper, or butter lightly.

BY HAND: To make the filling, in a bowl, combine the granulated sugar, flour, butter, cocoa, and cinnamon and mix together with a pastry blender or your fingers until fine crumbs form. Stir in the egg white just until evenly blended.

BY FOOD PROCESSOR: To make the filling, combine the granulated sugar, flour, butter, cocoa, and cinnamon. Process until fine crumbs form. Add the egg white and process just until the mixture is evenly blended.

On a lightly floured work surface, roll out the pastry into a rectangle about 14 inches (35 cm) long, 9 inches (23 cm) wide, and ¹/₄ inch (6 mm) thick. Spread the filling down the center third of the rectangle. Using a sharp knife, cut diagonal strips 1¹/₄ inches (3 cm) wide down the outside of the pastry on both sides of the filling, cutting almost through to the filling. Cut off the first and last strip on both sides so that a flap is formed at the top and bottom.

Fold the flaps over onto the filling. Starting at the top, fold the strips over the filling alternately from each side at an angle. When you get to the end, tuck the overhang of the last few strips underneath the braid to form a seal. Using a wide metal spatula, carefully transfer the pastry to the prepared pan. Place in a warm, draft-free spot, cover loosely with a kitchen towel, and let the braid rise until doubled in size, 30–40 minutes.

Position a rack in the middle of the oven, and preheat to 425°F (220°C).

Lightly brush the braid with the egg mixture. Sprinkle with sliced almonds and/or coarse sugar, or leave plain if using the Vanilla Glaze.

Bake the pastry for 15 minutes. Reduce the heat to 375°F (190°C) and continue baking until golden brown and puffed, 15–20 minutes longer. Check the braid during baking, and if it turns brown early, cover with aluminum foil during the last minutes of baking. Transfer to a wire rack and let cool on the pan for 10 minutes, then transfer the braid to the rack and let cool completely. If using, drizzle the braid with Vanilla Glaze just before slicing.

VARIATIONS

Frangipane Danish Braid
Omit the chocolate-streusel filling. Fill the braid with Frangipane (page 309).

Danish Braid with Berry Pastry Cream
Omit the chocolate-streusel filling. Mix ¹/₂ cup (4 fl oz/125 ml) Pastry Cream (page 309) with ¹/₄ cup (2¹/₂ oz/75 g) raspberry or blackberry jam. Fill the braid with the berry pastry cream mixture.

Danish Braid with Apricot Pastry Cream
Omit the chocolate-streusel filling. Mix ¹/₂ cup (4 fl oz/125 ml) Pastry Cream (page 309) with ¹/₄ cup (2 oz/60 ml) Apricot Filling (page 273). Fill the braid with the apricot pastry cream mixture.

MASTER RECIPE Croissants

For the croissant dough

¹/₂ oz (15 g) fresh cake yeast or 2 teaspoons active dry yeast

2 tablespoons sugar

3 tablespoons warm water (105°–115°F/40°–46°C)

1 teaspoon salt

2 tablespoons unsalted butter, melted and cooled

1 cup (8 fl oz/250 ml) cold whole milk

2¹/₂ cups (12¹/₂ oz/390 g) all-purpose (plain) flour

For the butter package

1 cup (8 oz/250 g) unsalted butter

2 tablespoons all-purpose (plain) flour

1 large egg beaten with 1 tablespoon whole milk

In a small bowl, dissolve the yeast and a pinch of the sugar in the warm water. Let stand until foamy, about 5 minutes.

BY HAND: In a large bowl, combine the remaining sugar, the salt, melted butter, milk, the yeast mixture, and ¹/₂ cup (2¹/₂ oz/75 g) of the flour, and mix with a wooden spoon until blended. Gradually add the remaining 2 cups (10 oz/315 g) flour ¹/₂ cup (2¹/₂ oz/75 g) at a time and mix just until the dough comes together in a sticky mass.

BY STAND MIXER: In the large bowl of a stand mixer fitted with the paddle attachment, combine the remaining sugar, the salt, melted butter, milk, and the yeast mixture and mix on medium speed until combined. Gradually add the flour ¹/₂ cup (2¹/₂ oz/75 g) at a time and mix just until the dough comes together in a sticky mass.

On a lightly floured work surface, roll out the dough into a rectangle about ¹/₂ inch (12 mm) thick. Transfer to a half-sheet pan, cover with plastic wrap, and refrigerate until chilled, about 40 minutes.

To make the butter package (page 256), using a rolling pin or the heel of your hand, beat or knead the butter on a work surface to flatten it and warm it to about 60°F (16°C). Sprinkle the butter with the flour and gently beat the butter with the rolling pin to press the flour into the butter. Shape the butter into a 6-by-8-inch (15-by-20-cm) rectangle. If the butter has become too warm, wrap and refrigerate just until firm but still pliable (60°F/16°C).

To laminate the dough (page 257), on a lightly floured work surface, roll out the dough into a 9-by-13-inch (23-by-33-cm) rectangle. With a short side facing you, place the butter on the lower half, leaving a ¹/₂-inch (12-mm) border on all sides. Fold over the upper half to cover the butter and press the edges together to seal. Then, with a folded side to your left, roll out the dough into a 10-by-24-inch (25-by-60-cm) rectangle. With a short side facing you, fold the bottom third up, then fold the top third down, as if folding a letter. This completes the first turn. Return to the pan, cover with plastic wrap, and refrigerate for 45 minutes.

Return the chilled dough to the lightly floured work surface with a folded side to your left and repeat the process to make 3 more turns, rolling, folding, and chilling the dough each time, for a total of 4 turns. After the final turn, refrigerate the dough for at least 4 hours or for up to overnight.

Mastering the making of croissant pastry is considered a great achievement in the baking world. Buttery layers rise into pastries that are crisp on the outside and moist on the inside. You can freeze the pastry before forming the croissants for longer storage. Wrap tightly with plastic wrap, place in an airtight plastic bag, and freeze for up to 1 month. If you have never had a freshly baked homemade croissant, you are in for a treat.

To form the croissants, roll out the pastry on a lightly floured work surface into a 9-by-18-inch (23-by-45-cm) rectangle. Cut in half lengthwise, and then cut each half crosswise into 4 squares, for a total of 8 squares. Cut each square in half on the diagonal.

Lightly butter 2 half-sheet pans. Working with 1 triangle at a time, gently stretch each triangle to about twice its original length. Then, gently stretch the wide end of the triangle. Lay the triangle on the work surface with the point facing you. Place your hands at the top on the wide end and gently roll the pastry toward you. Just before you get to the end, smear the tip against the work surface with your thumb. Continue to roll until the tip is on the underside. Place, tip side down, on a prepared pan. For the classic shape, turn the ends in slightly toward the center. Repeat with the remaining triangles, spacing them about 3 inches (7.5-cm) apart. Place in a warm, draft-free spot, cover loosely with a kitchen towel, and let the pastries rise until they double in size, about 1$^{1}/_{2}$ hours.

Position a rack in the middle of the oven, and preheat to 425°F (220°C).

Lightly brush the tops of the pastries with the egg mixture. Bake the pastries, 1 sheet at a time, until golden brown, 15–18 minutes. Transfer to a wire rack and let cool on the pan. Serve warm or at room temperature. Store in an airtight container at room temperature for up to 1 day.

WORKING WITH CROISSANT PASTRY

A few simple rules will help to guarantee your success when making croissant pastry:

■ Always use unsalted butter; it has a lower moisture content and superior flavor to salted butter.

■ Try to work with a block, rather than sticks, of butter.

■ Keep the butter-laden dough cold throughout the preparation. The butter must remain pliable but never become warm or sticky.

■ Finally, when rolling up the croissant, gently stretch the dough long enough to make 3 complete turns. Be careful not to tear the dough when stretching it.

Almond Croissants

Frangipane, a sweet almond filling, is swirled through each of these croissants, resulting in a delectable crunch with every bite. Other nuts, such as hazelnuts (filberts), pistachios, or pecans, can be substituted for the almonds. It is a good idea to store your nuts in the refrigerator or freezer to keep them fresh tasting whenever you decide to bake. You can make the frangipane ahead of time and store it in an airtight container in the refrigerator for up to 3 days.

Prepare the Croissant Dough up to the point where it is ready to roll out for baking (page 276). Lightly butter 2 half-sheet pans.

BY HAND: To make the frangipane, finely chop the nuts with a sharp knife. In a bowl, combine the nuts, brown sugar, and flour and, using a wooden spoon, stir until combined. Add the butter and egg and stir until a paste forms.

BY FOOD PROCESSOR: To make the frangipane, combine the nuts and brown sugar and process until the nuts are coarsely chopped. Add the flour, butter, and egg and process just until a paste forms.

On a lightly floured work surface, roll out the pastry into a 9-by-18-inch (23-by-45-cm) rectangle. Cut in half lengthwise, then cut each half crosswise into 4 squares, for a total of 8 squares. Cut each square in half on the diagonal.

Working with 1 triangle at a time, gently stretch each triangle to about twice its original length. Then, gently stretch the wide end of the triangle. Lay the triangle on the work surface with the point facing you. Using a small offset spatula, spread 1 tablespoon of frangipane over each triangle, leaving a $1/2$-inch (12-mm) border.

Place your hands at the top on the wide end and gently roll the pastry toward you. Just before you get to the end, smear the tip against the work surface with your thumb. Continue to roll until the tip is on the underside. Place the pastries, tip side down, on a prepared pan. Repeat with the remaining triangles, spacing them about 2–3 inches (5–7.5 cm) apart. Place in a warm, draft-free spot, cover loosely with a kitchen towel, and let the pastries rise until they double in size, about $1^1/2$ hours.

Position a rack in the middle of the oven, and preheat to 425°F (220°C). Lightly brush the tops of the pastries with the egg mixture. Bake the pastries, 1 sheet at a time, until golden brown, 15–18 minutes. Transfer to a wire rack and let cool on the pans. Store in an airtight container at room temperature for up to 1 day.

Croissant Dough (page 276)

For the frangipane

1 cup (5^1/2 oz/170 g) whole almonds, toasted (page 21)

^{1}/4 cup (2 oz/60 g) lightly packed golden brown sugar

2 tablespoons all-purpose (plain) flour

2 tablespoons unsalted butter, at room temperature

1 large egg

1 egg beaten with 1 tablespoon whole milk

Pain au Chocolat

Croissant Dough (page 276)

6 oz (185 g) bittersweet or semisweet (plain) chocolate

**1 egg beaten with
1 tablespoon whole milk**

Prepare the Croissant Dough up to the point where it is ready to roll out and shape for baking. Lightly butter 2 half-sheet pans.

Using a box grater or a food processor, coarsely grate or chop the chocolate.

On a lightly floured work surface, roll out the pastry into a 12-by-16-inch (30-by-40-cm) rectangle. Cut lengthwise into 3 equal strips, then cut each strip crosswise into 4 squares, for a total of 12 squares.

Working with 1 square at a time, place a rounded tablespoon of the grated chocolate in a strip in the middle of the square. Fold the bottom up a third of the way, then fold the top down so that it slightly overlaps the bottom flap. Pinch the seam to seal.

Place, seam side down, on a prepared pan. Repeat with the remaining squares and chocolate, spacing the rolls 2–3 inches (5–7.5 cm) apart. Place in a warm, draft-free place, cover loosely with a kitchen towel, and let the pastries rise until they double in size, about 1$\frac{1}{2}$ hours.

Position a rack in the middle of the oven, and preheat to 425°F (220°C).

Lightly brush the tops of the rolls with the egg mixture. Bake the pastries, 1 sheet at a time, until golden brown, 15–18 minutes. Transfer to a wire rack and let the pastries cool on the pans. Serve warm or at room temperature. Store in an airtight container at room temperature for up to 1 day.

Here is the French school-child's traditional afternoon treat: a flaky roll concealing a gooey stripe of bittersweet chocolate. Eat these pastries within a few hours of baking to ensure that the chocolate is still soft. To save some for another day, after forming and before baking, place them on a tray lined with parchment (baking) paper, cover the tray with plastic wrap, and freeze for up to 2 weeks. Thaw in the refrigerator overnight, then let rise and bake as directed.

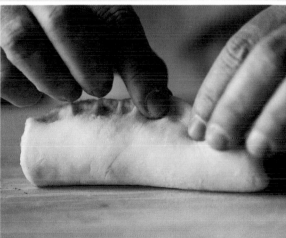

MASTER RECIPE Choux

¹/₂ cup (4 fl oz/125 ml)
whole milk

¹/₂ cup (4 fl oz/125 ml) water

6 tablespoons (3 oz/90 g)
unsalted butter, cut into
¹/₂-inch (12-mm) pieces

¹/₄ teaspoon salt

1 cup (5 oz/155 g)
unbleached all-purpose
(plain) flour

4 large eggs

In a saucepan over medium-high heat, combine the milk, water, butter, and salt and bring to a full boil. When the butter melts, remove the pan from the heat, add the flour all at once, and stir vigorously with a wooden spoon until blended. Return the pan to medium heat and continue stirring until the mixture leaves the sides of the pan and forms a ball. Remove from the heat and let cool for 3–4 minutes, or to 140°F (60°C) on an instant-read thermometer.

Meanwhile, in a small bowl, whisk 1 egg. When the batter has cooled, pour the egg into the batter and beat with the spoon until incorporated. Add the remaining 3 eggs one at a time by whisking each one first and then stirring it into the batter. After each egg is added, the mixture separates and appears shiny, but it returns to a smooth paste with vigorous beating. Let the paste cool for about 10 minutes before shaping.

Position 2 racks evenly in the oven, and preheat to 425°F (220°C). Line 2 half-sheet pans with parchment (baking) paper or aluminum foil.

To shape small puffs (ideal for profiteroles), fit a pastry (piping) bag with a ³/₁₆-inch (5-mm) plain tip and fill the bag with the paste. For each puff, pipe about 1 teaspoon of the paste onto a prepared pan, forming a mound about ¹/₂ inch (12 mm) in diameter. Space the mounds at least 2 inches (5 cm) apart to allow for expansion.

To shape large puffs (the perfect size for cream puffs), fit a pastry bag with a ⁵/₈-inch (1.5 cm) plain tip and fill the bag with the paste. For each puff, pipe about 1 tablespoon of the paste onto a prepared pan, forming a mound about 2 inches (5 cm) in diameter. Space the mounds at least 2 inches (5 cm) apart to allow for expansion.

To shape logs (good for éclairs), fit a pastry bag with a ³/₄-inch (2-cm) plain tip and pipe out logs 4 inches (10 cm) long and 1 inch (2.5 cm) wide. Space the logs at least 2 inches (5 cm) apart to allow for expansion.

Bake the puffs for 15 minutes, then reduce the heat to 375°F (190°C) and continue baking until golden brown, 5–10 minutes longer for the the small puffs and 15–20 minutes longer for the large puffs and logs.

Remove from the oven and immediately prick the side of each puff or log with the tip of a sharp knife. Return to the oven, leave the oven door open, and allow the pastries to dry out for 10–15 minutes. Let the pastries cool completely on the pans on wire racks before filling.

Choux (pronounced "shoo") are puff shells that are made from a thick batter (*pâte à choux*) of butter, flour, eggs, milk, and water. The mixture is cooked on the stove top and then fashioned into a variety of shapes and sizes and slipped into a hot oven to bake. The moist interior and crisp shells are ideal for savory or sweet fillings. Store the shells in an airtight container at room temperature for up to 1 day, or make them ahead and freeze them for up to 1 month.

Profiteroles with Ice Cream and Chocolate Sauce

40 small choux (page 282)

1 qt (1l) vanilla bean, coffee, or toasted almond ice cream

This elegant dessert is easy to assemble in stages. Have the small puffs baked and fill them with ice cream at the last minute, or fill them, arrange them in a single layer on a serving plate, slip the plate into a zippered plastic bag or wrap with plastic wrap, and freeze for up to 2 weeks. When ready to serve, thaw briefly if frozen and top with the warm chocolate sauce.

Bake and cool the small puff-shaped choux. Set aside.

To make the chocolate sauce, place the chocolate and corn syrup in the top of a double boiler placed over (not touching) barely simmering water. Heat, stirring often, until the chocolate melts. Add the half-and-half, butter, and vanilla and stir until blended.

To assemble, slit each puff horizontally almost through and fill with a small scoop of ice cream. Arrange 3 or 4 filled puffs on each dessert plate or bowl. Spoon the warm chocolate sauce over the puffs. Serve immediately.

For the chocolate sauce

6 oz (185 g) bittersweet chocolate, chopped, or semi-sweet (plain) chocolate chips

$^1/_3$ cup ($3^1/_2$ oz/105 g) light corn syrup

$^1/_3$ cup (3 fl oz/90 ml) half-and-half (half-cream) or whole milk

1 tablespoon unsalted butter

1 teaspoon vanilla extract (essence)

Éclairs

VARIATION

Caramel Glaze

Place 2 tablespoons unsalted butter, $^1/_4$ cup (2 oz/60 g) firmly packed dark brown sugar, and 1 tablespoon heavy (double) cream in the top of a double boiler placed over (not touching) hot water. Heat until hot, stirring until smooth. Remove from over the water and let cool slightly. Using a wooden spoon, beat in $^1/_2$ cup (2 oz/60 g) confectioners' (icing) sugar until thick enough to spread. Using an icing spatula, spread on the top half of the log.

There is nothing like biting into a freshly made éclair with cream oozing out of the center. With their thick, dark chocolate or caramel glaze, these delectables are nothing like the store-bought doughnuts that try to pass as true éclairs.

Bake and cool the log-shaped choux. Set aside. Have the whipped cream or pastry cream ready.

To make the chocolate ganache, combine the chocolate and butter in a heatproof bowl. In a small saucepan over medium-high heat, bring the milk to a boil. Remove from the heat and immediately pour over the chocolate and butter. Stir with a wire whisk until the chocolate and butter melt and are smooth. Place the ganache in a wide bowl.

Using a sharp, serrated knife, cut each choux log in half. Holding the top half upside down, dip the top surface into the ganache. Turn the dipped half right side up and place on a wire rack to set. Using a pastry (piping) bag fitted with a $^3/_4$-inch (2-cm) plain or star tip, pipe the cream into the bottom half of each log (page 213). Set the ganache-topped half on top of the cream. Serve at once, or refrigerate for 2 hours before serving.

10 log–shaped choux (page 282)

Whipped Cream (page 306) or Pastry Cream (page 309)

For the chocolate ganache

4 oz (125 g) bittersweet or semisweet (plain) chocolate coarsely chopped

$^1/_4$ cup (2 oz/60 g) unsalted butter, cut into $^1/_2$-inch (12-mm) pieces

$^1/_4$ cup (2 fl oz/60 ml) whole milk or freshly brewed coffee

Pistachio Baklava

For the syrup

³/₄ cup (6 oz/185 g) sugar

1 cup (8 fl oz/250 ml) water

2 tablespoons fresh lemon juice, strained

1 cinnamon stick

2 orange and 2 lemon zest strips (page 23)

³/₄ cup (9 oz/280 g) honey

For the filling

¹/₄ cup (2 oz/60 g) sugar

1 teaspoon grated orange zest

1 teaspoon grated lemon zest

4 cups (1 lb/500 g) pistachio nuts, finely chopped

1 lb (500 g) filo dough, thawed in the refrigerator if frozen

³/₄ cup (6 oz/185 g) clarified unsalted butter, melted and cooled (page 17)

The patrician dessert of the Greeks, baklava is traditionally made with walnuts or almonds, or a combination. Here, pistachio nuts and orange zest are a flavorful and colorful variation. When working with filo dough, always keep the tissue-thin sheets covered with a kitchen towel, or they will dry out and tear easily. You can purchase frozen filo at many supermarkets and at Middle Eastern markets, or find fresh filo at some Middle Eastern bakeries. Make the syrup first so that it will be cold when it is poured over the hot pastry, ensuring that it will be quickly absorbed. If desired, a whole clove may be inserted in the center of each pastry diamond before baking. This pastry freezes well, before or after baking.

Position a rack in the middle of the oven, and preheat to 325°F (165°C). Butter a 9-by-13-inch (23-by-33-cm) baking dish.

To make the syrup, in a saucepan over medium heat, combine the sugar, water, lemon juice, cinnamon stick, orange and lemon zest strips, and honey. Bring to a boil and cook, stirring, until the sugar dissolves. Remove from the heat and let cool completely. Remove and discard the cinnamon stick and citrus strips.

To make the filling, in a bowl, mash the sugar with the orange and lemon zest. Add the nuts and mix well. Set aside.

Place a sheet of parchment (baking) paper on a large, dry work surface. Unroll the filo sheets, lay them on the parchment, and cover them with a kitchen towel to prevent them from drying out. Line the prepared dish with 1 filo sheet. If the sheet hangs over the sides of the dish, fold the overhanging layer to fit. Brush the sheet with a thin coating of clarified butter. Repeat with 2 more sheets for a total of 3 sheets. Sprinkle lightly with about ¹/₂ cup (2 oz/60 g) of the nut mixture.

Cover the nuts with 2 more filo sheets, brushing each sheet with butter. Sprinkle the filo lightly with about ¹/₂ cup (2 oz/60 g) of the nut mixture. Repeat to use up the remaining filo and nuts, layering and buttering 2 filo sheets and topping with more of the nut mixture. For the final layer, top the baklava with 3 or 4 buttered filo sheets.

Using a sharp knife, and cutting only through the top layers of filo, cut on the diagonal across the dish, first from one corner and then from the opposite corner, into diamond-shaped pieces about 1¹/₂ inches (4 cm) on each side.

Bake the baklava until golden brown, 35–40 minutes. Cut the baklava into diamonds, and then pour the syrup over the baklava. Let cool on a wire rack to room temperature before serving. Store in an airtight container for up to 3 days.

VARIATIONS

Almond Baklava
Substitute 3¹/₂ cups (1 lb/500 g) almonds, finely chopped and lightly toasted (page 21), for the pistachio nuts in the filling.

Walnut Baklava
Substitute 3¹/₂ cups (1 lb/500 g) walnuts, finely chopped and lightly toasted (page 21), for the pistachio nuts in the filling.

Apple Strudel

Commercial filo dough makes it easy to bake strudel at home. The paper-thin pastry sheets used for strudel were originally made at home with a flour-and-water dough that was rolled out with a broom stick into sheets a yard (1 m) wide. Then the strudel was assembled on a towel, and the edge of the towel was lifted to roll up the strudel for baking. For this recipe, use a tart apple, such as a Granny Smith, and slice it ultrathin with a sharp knife, a mandoline, or the slicer attachment of a food processor. If you have purchased frozen filo and thawed it in the refrigerator, let it warm to room temperature in the package for 2 hours before using.

Position a rack in the middle of the oven, and preheat to 375°F (190°C). Butter a half-sheet pan.

To make the filling, in a bowl, toss together the apples, granulated sugar, raisins, almonds, lemon zest, and lemon juice until evenly mixed.

Place a sheet of parchment (baking) paper on a large, dry work surface. Unroll the filo sheets, lay them on the parchment, and cover them with a kitchen towel to prevent them from drying out. Lay out 1 filo sheet on a separate piece of parchment, brush with a little of the clarified butter, and repeat with the remaining filo sheets, brushing each one with butter. Spoon the apple mixture in a strip along the length of one side, leaving a 2-inch (5-cm) border. Fold in the short sides and, starting from the border, roll up into a log. Place, seam side down, on the prepared pan.

Bake the strudel until the apples are tender when pierced with a toothpick and the filo is golden brown, 30–35 minutes. Transfer to a wire rack and let the strudel cool slightly in the pan.

Using a fine-mesh sieve, dust lightly with confectioners' sugar. Serve warm, cut into thick slices.

For the filling

6 large tart apples, peeled, cored, and very thinly sliced

1/2 cup (4 oz/125 g) granulated sugar

1/3 cup (2 oz/60 g) golden raisins (sultanas) or dried currants

1/3 cup (1 1/2 oz/45 g) slivered blanched almonds

2 teaspoons grated lemon zest

1 1/2 tablespoons fresh lemon juice, strained

6 sheets filo dough, thawed in the refrigerator if frozen

6 tablespoons (3 oz/90 g) clarified unsalted butter, melted and cooled (page 17)

Confectioners' (icing) sugar for dusting

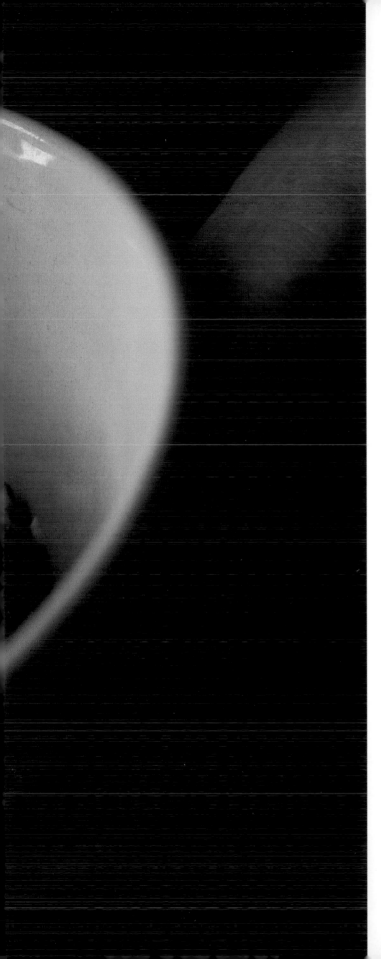

Custards
and Soufflés

About Custards and Soufflés

Custards and soufflés, both built on a mixture of eggs and milk or cream, are all about texture—smooth and satiny on one hand and light and airy on the other. These decadent desserts are elegant enough for a dinner party, but comforting enough for a family get-together.

Custards are among the most endearing of all comfort foods. They owe their legendary silkiness to the slow cooking of eggs and cream or milk until the ideal consistency is achieved. Soufflés, on the other hand, are airy creations that rely on a billowy mountain of beaten egg whites for their signature loft.

Stirred custards are cooked on the stove top. Cream or milk and eggs are combined in a heatproof bowl and then stirred over gentle heat with a wooden spoon until the mixture thickly coats the back of the spoon and a finger drawn along its back side leaves a clear trail. When these stove-top custards are fully cooked, they are thick yet pourable. They are the basis for such classic dessert sauces as crème anglaise and sabayon, and are used to bind bread puddings. They are also used as a base for ice creams.

Baked custards are cooked in the oven. Typically, cream or milk is heated on the stove top and then whisked into a mixture of beaten eggs and sugar until the sugar dissolves. The mixture is then strained into molds, usually individual porcelain ramekins, brûlée dishes, or custard cups, and baked gently in a water bath.

A water bath is created by placing the ramekins or cups in a large baking pan or dish and then carefully filling the pan or dish with hot water to reach about halfway up the sides of the molds. This insulates the custards from the direct heat of the oven, ensuring the even, gentle cooking that is necessary to baking a successful, silky, creamy custard.

Crème caramel, *pots de crème*, and crème brûlée, all of them baked custards, are perfectly done if the custard jiggles slightly when its baking vessel is gently shaken. It is very important not to overbake custards, particularly chocolate custards, or they will become grainy and curdled and the ingredients may separate, resulting in a watery consistency.

Soufflés are decadent treats that start out with a flavored base that is then folded into whipped egg whites and baked in a hot oven. Pastry cream, which is milk and a little flour cooked together and then combined with egg yolks, serves as the base for some soufflés. Others rely on a base of fruit syrup, fruit purée, fruit preserves, or fruit curd.

Savory soufflés often start with a cooked butter and flour mixture, known as a roux.

The flavoring—cheese, vegetables, herbs—is stirred into the roux, the mixture is combined with egg yolks, and then the whites are folded into the base.

Soufflés are most often and most successfully baked in individual or large white porcelain ramekins. But they can be baked in almost any straight-sided, relatively deep ceramic vessel. However, if you decide to use a dish other than what is specified in a recipe, make sure that it has the same volume.

Because both custards and soufflés typically call for relatively few ingredients, always buy the very best that your budget can afford, whether it be farm-fresh organic eggs and cream, the finest European or American chocolate, or a bottle of Grand Marnier. You and your guests will be rewarded.

TROUBLESHOOTING CUSTARDS AND SOUFFLÉS

What happened	Why it happened
Custard is lumpy.	Custard was overcooked on stove top or was not strained.
Custard is grainy or watery.	Custard was overbaked.
Custard is too wet in center.	Custard was underbaked.
Bread pudding is dry.	Bread did not sit long enough to absorb the custard before being baked.
Soufflé did not rise.	Soufflé batter was overfolded and air was knocked out, or oven was not hot enough.
Soufflé is dry.	Egg whites were overwhipped, or soufflé was overbaked.

Crème Brûlée

2 cups (16 fl oz/500 ml) heavy (double) cream

6 large egg yolks

1/2 cup (4 oz/125 g) granulated sugar

1/2 teaspoon vanilla extract (essence)

1/3 cup (2 1/2 oz/75 g) firmly packed golden brown sugar

Position a rack in the middle of the oven, and preheat to 300°F (150°C). Butter four 3/4-cup (6–fl oz/180-ml) brûlée dishes or ramekins. Line a shallow baking pan with a small kitchen towel.

In a saucepan over medium heat, warm the cream until small bubbles appear along the edges of the pan, then remove from the heat. In a bowl, whisk together the egg yolks and granulated sugar until the sugar dissolves and the mixture is pale yellow. Slowly pour in the hot cream while whisking constantly. Stir in the vanilla. Pour the custard through a fine-mesh sieve into a pitcher. Divide the custard evenly among the brûlée dishes.

Place the dishes in the towel-lined pan and pour hot water into the pan to reach halfway up the sides of the dishes. Cover the pan with aluminum foil.

Bake the custards until they are set but still jiggle slightly when the dishes are shaken, 35–40 minutes. Carefully transfer the baking pan to a wire rack, let the custards cool slightly, and then lift the brûlée dishes out of the water bath. Cover with plastic wrap placed directly on the surface of the custards to prevent a skin from forming. Refrigerate until well chilled, about 3 hours or up to overnight.

Just before serving, sprinkle the brown sugar evenly over the tops of the chilled custards to form an even layer 1/8 inch (3 mm) thick. Use a small kitchen torch to caramelize the sugar. Set the sugar-topped custards on a work surface and ignite the torch. Adjust the intensity of the flame. Hold the flame close to the surface of the custard until the sugar begins to melt quickly. Move the flame gradually in small circles over the surface of the custard, heating the sugar until it is evenly melted and golden brown.

Alternatively, preheat the broiler (grill). Place the brûlée dishes on a half-sheet pan and slip the pan under the broiler 2–3 inches (5–7.5 cm) from the heat source. Broil (grill) until the sugar melts and caramelizes, 1–2 minutes, watching constantly and turning the pan if necessary to broil evenly.

Serve the custards immediately.

A brittle caramel crust seals the top of this ultrarich custard. When tapped with a spoon, the brown sugar topping shatters open, revealing the silken pudding. This crust can be made three ways: The sugar can be sprinkled or sifted over the top and then caramelized with a kitchen torch or under a broiler (grill), or the sugar can be caramelized in a pan (page 297) and poured over the top. Be careful not to overbake these delicate, creamy custards or they will curdle and become grainy.

Orange Crème Caramel

This beloved dessert can be found in many countries, either plain or with various flavorings, including orange, lemon, coffee, chocolate, maple, and butterscotch. Whole milk and eggs produce a satisfying result, but for a richer custard, use egg yolks and half-and-half. When making the caramel, do not stir it once the sugar has dissolved, or sugar crystals may form. The caramel will harden quickly once it is poured into the molds, but will return to a liquid once the custards have been baked.

Position a rack in the middle of the oven, and preheat to 325°F (165°C). Butter eight ³/₄-cup (6–fl oz/180-ml) ramekins or custard cups or a 1¹/₂-qt (1.5-l) metal mold. Line a shallow baking pan with a small kitchen towel.

To make the caramel, in a heavy saucepan over medium heat, combine the sugar, water, and corn syrup and stir until the sugar dissolves. As soon as the sugar dissolves, stop stirring and wash down any sugar crystals from the sides of the pan with a pastry brush dipped in clean water. Cook the sugar until it turns amber, 5–7 minutes. Divide the hot caramel evenly between the prepared ramekins or pour into the large prepared mold. Quickly tilt the ramekins or mold so the caramel covers the bottom and partway up the sides. The caramel will harden.

To make the custard, in a saucepan over medium heat (you can use the same saucepan that you used for the caramel), warm the milk until small bubbles appear along the edge of the pan, then remove from the heat. In a bowl, whisk the eggs until blended, then whisk in the sugar, orange zest, and salt. Slowly pour in the hot milk and the liqueur while whisking continuously until the sugar dissolves. Pour the custard through a fine-mesh sieve into a pitcher. Divide the custard evenly among the caramel-lined ramekins or pour into the mold.

Place the ramekins or mold in the towel-lined pan and pour hot water into the pan to reach halfway up the sides of the ramekins or mold. Bake until set but the custard still jiggles slightly when a mold is shaken, 35–40 minutes for the ramekins or 45–55 minutes for the large mold. Carefully transfer the baking pan to a wire rack, let the custard(s) cool slightly, and then transfer to a rack and let cool completely. Cover and refrigerate for about 3 hours before serving.

To unmold, run a thin, sharp knife around the edge of the custard(s). Place a serving plate on top of each ramekin or the mold, and invert together. Gently lift off the ramekin or mold. Serve immediately.

For the caramel

²/₃ cup (5 oz/155 g) sugar

¹/₄ cup (2 fl oz/60 ml) water

¹/₂ teaspoon light corn syrup
or fresh lemon juice

For the custard

3 cups (24 fl oz/750 ml)
whole milk or half-and-half
(half-cream)

6 large whole eggs, or
4 large whole eggs plus
4 large egg yolks

²/₃ cup (5 oz/155 g) sugar

1 tablespoon grated
orange zest

¹/₈ teaspoon salt

2 tablespoons orange liqueur

Chocolate Pots de Crème

1 cup (8 fl oz/250 ml) heavy (double) cream

1¹/₂ cups (12 fl oz/375 ml) whole milk

6 oz (185 g) bittersweet or semisweet (plain) chocolate, finely chopped

6 large egg yolks

¹/₄ cup (2 oz/60 g) sugar

1 teaspoon vanilla extract (essence), or 2 tablespoons Grand Marnier or framboise

Whipped Cream (page 306), optional

Position a rack in the middle of the oven, and preheat to 325°F (165°C). Butter six ³/₄-cup (6–fl oz/180 ml) ramekins or eight ¹/₂-cup (4–fl oz/125 ml) *pot de crème* pots. Line a shallow baking pan with a small kitchen towel.

In a saucepan over low heat, combine the cream, milk, and chocolate and heat, whisking constantly, until the chocolate melts and the liquid is warm. Do not allow the mixture to boil. Remove from the heat.

In a bowl, whisk together the egg yolks and sugar until blended. Slowly pour in the hot chocolate mixture while whisking constantly until blended and the sugar dissolves. Pour the custard through a fine-mesh sieve into a 1-qt (1-l) measuring pitcher. Skim off any bubbles from the surface. Divide the custard evenly among the prepared ramekins or pots. Place the molds in the towel-lined pan and pour hot water into the pan to reach halfway up the sides of the molds. Cover the pan with aluminum foil.

Bake the custards until they are set but still jiggle slightly when the ramekins are shaken, 40–45 minutes. Carefully transfer the baking pan to a wire rack, let the custards cool slightly, and then lift the ramekins out of the water bath. Cover and refrigerate the custards until well chilled, at least 2 hours or up to overnight. Serve the custards topped with whipped cream, if desired.

Use a good-quality bittersweet or semisweet chocolate for this elegant, silken chocolate pudding enriched with egg yolks and cream. Because bittersweet chocolate melts at around 125°F (52°C), it is particularly important to bake these custards in a water bath, which insulates them from the harsh heat of the oven, or they may turn grainy. Traditionally, small lidded porcelain pots, called *pots de crème*, are used, but you can also use ramekins or custard cups. If desired, flavor the whipped cream with cognac or Grand Marnier.

Currant Bread Pudding

After being out of style for decades, old-fashioned bread pudding has once again become fashionable. Egg bread, such as brioche or challah, produces a particularly light, airy texture and rich flavor. Crème anglaise, the classic vanilla custard sauce, elevates the homey pudding to a special-occasion dessert. The currants can be replaced with other dried fruits, such as cherries, diced apricots, or cranberries, or even chopped semisweet chocolate or toasted nuts.

Position a rack in the middle of the oven, and preheat to 350°F (180°C).

Lightly butter a 2-qt (2-l) baking dish. Line a shallow baking pan with a small kitchen towel.

Trim the crusts from the bread and cut the bread into ¹/₂-inch (12-mm) cubes. You need about 3 cups (6 oz/185 g), lightly packed. Scatter the bread in the prepared baking dish and sprinkle with the currants.

In a large bowl, whisk together the eggs, sugar, vanilla, nutmeg, and salt until blended, then whisk in the milk. Pour the mixture through a fine-mesh sieve over the bread and set aside for 20 minutes to moisten the bread. Tilt the dish occasionally to keep the bread evenly covered with the liquid.

Place the baking dish in the towel-lined pan and pour hot water into the pan to reach halfway up the sides of the dish. Bake until a knife inserted into the center comes out clean, 40–45 minutes. Carefully remove the baking dish from the water bath and let cool completely on a wire rack. Serve at room temperature or refrigerate to chill for up to 3 hours.

Top each serving with whipped cream or crème anglaise, if desired.

8 thin slices day-old Challah (page 62), Brioche (page 60), or top-quality white bread, about ¹/₂ lb (250 g) total weight

¹/₂ cup (3 oz/90 g) dried currants

3 large eggs

¹/₂ cup (4 oz/125 g) sugar

1 teaspoon vanilla extract (essence)

¹/₄ teaspoon freshly grated nutmeg

¹/₈ teaspoon salt

2 cups (16 fl oz/500 ml) whole milk

Whipped Cream or Crème Anglaise (page 306), optional

Grand Marnier Soufflé

Unsalted butter and sugar for preparing dish

$^1/_2$ cup (4 fl oz/125 ml) whole milk

$1^1/_2$ tablespoons all-purpose (plain) flour

5 tablespoons (3 oz/90 g) sugar

4 large eggs, separated

1 tablespoon unsalted butter

2 teaspoons grated orange zest

$^1/_4$ cup (2 fl oz/60 ml) Grand Marnier

$^1/_8$ teaspoon salt

$^1/_4$ teaspoon cream of tartar

Crème Anglaise (page 306), optional

This dramatic soufflé is always a showstopper. You can make it especially light by adding an extra egg white. Rubbing a little sugar into the orange zest brings out its oils and enhances the orange flavor of the finished soufflé.

Position a rack in the lower third of the oven, and preheat to 400°F (200°C) for individual soufflés or 375°F (190°C) for a large soufflé.

Butter four 1-cup (8–fl oz/250-ml) ramekins or a 1-qt (1-l) soufflé dish and dust the bottom and sides with sugar.

In a saucepan over medium heat, warm the milk until bubbles appear along the edge of the pan, then remove from the heat. In a bowl, stir together the flour and 3 tablespoons of the sugar. Slowly pour in the hot milk while whisking constantly. Return the mixture to the pan, place over medium heat, and bring to a boil, stirring constantly. Boil for 1–2 minutes.

Meanwhile, in a medium bowl, whisk the egg yolks until pale in color and thick. Slowly pour the hot milk mixture into the yolks while whisking constantly. Return the mixture to the pan. Cook over low heat, stirring, until thickened and the mixture coats the back of a spoon, about 3 minutes. Remove from the heat and stir in the butter. In a small bowl, using the back of a spoon, mash the orange zest with a pinch of the sugar, then whisk into the egg yolk mixture along with the Grand Marnier.

BY HAND: In a large, clean bowl, whisk together the egg whites, salt, and cream of tartar with a balloon whisk until soft peaks form. Slowly add the remaining 2 tablespoons of sugar and beat until stiff, glossy peaks form (page 27).

BY MIXER: In a large, clean bowl, using a stand mixer fitted with the whip attachment or a hand mixer, beat the egg whites, salt, and cream of tartar on medium-high speed until soft peaks form. Slowly add the remaining sugar and beat until stiff, glossy peaks form (page 27).

Using a rubber spatula, fold one-fourth of the beaten egg whites into the egg yolk mixture to lighten it. Then gently fold in the remaining whites just until no white streaks remain. Spoon into the prepared dish(es). Run your thumb around the rim of the dish to form a shallow groove. This will give the soufflé a "hat."

Bake the soufflé until set, puffed, and the center still jiggles when the dish is shaken, 8–10 minutes for the individual soufflés or 25–30 minutes for the large soufflé. Serve immediately with crème anglaise, if desired.

VARIATION

Raspberry Soufflé

Substitute 2 teaspoons grated lemon zest and 2 tablespoons framboise or kirsch for the orange zest and Grand Marnier. Fold in $1^1/_4$ cups (5 oz/155 g) raspberries just after folding in the egg whites.

Chocolate Soufflé

Soufflés have the reputation of being tricky to prepare, yet they are surprisingly easy as long as you handle the egg whites properly. Let the egg whites warm to room temperature before beating, and then beat them just until they hold stiff, upright, glossy peaks. This ensures that they will expand to their maximum in the oven.

Position a rack in the lower third of the oven, and preheat to 375°F (190°C) for a large soufflé or 400°F (200°C) for individual soufflés. Butter a 1¹/₂-qt (1.5-l) soufflé dish or six 1-cup (8–fl oz/250-ml) ramekins and dust the bottom and sides with sugar.

Place the chocolate in the top of a double boiler placed over (not touching) barely simmering water. Heat, stirring often, until the chocolate melts. Remove from over the water and set aside to cool slightly.

BY HAND: In a large, clean bowl, whisk together the egg whites, salt and cream of tartar with a balloon whisk until soft peaks form. Slowly add ¹/₄ cup (2 oz/60 g) sugar and beat until stiff, glossy peaks form (page 27).

BY MIXER: In a large bowl, using a stand mixer fitted with the whip attachment or a hand mixer, beat the egg whites, salt, and cream of tartar on medium-high speed until soft peaks form. Slowly add ¹/₄ cup (2 oz/60 g) sugar and beat until stiff, glossy peaks form (page 27).

In another bowl, whisk the egg yolks until thick and pale in color. Whisk in the remaining ¹/₂ cup (4 oz/125 g) of the sugar and the vanilla. Using a rubber spatula, fold in the melted chocolate.

Fold one-fourth of the beaten egg whites into the chocolate mixture to lighten it. Then gently fold in the remaining whites just until no white streaks remain. Spoon into the prepared dish(es). Run your thumb around the rim of the dish to form a shallow groove along the edge. This will give the soufflé a "hat."

Bake the soufflé until set, puffed, and the center still jiggles when the dish is gently shaken, 25–30 minutes for the large soufflé or 8–10 minutes for the individual soufflés. Serve immediately with whipped cream, crème anglaise, or ice cream, if desired.

Unsalted butter and sugar for preparing dish

8 oz (250 g) bittersweet or semisweet (plain) chocolate, chopped

6 large eggs, separated

¹/₈ teaspoon salt

¹/₂ teaspoon cream of tartar

³/₄ cup (6 oz/185 g) sugar

1 teaspoon vanilla extract (essence), or 1 tablespoon Cointreau

Whipped Cream or Crème Anglaise (page 306), or vanilla bean ice cream (optional)

Goat Cheese and Chive Soufflé

Unsalted butter and grated Parmesan cheese for preparing dish

$1/2$ lb (250 g) fresh goat cheese or natural cream cheese, at room temperature

$1/4$ cup (2 oz/60 g) sour cream

5 large eggs, separated

1 teaspoon Dijon mustard

$1/2$ teaspoon salt

$1/4$ teaspoon freshly grated nutmeg

$1/4$ teaspoon ground white pepper

3 tablespoons minced fresh chives

$1/4$ teaspoon cream of tartar

3 tablespoons grated Parmesan cheese

Perfect for a special brunch or luncheon, this creamy soufflé is lovely accompanied with a spinach salad tossed with toasted pine nuts. Dusting the dish with grated Parmesan cheese will help the soufflé to rise tall and stately. The soufflé may be assembled up to an hour in advance. Once it is baked, it should be served promptly, as it deflates quickly. It is fine to let your guests wait for the soufflé, but do not let the soufflé wait for anyone.

Position a rack in the lower third of the oven, and preheat to 425°F (220°C). Butter a $1^{1}/_{2}$-qt (1.5-l) soufflé dish or six 1-cup (8–fl oz/250 ml) ramekins and dust the bottom and sides with Parmesan cheese.

BY HAND: In a large bowl, using a whisk, cream the goat cheese until light. Beat in the sour cream, egg yolks, mustard, salt, nutmeg, white pepper, and chives until combined. In another large, clean bowl, whisk together the egg whites and cream of tartar with a balloon whisk until stiff, glossy peaks form (page 27).
BY MIXER: In a large bowl, using a stand mixer fitted with the paddle attachment or a hand mixer, cream the goat cheese on medium-high speed until light. Beat in the sour cream, egg yolks, mustard, salt, nutmeg, white pepper, and chives until combined. In another large, clean bowl, using the stand mixer fitted with the whip attachment or the hand mixer, beat together the egg whites and cream or tartar on medium-high speed until stiff, glossy peaks form (page 27).

Using a rubber spatula, fold one-fourth of the beaten egg whites into the cheese mixture to lighten it. Then gently fold in the remaining egg whites just until no white streaks remain. Spoon into the prepared dish(es) and smooth the top. Sprinkle the top with the Parmesan cheese.

Bake the soufflé until set, puffed, and the center still jiggles when the dish is shaken, 20–25 minutes for a large soufflé or 8–10 minutes for the individual soufflés. Serve immediately.

SOUFFLÉ COLLARS

Soufflé collars give your soufflé dish or ramekin extra height and help ensure that your souffle rises well above the rim.

To make a soufflé collar, cut equal strips of parchment (baking) paper. The strips should be wide enough to stand 2–3 inches (5–7.5 cm) above the rim of the dish when folded in half, and long enough to wrap around the dish with a slight overlap. For individual soufflé dishes, cut the strips to about 5 inches (13 cm) wide by about 12 inches (30 cm) long. Fold the parchment in half and tuck one end into the other. Place around the dish and tighten. Secure the parchment by tying it with a piece of kitchen string.

Sauces, Toppings, and Fillings

This section contains basic recipes for widely used dessert sauces, such as coulis and crème anglaise; dessert toppings, such as plain and flavored whipped cream; frostings and glazes, such as buttercream and chocolate glaze; and fillings, such as pastry cream and frangipane.

Berry Coulis

2 cups (8 oz/250 g) fresh or thawed, frozen raspberries or strawberries

Sugar

Juice of 1/2 lemon, strained

If using fresh strawberries, remove the hulls. Using a food processor or blender, purée the berries until smooth. Strain the purée through a fine-mesh sieve into a bowl. Season to taste with sugar, then stir in the lemon juice to heighten the flavor of the berries.

Makes about 1 cup (8 fl oz/250 ml)

Crème Anglaise

4 large egg yolks

1/3 cup (3 oz/90 g) sugar

1 1/2 cups (12 fl oz/375 ml) half-and-half (half-cream) or whole milk

1 teaspoon vanilla extract (essence)

In a bowl, whisk together the egg yolks and sugar until blended and thick. In the top of a double boiler over (not touching) simmering water, heat the half-and-half until it is steaming. Pour the hot half-and-half into the egg mixture while whisking constantly. Return the mixture to the top of the double boiler over (not touching) simmering water. Cook, stirring, until the mixture thickly coats the back of the spoon, about 3 minutes. Pour through a fine-mesh sieve into a bowl. Let cool, then stir in the vanilla. Serve at room temperature or chill before using.

Makes about 1 1/2 cups (12 fl oz/375 ml)

Whipped Cream

1 cup (8 fl oz/250 ml) heavy (double) cream

2 tablespoons confectioners' (icing) sugar

1 teaspoon vanilla extract (essence)

BY HAND: In a large bowl, combine the cream, sugar, and vanilla. Using a balloon whisk, beat until medium peaks form (page 27).

BY MIXER: In a large bowl, combine the cream, confectioners' (icing) sugar, and vanilla. Using a stand mixer fitted with the whip attachment or a hand mixer, beat on medium-high speed until medium peaks form (page 27).

Makes about 2 cups (16 fl oz/500 ml)

Raspberry Whipped Cream

1 cup (8 fl oz/250 ml) heavy (double) cream

2 tablespoons seedless raspberry preserves

2 teaspoons framboise

BY HAND: In a large bowl, combine the cream, preserves, and framboise. Using a balloon whisk, beat until soft peaks form (page 27).

BY MIXER: In a large bowl, combine the cream, preserves, and framboise. Using a stand mixer fitted with the whip attachment or a hand mixer, beat on medium-high speed until soft peaks form (page 27).

Makes about 2 cups (16 fl oz/1 l)

Vanilla Meringue Buttercream

6 large egg whites

1 1/4 cups (10 oz/315 g) sugar

2–2 1/2 cups (1–1 1/4 lb/500–625 g) unsalted butter, at room temperature

1 tablespoon vanilla extract (essence)

Combine the egg whites and sugar in a deep stainless-steel bowl or in the bowl of a stand mixer. Stir gently with a sturdy wire whisk to mix.

Choose a saucepan in which the bowl will fit snugly in the rim, fill it halfway with water, and bring to a simmer. Set the bowl holding the egg whites and sugar over (not touching) the simmering water. Stir gently with the whisk for a few minutes until the mixture is quite warm (160°F/75°C on an instant-read thermometer) and the sugar has dissolved. Remove from the heat.

BY HAND: Using a balloon whisk, whip the mixture as fast as you can until it becomes stiff and glossy. You should be able to turn the bowl upside down without the whipped egg whites falling.

Add 2 cups (1 lb/500 g) of the butter and continue to whip as fast as you can until the frosting pulls away from the sides of the bowl, adding more butter as needed to correct the consistency. The mixture should be smooth and satiny. If it looks curdled and the mixing bowl feels cold, warm it slightly over hot water and beat it again until it looks shiny and smooth. Beat in the vanilla.

BY MIXER: Using a stand mixer fitted with the whip attachment or a hand mixer, beat the mixture on high speed until it becomes stiff and glossy. You should be able to turn the bowl upside down without the whipped egg whites falling.

Add 2 cups (1 lb/500 g) of the butter and continue to beat at high speed until the frosting pulls away from the sides of the bowl, adding more butter as needed to correct the consistency. The mixture should be smooth and satiny. If it looks curdled and the mixing bowl feels cold, warm it slightly over hot water and beat it again until it looks shiny and smooth. Beat in the vanilla.

Makes about 2 cups (16 fl oz/500 ml), enough to frost a 9-inch (23-cm) cake

Rich Vanilla Buttercream

6 large egg yolks

³/₄ cup (6 oz/185 g) sugar

¹/₂ cup (4 fl oz/125 ml) water

1 cup (8 oz/250 g) unsalted butter, at room temperature

2 teaspoons vanilla extract (essence)

1 cup (8 oz/250 g) Pastry Cream (page 309), cooled

With a sturdy wire whisk, stir the egg yolks lightly in the bowl of a stand mixer or another deep bowl. Set aside.

In a small, heavy saucepan over medium-high heat, combine the sugar and water and bring to a boil. Cover and allow to boil for 1 minute. (The steam created in the pan will wash the sugar crystals down the pan sides.) Uncover and continue to boil until the syrup reaches the soft-ball stage, or 239°F (115°) on a candy thermometer, about 5 minutes. (To test without a thermometer, scoop up a few drops of the syrup with a wooden spoon and immerse the spoon in a glass of ice water. When you trap the drops between your fingertips, you should be able to form them into a soft, pliable ball.)

BY HAND: Once the syrup is at the soft-ball stage, begin whisking the yolks with the whisk. While whisking continuously, slowly pour the

hot syrup onto the yolks. Be careful not to burn yourself with the hot syrup. Whisk vigorously until all of the syrup is incorporated. Switch to a balloon whisk and continue to whisk until cool and thick.

Still using the balloon whisk, beat the butter into the cooled egg mixture until smooth and satiny. If the mixture looks curdled and the bowl feels cold, warm it slightly over hot water and beat the mixture again until it looks smooth and shiny. Beat in the vanilla and the pastry cream.

BY MIXER: Once the syrup is at the soft-ball stage, begin beating the yolks with a stand mixer fitted with the whip attachment or a hand mixer set on medium speed. While beating continuously, slowly pour the hot syrup onto the yolks. Be careful not to burn yourself with the hot syrup. Beat until all of the syrup is incorporated, then continue to beat until cool and thick.

Beat the butter into the cooled egg mixture until smooth and satiny. If the mixture looks curdled and the bowl feels cold, warm it slightly over hot water and beat the mixture again until it looks shiny and smooth. Beat in the vanilla and the pastry cream.

Makes about 2 cups (16 fl oz/500 ml), enough to frost a 9-inch (23-cm) cake

VARIATIONS

Rich Almond Buttercream
Substitute 1 teaspoon almond extract (essence) for the vanilla extract.

Rich Liqueur-Flavored Buttercream
Substitute 2–3 tablespoons liqueur such as Grand Marnier, rum, Cointreau, framboise, kirsch, Kahlúa, or brandy for the vanilla.

Rich Espresso Buttercream
Substitute 2 tablespoons instant espresso powder dissolved in 2 teaspoons hot water for the vanilla.

Rich Citrus Buttercream
Substitute the grated zest and juice of 2 lemons or 1 orange for the vanilla extract.

Rich Chocolate Buttercream
Add 3–4 oz (90–125 g) semisweet (plain), bittersweet, milk, or white chocolate, melted and cooled (page 21), with the vanilla extract.

Sour Cream Chantilly

1 cup (8 oz/250 ml) sour cream

2 cups (16 fl oz/500 ml) heavy (double) cream

2 tablespoons sugar

2 teaspoons vanilla extract (essence)

BY HAND: In a large bowl, combine the sour cream, heavy cream, sugar, and vanilla. Using a balloon whisk, beat until medium peaks form (page 27).

BY MIXER: In a large bowl, combine the sour cream, heavy cream, sugar, and vanilla. Using a stand mixer fitted with the whip attachment or a hand mixer, beat on medium-high speed until medium peaks form (page 27).

Makes about 6 cups (48 fl oz/1.5 l), enough to frost a 9-inch (23-cm) cake

VARIATIONS

Almond-Flavored Chantilly
Substitute ¹/₂ teaspoon almond extract (essence) for the vanilla extract.

Liqueur-Flavored Chantilly
Substitute 1–2 tablespoons liqueur such as Grand Marnier, rum, Cointreau, framboise, kirsch, Kahlúa, or brandy for the vanilla.

Fruit-Flavored Chantilly
Substitute ¹/₃ cup (3¹/₂ oz/105 g) seedless preserves or marmalade of choice for the sugar. Stir into the cream mixture.

Espresso Buttercream

4 large egg yolks

$^1/_2$ cup (4 oz/125 g) sugar

$^1/_4$ cup (2 fl oz/60 ml) water

1 cup (8 oz/250 g) unsalted butter, at room temperature

2 tablespoons instant espresso powder dissolved in 1 tablespoon hot water

1 tablespoon Kahlúa (optional)

With a wire whisk, stir the egg yolks gently in the bowl of a stand mixer or another deep bowl. Set aside.

In a small, heavy saucepan over medium-high heat, combine the sugar and water and bring to a boil. Cover and allow to boil for 1 minute. (The steam created in the pan will wash the sugar crystals down the pan sides.) Uncover and continue to boil until the syrup reaches the soft-ball stage, or 239°F (115°) on a candy thermometer, about 5 minutes. (To test without a thermometer, scoop up a few drops of the syrup with a wooden spoon and immerse the spoon in a glass of ice water. When you trap the drops between your fingertips, you should be able to form them into a soft, pliable ball.)

BY HAND: Once the syrup is ready, begin whisking the yolks with the wire whisk. While whisking continuously, slowly pour the hot syrup onto the yolks. Be careful not to burn yourself with the hot syrup. Whisk vigorously until all of the syrup is incorporated. Switch to a balloon whisk and continue to whisk until cool and thick. Still using the balloon whisk, beat the butter into the cooled egg mixture until smooth and satiny. If the mixture looks curdled and the bowl feels cold, warm it slightly over hot water and beat the mixture again until it looks smooth and shiny. Beat in the espresso and the Kahlúa, if using.

BY MIXER: Once the syrup is ready, begin beating the yolks with a stand mixer fitted with the whip attachment or a hand mixer set on medium speed. While beating continuously, slowly pour the hot syrup onto the yolks. Be careful not to burn yourself. Beat until all of the syrup is incorporated, then continue to beat until cool and thick.

Beat the butter into the egg mixture until smooth and satiny. If the mixture looks curdled and the bowl feels cold, warm it over hot water and beat the mixture again until it looks shiny and smooth. Beat in the espresso and Kahlúa.

Makes about 2 cups (16 fl oz/500 ml), enough to frost a 9-inch (23-cm) cake

VARIATIONS

Almond Buttercream

Substitute $^1/_2$ teaspoon almond extract (essence), 2 tablespoons amaretto (optional), and $^1/_4$ cup almonds, toasted (page 21) and finely chopped for the espresso and Kahlúa.

Chocolate-Orange Buttercream

Substitute 3 oz (90 g) bittersweet chocolate, melted and cooled (page 21), and the grated zest of 1 orange for the espresso and Kahlúa.

Chocolate Glaze

12 oz (375 g) semisweet (plain) chocolate, finely chopped

1 cup (8 oz/250 g) unsalted butter

2 tablespoons corn syrup

Place the chocolate, butter, and corn syrup in the top of a double boiler placed over (not touching) barely simmering water and heat until the chocolate and butter melt, stirring often. Remove from the heat and pour the glaze through a fine-mesh sieve. Let cool to 92°F (33°C) before using.

Makes about 1$^1/_2$ cups (12 fl oz/375 ml)

Vanilla Cake Syrup

$^1/_3$ cup (3 oz/90 g) sugar

$^1/_3$ cup (3 fl oz/80 ml) water

Juice of $^1/_2$ lemon, strained

2 teaspoons vanilla extract (essence)

In a small saucepan over high heat, combine the sugar and water and bring to a boil. As soon as the sugar dissolves, remove the pan from the heat and stir in the lemon juice and vanilla. Let cool before using.

Makes about 1 cup (8 fl oz/250 ml), enough for one 9-inch (23-cm) cake

VARIATIONS

Flavored Cake Syrups

Substitute one of the following flavorings for the vanilla extract.

$^1/_2$–1 teaspoon almond extract (essence)

1–2 tablespoons Grand Marnier, rum, Cointreau, kirsch, framboise, Kahlúa, brandy, or other spirit

1–2 teaspoons orange-flower water or rose water

Juice of 2 lemons or 1 orange, strained

2 teaspoons instant espresso powder and 1 tablespoon Kahlúa or brandy

Infused Cake Syrups

Substitute one of the following for the vanilla extract. Cover and let stand for 10–15 minutes. Strain through a fine-mesh sieve before using.

3 cinnamon sticks

1 vanilla bean, split lengthwise, seeds scraped into syrup, and then pods added

1-inch (2.5-cm) piece fresh ginger, peeled

2 tablespoons whole-leaf black or green tea

$^1/_4$ cup ($^1/_4$ oz/7 g) crushed fresh spearmint or peppermint leaves

Ganache Filling

6 oz (185 g) bittersweet or semisweet (plain) chocolate, finely chopped

2 tablespoons unsalted butter

$^1/_2$ cup (4 fl oz/125 ml) heavy (double) cream

Combine the chocolate and butter in a heatproof bowl. In a small saucepan over medium-high heat, bring the cream just to a boil. Remove from the heat and immediately pour over the chocolate and butter. Stir with a wire whisk until the chocolate and butter melt and are smooth. Let cool until spreadable.

Makes about 1$^1/_3$ cups (11 fl oz/340 ml)

Ganache Mousse

4 oz (125 ml) bittersweet or semisweet (plain) chocolate, finely chopped

$^1/_4$ cup (2 fl oz/60 ml) whole milk

$^1/_2$ cup (4 fl oz/125 ml) heavy (double) cream

Put the chocolate in a heatproof bowl. In a small saucepan over medium-high heat, bring the milk just to a boil. Remove from the heat and immediately pour over the chocolate. Stir with a wire whisk until the chocolate melts and the mixture is smooth. In a clean bowl, using a balloon whisk, whip the cream just until soft peaks form (page 27). With a rubber spatula, gently fold the cream into the chocolate just until the two mixtures are incorporated. Do not overfold, or the filling will be gritty. Cover with plastic wrap and refrigerate until firm and spreadable, about 1 hour, or for up to 3 days.

Makes about 1$^3/_4$ cups (14 fl oz/430 ml)

Pastry Cream (Crème Pâtissière)

1$^1/_2$ cups (12 fl oz/375 ml) whole milk

1 vanilla bean, halved lengthwise and scraped (page 19)

4 large egg yolks

$^1/_2$ cup (4 oz/125 g) sugar

2 tablespoons cornstarch (cornflour)

2 tablespoons unsalted butter

In a saucepan over medium heat, warm the milk and the vanilla bean pod and scrapings until small bubbles appear along the edges of the pan. Remove from the heat, them remove the vanilla bean pod. In a bowl, whisk together the egg yolks, sugar, and cornstarch until smooth. Slowly whisk in the hot milk until blended. Pour the mixture back into the saucepan and place over medium-low heat. Cook, whisking constantly, until the mixture comes to a boil and thickens, about 3 minutes. Continue cooking, whisking constantly, for 1 minute longer. Pour through a fine-mesh sieve into a clean bowl. Stir in the butter until melted and smooth. Cover the bowl with plastic wrap, pressing it directly onto the surface of the cream to prevent a skin from forming. Poke a few holes in the plastic with the tip of a knife to allow steam to escape. Refrigerate until well chilled, at least 2 hours or for up to 2 days.

Makes about 1$^1/_2$ cups (12 fl oz/375 ml)

VARIATION

Crème Diplomat
Using a stand mixer fitted with the whip attachment or a hand mixer on medium speed, whip $^1/_4$ cup (2 fl oz/60 ml) heavy (double) cream until soft peaks form (page 27). Fold the cream into the chilled pastry cream. Refrigerate to chill until ready to use.

Lemon Curd

Zest of 2 lemons, in wide strips

Juice of 2 lemons, strained

6 tablespoons (3 oz/90 g) sugar

2 large whole eggs, plus 3 large egg yolks

$^1/_4$ cup (2 oz/60 g) unsalted butter

In a large heatproof bowl, combine the lemon zest and juice, sugar, eggs, and butter and place over (not touching) gently simmering water in a saucepan. Whisk steadily until the sugar dissolves and the butter melts, then continue to whisk until the curd coats the back of a spoon, about 3 minutes. Do not let the curd boil.

Remove from the heat. With a rubber spatula, push the curd through a medium-mesh sieve into a clean, dry bowl. Cover with plastic wrap, pressing it directly onto the surface of the curd to prevent a skin from forming. Poke a few holes in the plastic with the tip of a knife to allow steam to escape. Refrigerate until well chilled, about 3 hours, or for up to 5 days.

Makes about $^3/_4$ cup (6 fl oz/180 ml)

Frangipane

1 cup (5$^1/_2$ oz/170 g) almonds, toasted (page 21)

$^1/_4$ cup (2 oz/60 g) firmly packed brown sugar

2 tablespoons all-purpose (plain) flour

2 tablespoons unsalted butter, at room temperature, cut into small cubes

1 large egg

In a food processor, combine the nuts and sugar and process until the nuts are coarsely chopped. Add the flour, butter, and egg and process just until a paste forms. Store in an airtight container in the refrigerator for up to 3 days.

Makes about 1 cup (8 oz/250 g)

Glossary

ALMOND PASTE A mixture of ground blanched almonds, sugar, and liquid glucose or corn syrup. Similar to marzipan, almond paste contains more nuts and is thus coarser, stiffer, and has a stronger almond flavor.

AMARETTO An almond-flavored liqueur originally from the Italian town of Saronno, where it is made from bitter almonds. Elsewhere, makers use apricot kernels, which have a similar taste.

ASIAGO CHEESE Traditionally a sheep's milk cheese from the foothills of the Italian Dolomites, but now more commonly a pleasantly sharp cow's milk cheese that is available young (milder) and aged (sharper).

BAKING The cooking of food in the dry heat of an oven. While baking breads and desserts requires more precision than most other home cooking, anyone outfitted with a handful of ingredients and the proper equipment can produce towering cakes, crisp cookies, bubbling fruit pies, and golden breads. And, as with most things, baking becomes easier with practice.

BÂTARD A large loaf of French white bread with a dark crust and an oblong shape. Also known as *bâtarde*.

BATTER A smooth mixture that is thin enough to pour or spoon. Most batters consist of flour, eggs, and a liquid such as milk. Many also contain sugar and butter. Batters have a thinner consistency than doughs.

BEAT To mix vigorously until a single ingredient, such as eggs, or a mixture, such as a cake batter, is smooth, well blended, and aerated. Beating is often accomplished with an electric mixer, although it also can be done by hand with a spoon, whisk, or fork.

BLANCHED ALMONDS Almonds that have had their skins removed.

BUNDT PAN A style of cake pan with fluted sides, a rounded bottom, and a central tube.

BUTTERCREAM A light, fluffy mixture of butter, sugar, and eggs or custard used as a cake frosting or a filling. It can be flavored in myriad ways, including coffee, chocolate, and citrus.

CARAMELIZE To heat sugar until it melts and turns light to dark brown, or to cook other foods until their natural sugars caramelize, developing more complex flavors.

CHANTILLY CREAM Sweetened and sometimes flavored (vanilla or other extract/essence, liqueur) whipped cream.

CHOCOLATE JIMMIES Tiny, cylinder-shaped candies used to decorate sweets such as cupcakes and ice cream.

CLOTTED CREAM A specialty of Devonshire, England, this extra-rich cream is traditionally made by gently heating milk until a crust develops on the surface and the liquid beneath it thickens. High in milk fat, it is an English teatime staple, topping bread or scones.

COCCODRILLO Italian for "crocodile"; this is the name used for an oblong yeast bread with a rough surface.

COCONUT MILK Made by soaking grated coconut in water, coconut milk has a rich, nutty flavor. It is widely available in cans and sometimes frozen in Asian stores and many supermarkets. It comes in lowfat and regular versions. Do not confuse this unsweetened product with canned sweetened coconut cream.

COINTREAU An orange-flavored French liqueur.

CORE To remove the central core, or seeds and stem, of a fruit or vegetable.

CORN SYRUP This syrup, made from cornstarch, is available in light and dark versions, the latter with a deeper flavor. It is used to add sweetness, moisture, and chewiness.

COULIS A thick, sieved purée made of raw or cooked fruits (or vegetables if making for a savory course) and served as a sauce.

CREAM CHEESE A mild, tangy fresh cheese made from cow's milk high in milk fat. Some bakers prefer "natural" cream cheese for its taste and because it does not contain stabilizers or additives present in most commercial brands.

CREAM OF TARTAR This powdery, white substance, technically known as potassium tartrate, is a by-product of wine making. It stabilizes and promotes volume when whipping egg whites; delivers greater loft and whiter, finer crumbs in cakes; and enhances creaminess in frostings.

CRIMP To seal together the edges of two pieces of pastry dough by pressing the dough with the tines of a kitchen fork, the side of a knife, or a pastry crimper. Crimping differs from fluting in that you use a tool to seal the dough, whereas fluting calls for using your fingers to seal and form a decorative edge.

CRYSTALLIZED FLOWERS Edible flowers that are coated with a sugar syrup, transforming them into elegant decorations. Also called candied or iced flowers, they are sold in specialty-baking stores.

CRYSTALLIZED GINGER Ginger that has been preserved in sugar syrup and then dusted with sugar. It adds a sweet-spicy flavor to cookies, fruit fillings, quick breads, and cakes.

CURD A flavorful concoction made by cooking together citrus juice—lemon, orange, lime, grapefruit—egg yolks, sugar, and butter until thick and creamy. Used as a filling or topping.

CURDLING Usually, but not always, a sign that something has gone wrong. Visual evidence of curdling includes sauces or custards that separate, commonly the result of overheating eggs, which causes their proteins to solidify and clump. To avoid curdling, heat mixtures containing eggs gently and slowly, just to the point of thickening. If eggs are to be added to hot liquids, temper them first by mixing in a little of the hot liquid to warm them. Fat also prevents curdling. When making recipes that call for milk or cream plus an acidic ingredient, be wary of substituting a lower-fat version of the milk or cream. Sometimes curdling is desired, such as when cream is mixed with an acid such as buttermilk, which then thickens to become homemade crème fraîche.

DÉTREMPE French term used for the supple dough of flour, water, salt, and a small amount of butter in which a large, pliable block of butter is wrapped for making puff pastry.

DISK Dough—usually pie or cookie dough—shaped into a thick, flattened round.

DUST To sprinkle food or a work surface with a light layer of a powdery ingredient such as confectioners' (icing) sugar, flour, or unsweetened cocoa powder.

EDIBLE GOLD LEAF A fragile but spectacular garnish. Sold in paper-thin sheets, it is available from shops specializing in cake-decorating supplies. It is also sold in Indian markets, where it is called *varak* or *vark*. Because of its delicate nature, do not handle it with your hands; instead, apply it directly to the food item, such as pastry, with an artist's brush.

ESPRESSO POWDER, INSTANT Made from coffee beans, this extremely fine powder dissolves instantly in hot water. It is used to deliver an intense coffee flavor to such dessert preparations as pastry cream, buttercream frosting, and custard.

FERMENTATION A chemical change that occurs when yeast and bacteria are permitted to multiply in food, breaking down large sugar or starch chains into smaller molecules and creating carbon dioxide and alcohol in the process. In the case of bread, the gas produced during fermentation is trapped, which makes the dough rise.

FILO DOUGH These large, paper-thin dough sheets create the flaky layers of many Middle Eastern and Greek sweet and savory pastries, including the well-known baklava. The machine-rolled frozen filo sold in supermarkets is a good alternative to the fresh sheets available at Middle Eastern markets. Always bring the sheets to room temperature before using them, work quickly, and keep the sheets covered with a kitchen towel until just before using to prevent them from drying out.

FOUGASSE A decorative flatbread popular in France's Provence region. It is typically shaped like a leaf and flavored with olive oil and herbs.

FRAMBOISE A raspberry-flavored French brandy, the name of which is taken from framboise, French for "raspberry."

FROSTING A thick, fluffy mixture, such as buttercream, used to coat the outside of a cake. The term is often used interchangeably with icing, although the latter is usually shinier and thinner. Frostings are also used to fill cakes.

GALETTE A round, flat French tart or cake usually made from a flaky-pastry dough or puff pastry and holding a sweet or savory filling.

GANACHE A smooth mixture of melted chocolate and cream. While still barely warm, it is poured over cakes and tortes to form a smooth glaze. Cooled ganache can be whipped and used as a filling for cakes, pastries, and chocolate truffles.

GLAZE Thinner than either a frosting or icing, a glaze is poured, drizzled, or brushed on cakes, tarts, and pastries. Many glazes harden once they are applied, becoming smooth and shiny.

GLUTEN The weblike structure that forms in a dough due to the protein present in wheat flours and in very small amounts in rye and oat flours. Gluten is what makes dough elastic and extensible when kneaded. You can control the amount of gluten by the type of flour you use and how much you manipulate the dough or batter before baking.

GOAT CHEESE Made from pure goat's milk or a blend of goat's and cow's milk. Fresh goat cheese is mild, creamy, and only slightly tangy. As goat cheeses age, they harden and their flavor sharpens

GRAND MARNIER Regarded as one of the finest of the many orange liqueurs available, this deep amber French product is made by blending Cognac and a distilled essence of bitter orange peels.

GRAPPA A potent Italian brandy made from what remains of grapes (pomace, skins, stems, and seeds) after they have been pressed for wine making.

GRUYÈRE CHEESE A smooth, creamy cow's milk cheese produced in Switzerland and France and appreciated for its mild, nutty flavor.

HALF-SHEET PAN Also known as a baking sheet, a baking pan that measures 12 by 17 inches (30 by 43 cm) and has 1-inch (2.5-cm)

sides, half the size of a commercial sheet pan, thus its name. The smaller-sized jelly-roll pan, used to make flat sponge cakes that are spread with jelly or another filling and rolled, is traditionally 10 by 15 inches (25 by 38 cm) with $^1/_2$-inch (12-mm) sides.

HULL To remove the dry outer covering of a fruit, seed, or nut, or to remove the leafy base where a stem connects to a fruit.

ICING Used to coat and/or fill a cake, an icing is similar to a frosting, and the two terms are frequently used interchangeably. An icing is generally thinner and glossier.

KAHLÚA A popular and distinctive Mexican coffee liqueur flavored with herbs and vanilla.

KIRSCH A cherry-flavored colorless brandy, the best of which are made by producers in Germany, France, and Switzerland, where the wild black cherry, native to the Rhine Valley, is used.

KNEAD To fold and press dough repeatedly to develop the structure of bread (the gluten protein webbing) and other baked goods.

LAVENDER FLOWERS, DRIED When fresh, these small blossoms of the lavender plant are light purple; when dried, they take on a gray cast. The flowers have a sweet and mildly lemony flavor and fragrance.

LEVAIN A natural sourdough starter that begins with a *chef*, a mixture of flour and water (or other liquid), which is left to ferment for a few days. Then flour is added to the soured dough, and it becomes a *levain*, or "leavening."

MACERATE To soak a food, usually fruit, in sugar and/or a flavorful liquid, such as a liqueur, draw out the juices, enhance its flavor, and sometimes soften its texture.

MALT SYRUP A thick syrup made from maltose sugar extracted from sprouted barley. Be sure to buy the sweeter plain-flavored syrup, not the bitter hop-flavored syrup used by brewers.

MANDOLINE A flat, rectangular tool used for slicing foods quickly and with precision and uniformity. Mandolines come with an assortment of blades.

MASCARPONE CHEESE A soft, rich, smooth fresh Italian cheese made from cream, with a texture reminiscent of sour cream. Sold in plastic tubs. Found in most upscale markets.

MERINGUE Sweet, white, and fluffy, this delicate mixture is produced by beating together egg whites and sugar. A meringue can be soft, glossy, and smooth for spooning onto pies and other desserts, or hard, made with more sugar and baked until crisp, light, and dry.

MICROPLANE The brand name for a line of graters, including a narrow model, 12-inches (30-cm) long, ideal for use on citrus zest.

MORELLO CHERRY A dark red, sour (or tart) cherry sold jarred or canned, packed in syrup.

MOUSSE An airy, rich concoction of sweet or savory ingredients. It may be a suspension of fruit in whipped cream served as an elegant dessert, or softly whipped cream folded into melted chocolate for using as a cake filling. Some chilled mousses, also known as cold soufflés, contain beaten egg whites for extra height and lightness. A mousse that includes egg yolks, such as a classic French chocolate mousse, has a dense and creamy texture.

NUTMEG The brown, oblong seed of a tropical evergreen tree, a whole nutmeg resembles an unshelled pecan. When harvested, the seeds have a brilliant red, lacy membrane covering them, which is removed and dried to become

mace. In baking, nutmeg's warm sweetness complements spice cakes, cookies, and fruit desserts. Both whole and ground nutmeg are widely available. For the best flavor, use freshly grated nutmeg rather than the preground spice.

PASTRY A term used to refer to various doughs, such as puff pastry and pie pastry; individual pastry creations, such as napoleons and éclairs; and an entire category of baked items, including everything from baklava to choux to croissants.

PASTRY CREAM A basic custard with many applications in dessert making. It is used as a filling for cakes, tarts, cream pies, and pastries, including éclairs and napoleons. The main ingredients are milk, eggs, sugar, flour or cornstarch (cornflour), and a flavoring—traditionally vanilla.

PIE PANS AND DISHES Metal pie pans or glass or ceramic pie dishes in 9- and 10-inch (23- and 25-cm) sizes are standard. Always follow recipe directions that indicate metal or glass, as temperature and timing are determined by the material used.

PINE NUTS Seeds of a type of pine tree, which nestle in the scales of the cones, pine nuts are small and rich, with an elongated, slightly tapered shape and a resinous, sweet flavor.

PIPE To make decorative effects on cakes and other baked goods by spooning frosting, whipped cream, or a similar mixture into the wide end of a pastry (piping) bag and then forcing, or piping, it out of the bag's narrow tip.

POACH To cook foods gently in not-quite-simmering water or other liquid.

POLENTA Refers to both a milled grain, Italian cornmeal, and the cooked dish made from the grain. In baking, the grain is used in breads, cakes, and cookies.

PROOFING Refers to the rise, or fermentation period, of a yeast dough after it has been shaped. It is also used to describe the test that yeast undergoes—mixed with warm water and allowed to stand for a few minutes—to determine if it is active.

PROSCIUTTO DI PARMA An Italian ham that is seasoned, salt-cured, and air-dried. It is prized for its distinctive fragrance and subtle flavor. Aged from 10 months to 2 years, prosciutto from Parma in the Italian region of Emilia-Romagna is considered by most culinary observers to be the best available.

PUNCH DOWN To press down a yeast dough that has completed its first rise, before it is allowed to rise a second time. This step redistributes the yeast to give it a fresh food supply as it continues to ferment and raise the dough. It also expels larger carbon dioxide bubbles that have already been created by the fermenting yeast, resulting in a more even crumb in the finished loaf. To punch down dough, press down on the mass with both hands. Bread dough that is removed from the bowl and shaped before the second rise—or that does not call for a second rise—does not need to be punched down; simply handling the dough achieves the same result.

PURÉE To reduce solid food to a smooth, thick consistency by blending, mashing, or pushing it through a sieve or similar tool.

QUICK BREADS Breads that rise through the action of baking powder and/or baking soda (bicarbonate of soda), unlike yeast breads, which depend on yeast for their expansion. Quick breads require less mixing than yeast breads, are usually higher in fat and sugar, and have denser, moister textures.

RICOTTA CHEESE A whey-based Italian cheese made by heating the whey left over from making sheep's, goat's, or cow's milk cheeses. Most of the ricotta available outside of Italy is made from cow's milk, either whole or part-skim, and is sold packed into plastic containers.

RISE To increase the volume of a mixed batter or dough, an action brought on by the use of a leavener, such as yeast, baking powder, or baking soda (bicarbonate of soda).

ROLL OUT To flatten dough using a rolling pin. Pie dough and cookie dough are rolled out on a work surface, such as a countertop or pastry board, which is floured to prevent sticking.

SABAYON A custard-based sauce flavored with dessert wine; also known as zabaglione.

SIFT To pass an ingredient through a sifter or sieve to aerate it, give it a uniform consistency, and eliminate any large particles.

SLASH Using a sharp knife or similar tool, to make one or more shallow cuts in the top of a loaf of bread or a roll before baking. These slashes enhance and increase crust area and promote more even rising in the oven.

SOURDOUGH Yeast bread with a tangy flavor, the result of a sourdough starter, or fermented mixture of flour, water, and yeast.

SPONGE A portion of dough that is prepared ahead of time and allowed to ferment—developing a spongy consistency—before being mixed with the remaining ingredients. It is usually a combination of flour, water, and yeast.

SPRINGFORM PAN A deep, round cake pan with sides secured by a clamp. It is especially good for baking cheesecakes and other solid cakes, as the sides expand when the clamp is released, making the cake easy to remove.

STARTER Yeast starters and sourdough starters are used to leaven bread; they may be made at home or purchased. A yeast starter is a mixture of flour, water, sugar, and yeast that has been allowed to ferment. A portion of the starter is used as the leavener for yeast bread dough, and the remaining starter is kept alive indefinitely by replenishing it with equal parts flour and water. A sourdough starter is made without any (or with a very small amount of) baker's yeast. Instead, a mixture of flour and water, and some-times a crushed vegetable or fruit, is allowed to sit at room temperature, where it captures the wild yeasts always present in the atmosphere.

STREUSEL A crumbly mixture of flour, butter, and sugar used to top cakes, pies, breads, and other baked goods. Nuts, rolled oats, and/or ground spices are sometimes included for additional flavor and texture.

SWEET MARSALA A fortified dessert wine first made around the Sicilian port of Marsala and used to flavor cakes and custards.

TUBE PAN Any cake pan with a central tube, a feature that helps the center of a cake to rise and bake evenly. Among the popular styles are an angel food cake pan, with a tall central tube and removable bottom, and a Bundt pan, with fluted sides and a rounded base.

WHEAT BRAN The outer layer of the wheat kernel that is removed during milling. Often sold in bulk in markets and health-food stores, wheat bran imparts flavor and fiber to breads and other baked goods.

YEAST BREADS Breads that are leavened with yeast, a living organism, unlike quick breads, which get their lift from chemical leaveners. Yeast breads require several minutes of knead-ing to develop their texture and structure.

Index

OXMOOR HOUSE INC.

Oxmoor House

Oxmoor House books are distributed by Sunset Books
80 Willow Road, Menlo Park, CA 94025
Telephone: 650-321-3600 Fax: 650-324-1532
Vice President/General Manager: Rich Smeby
Director of Special Sales: Gary Wright

Oxmoor House and Sunset Books are divisions of
Southern Progress Corporation

WILLIAMS-SONOMA, INC.
Founder & Vice-Chairman: Chuck Williams

WELDON OWEN INC.
Chief Executive Officer: John Owen
President: Terry Newell
Chief Operating Officer: Larry Partington
Vice President International Sales: Stuart Laurence
Creative Director: Gaye Allen
Associate Creative Director: Leslie Harrington
Publisher: Hannah Rahill
Editor: Kim Goodfriend
Consulting Editor: Jennifer Newens
Copy Editor: Sharon Silva
Assistant Editor: Donita Boles
Art Directors: Carl Hodson and Charlene Charles
Designer: Charlene Charles
Production Director: Chris Hemesath
Color Specialist: Teri Bell
Production and Shipping Coordinator: Libby Temple
Proofreaders: Desne Ahlers and Carolyn Miller
Indexer: Ken DellaPenta
Photographer: Noel Barnhurst
Photographer Assistants: Noriko Akiyama
and Heidi Ladendorf
Food Stylist: Sandra Cook
Food Stylist Assistants: Elizabet Der Nederlanden
and Melinda Barsales

THE ESSENTIALS SERIES
Conceived and produced by
WELDON OWEN INC.
814 Montgomery Street, San Francisco, CA 94133
Telephone: 415-291-0100 Fax: 415-291-8841

In Collaboration with Williams-Sonoma, Inc.
3250 Van Ness Avenue, San Francisco, CA 94109

A WELDON OWEN PRODUCTION
Copyright © 2003 Weldon Owen Inc.
and Williams-Sonoma, Inc.

First printed in 2003
10 9 8 7

ISBN 0-8487-2779-7

Printed by Midas Printing Limited
Printed in China